0102476

Sissinghurst

Sissinghurst

AN UNFINISHED HISTORY

Adam Nicolson

VIKING

VIKING

Published by the Penguin Group

Penguin Group (USA) Inc., 375 Hudson Street, New York, New York 10014, U.S.A.
Penguin Group (Canada), 90 Eglinton Avenue East, Suite 700, Toronto, Ontario,
Canada M4P 2Y3 (a division of Pearson Penguin Canada Inc.) · Penguin Books Ltd,
80 Strand, London WC2R 0RL, England · Penguin Ireland, 25 St. Stephen's Green,
Dublin 2, Ireland (a division of Penguin Books Ltd) · Penguin Books Australia Ltd,
250 Camberwell Road, Camberwell,Victoria 3124, Australia (a division of Pearson
Australia Group Pty Ltd) · Penguin Books India Pvt Ltd, 11 Community Centre,
Panchsheel Park, New Delhi–110 017, India · Penguin Group (NZ), 67 Apollo Drive,
Rosedale, North Shore 0632, New Zealand (a division of Pearson New Zealand Ltd)
Penguin Books (South Africa) (Pty) Ltd, 24 Sturdee Avenue,
Rosebank, Johannesburg 2196, South Africa

Penguin Books Ltd, Registered Offices: 80 Strand, London WC2R 0RL, England

First American edition
Published in 2010 by Viking Penguin, a member of Penguin Group (USA) Inc.

1 3 5 7 9 10 8 6 4 2

Illustration credits appear on page 327.

LIBRARY OF CONGRESS CATALOGING IN PUBLICATION DATA
Nicolson, Adam,———
Sissinghurst, an unfinished history : the quest to restore a working farm
at Vita Sackville-West's legendary garden / by Adam Nicolson
p. cm.
Includes bibliographical references and index.
ISBN 978-0-670-02173-4
1. Sissinghurst Garden (England)—History. 2. Historic farms—Conservation
and restoration—England. 3. Family farms—England—History. 4. Farm life—
England—History. I. Title. II. Title: Quest to restore a working farm
at Vita Sackville-West's legendary garden.
SB466.G8N53 2010
630.9422'38—dc22
2009050258

Printed in the United States of America   Set in Goudy Old Style
Designed by BTDNYC
Photo insert designed by Francesca Belanger

for Sarah

with all my love

and for

Sally Bushell, Jonathan Light, Sue Saville, and Fiona Reynolds

with many thanks for their longstanding

support and encouragement

Contents

1. Sissinghurst   1

2. Inheritance   42

3. The Idea   63

4. Origins   73

5. Testing   97

6. Occupation   115

7. Rejection   141

8. Glory   156

9. Disintegration   190

10. Acceptance   216

11. Admiration   231

12. Renewal   270

   Acknowledgments   323

   Illustration Credits   327

   Note on Sources   329

   Index   333

CHAPTER *1*

Sissinghurst

I HAVE LIVED AT SISSINGHURST, ON and off, for the last forty-five years. For my entire conscious life it has been what I have thought of as home, even when living away, in London, or abroad. For all my attachment to other places, this has always seemed like the root. I belong to it. It is the land I have walked over, looked out over, driven through, smoked my first cigarette in, planted my first tree in, bicycled over, slept in, and lived in all my life. It is where I came to understand what a tree was, what a friend was, what a hideout was, what a landscape was, how entrancing streams were as they made their way in and out of the margins of a wood, and what solitariness, nature, and love might be.

If I think of a view, or of mist on an autumn morning, the way it lies in a valley like a scarf, or the way a stream when blocked makes a reedy place upstream of the blockage, where after time willows grow in the wetness and make a dark summer tent over the bog; or the way wildflowers peak and then collapse as spring deepens into summer; if I think of geese belling across winter fields; or of being alone, or of the transition from childhood to adolescence, of the relationship of a place to its history or its future: every one of those things, strung out across my life, like lights marking a channel, is tied to and founded on Sissinghurst. It is the shape of what I am. I do not own it but it is my place. Anything else can only ever be an approximation to it.

There is a tree in the garden, an oak, growing on the edge of the moat, that my sister Juliet and I planted together when she was four and I was one. It is nearly fifty years old but, in its tree life, still in its teens. One or two of the lower branches have been pruned, to improve its shape, and the bark of the oak is creeping back, in pillowed, almost animal ridges, across the scars that the saw has left. But the rest of the tree—it is a strange hybrid, a sycamore oak, which has oak leaves but drops sycamore seeds in the autumn, the single wings helicoptering to the autumn grass—the rest of the tree is in the first glowing moment of adulthood, no leaning in the trunk, a full head of hair, if you can say that about a tree, a kind of bushy-brushed wholeness to it, its trunk like the trunk of a young man. It is now part of the Sissinghurst landscape, rooted, solid, essential, inevitably there, and I feel in my heart as much part of this place as that tree. My nutrients come from this soil.

WHEN I WAS A BOY here in the 1960s, my father used to take us, my sisters and me, down to the stream that runs through the wood, usually after lunch in the winter, to have a boat race. We chose small, fat sticks for boats, to be thrown into the stream where it entered the wood below a marshy patch in the Dog Field. He cut long wands from the hazels for what he called "hoikers"—the only way, if your stick got caught in the deep trench of the stream, that you could hoik it back into the main flow. No cheating was allowed, nor hurrying on of your stick if it happened to be drifting in a treacle-slow section of the current. It had to be stuck and immobile before you could push it back into the race with the hoiker. The finishing line was the chestnut bridge by the outflow from the lake. All of us cheated when he wasn't looking.

Or there were clearance weekends and bonfires, the brambles and dead wood lopped and slashed away with billhooks and bowsaws, all piled onto a smoky fire, the smoke finding its way out through the roof of the coppiced chestnuts as if through the thatch of a medieval hall. He would send me down to the wood sometimes to start the fire on my own before he came to join me. Start it small, he said, but make it as big as you can. Once he raced me to Bettenham, the neighbor farm to Sissinghurst, half a mile away, him on foot, me on a bike. I remember him now, stampeding down the track ahead of me, uncatchable and distant, however hard I pedaled.

Sissinghurst is embedded in the most explorable and boy-friendly of all landscapes, a part of Kent, no more than fifty miles south of London, called the Weald. That is an ancient Saxon or Germanic word meaning "forest," but over the twelve or thirteen centuries since the Saxons arrived here, that huge stretch of woodland has been cut up and largely cleared so that the Weald now is a patchwork of small woods and farms, with streams curling between them and lanes connecting one to another. It is a stretch of country that is accessible to London and its commuters but has an enormously deep past and is still full of hidden secrets. A sense of invitation is plastered all over it, and on summer mornings, at breakfast, on the bleached and knotty deal of the kitchen table, my father would pore with me over a two-and-a-half-inch map of it, exploring its possibilities with our fingers: the gridlines pale blue, the occasional contours a browny orange, the stipple of the scattered farms, each with the blue spot of a farmyard pond. Why don't you go and see what the Hammer Brook is like here—a bridge four miles away downstream—or here, where it joins the Beult? You see where it says "Roman Road" there, where it goes down the contours of that hill? Or look, a Roman ford—miles away, south of Benenden, into another parish—why don't you see if you can go and find that?

So I did, alone on my bike for hours and days at a time, looking for these places that he had made precious and important to me. I learned to read the map, which I kept folded in my pocket. I found the Roman road dropping south through woodland beyond Benenden: he must have known it but never told me he did, a place reverberating with the past, a huge trench as straight as it should be, just wobbling here and there like a piece of furniture two thousand years old, half a mile long, exactly preserved and deeply creased into the Wealden hill. I remember it now, its runnel filled with autumn leaves, the hornbeams and hazels on its banks, unvisited, unknown, the most wonderful and vivid antiquity I had ever seen. At the bottom of the valley, on a tiny tributary of the Rother no more than two feet wide, trickling to the south, with ferns and moss around them, I found the smooth dark stones of the Roman ford, scattered in the stream bed, as neglected as they had been since the Romans left fifteen hundred years before.

I would return from these expeditions, excited and exhausted, unaware of the riches I was gathering. Only now do I see this as the best education a child could have: the private discovery of a stretch of country rich in buried meanings, so easily and fluently to hand, to be discovered with nothing more than a map and a bike. Seeing, I suppose, how much I loved it all, the finding of the way, the connections made in three dimensions that the map had hinted at and led one to, we started going on longer expeditions. One June morning, early, when the world was heavy with summer and greenness, we went for a long walk together through the flat, oak-hedged grasslands of the Low Weald toward Biddenden. I was about eleven and we walked from one fifteenth-century Wealden farmhouse to another, maybe twelve miles or so through the cold morning, the leaves gray with dew, the sun blinking through them, admiring the close-set studs, the pitch of the roofs designed for thatch, now tiled, the rooted richness of this country.

It is not the buildings I remember, though, but a long hay meadow on the Hammer Brook, a mile or two upstream, just the other side of Hammer Mill, which we came to as we circled back to Sissinghurst and breakfast. I had never guessed that an air of perfection was not something to be dreamt about, but could be experienced on your skin, as a living, seen reality. I thought then and can still imagine now that the meadow was the most beautiful thing I had ever seen. One side of the long narrow green space, perhaps four hundred yards from end to end, all of it walled in by the fresh green of the springtime wood, followed the brook's meandering path. The other took a long straight line against the trees. We were there the morning after the farmer, Mr. Hall, had mown the grass. He had begun by following the stream in his tractor and had laid his swathes in repeated, rippling slices that mimicked the stream itself, as if the wavy hair of the field had been combed flat but kept its wave, gleaming early that brilliant morning, like oiled braids, with the pale stubs of the shorn grass between each mown tress, the buttercups laid in with the grass as a summer wreath, a vision of perfection for that moment only, before Mr. Hall came back with his tractor later that morning and began to turn and stir the grass with his tedder into the lifted ridges in which he needed it to dry.

April 1973: *My father and I on the Hammer Brook.*

We did other things: my father bought a double canoe and for three days we followed the Hammer Brook from where the Bettenham track crossed it, along its winding trench to the river Beult and then on to the Medway until we reached salt water at Rochester. We did the same on the Stour from Great Chart to Sandwich, taking with us this time, in a deliberate act of matchmaking, my cousin Robert Sackville-West, so that we would become friends, as we have remained for life. We walked to the North Downs across the Low Weald and then along the Pilgrim's Way. We went to see where William the Conqueror had landed and then Julius Caesar. It was as if my father was conquering Kent for me, not the Kent of commuter modernity but an older place, one in which nature and culture were more intimately bound together and of which Sissinghurst itself always seemed to be the center and the exemplar.

Nowhere felt deeper or more like a vein under the skin than down in the bed of the Hammer Brook. It was an entrancing and different world, a green, wet womb, a place of privacy and escape. Along the banks, the alders and hazels were so thick that the wavering line of the stream was like a strip of wood run wild. Once beneath them, you were in a liquid tunnel, arched over with leaves, gloomy in its hollows, suddenly bright where the sun broke through, seductively cool when the day was burning on the fields outside. Where the shade was particularly thick, in the depth of the little wood, the sunlight still found its way between the alders and the maples, making spots of light no bigger than a hand or a face, dropped across the darkness as if by a brush, looking like the speckling on the skin of a trout, or those pools of light hair you find on the flanks of a young deer.

The water flowed in riffles over the shallow bed, the gravel banks stained orange with the iron seeping from the ground. Green hanks of starwort sprouted from the stream floor. Occasionally, a small group of trout found its way from pool to pool, dark bodies in the sun, where curtains of the light dropped through the speck-filled water. In this tiny Wealden river, they were not the slick creatures of Wiltshire chalk streams, but flighty, on the edge of viability, darting away even from the shadow of a big dragonfly, a skimmer, maneuvering in the air not far above them. There were pike here and they must have been fearful of those jaws, but I have stood on the bank and watched a family of about twelve trout, the spotted bodies in the golden water, not hanging as they do in a big stream, but actively seeking prey, a gang of fish on the hunt, the big swaying adults, the slighter young ones, all of them roo-tling like pigs in the stones of the bed.

1930s: *Haycart on the track by the moat. Oast, barn, and piggery in the distance.*

It was a world that encouraged slowness, detail, attention. Downstream of each of the gravel banks, at the head of the still pools, I watched the current circle back on itself in tiny transient spirals, no more than a millimeter deep, slowly whirling through the leopard-spot patterns of light and shade. Nothing showed that the water was moving unless there happened to be the fleck of a seed pod or a fly caught in the surface, making its waltzing, turning progress downriver. Through it all a drowsy current moved, with amber-lit sandbanks far below, and sometimes a drifting leaf caught under a stone, waving up from its bed.

Then, rarely, as a treasure from nowhere, something different: I remember the first time I saw it here. I was standing in the river, the water running up against my boots and dragging at them, so that the rubber was wobbling with the pull of the current and the tops of the boots were opening and closing like a pair of lips. I had the dog with me, splashing in the shallows, shaking the drops from his muzzle so that his own lips were slapping against his teeth. Then from nowhere it came past us: a kingfisher searing through the gloom, making its turns along this river sunk beneath the fields on either side, a soundless riff played on the river air.

That swerve, a taut, cut line of wing through air, with so much verve to it, as if running the length of an electric wire, was a form of quickness the life of a plodding mammal could never approach, a magnesium strip in the light and dark of the river, traveling through those patches so that it seemed to flash as it passed, a stroboscopic flicking on and off of the color, but with a continuity, a driven line, leaving only an afterburn on the mind's eye, an undersurface glamour in the shadows of the stream.

I used to leave the house in my windcheater and gumboots and head out to the woods and tracks that cross Sissinghurst from north to south and east to west. The woods seemed enormous then. Their far boundaries were a long way from the house. They felt inexhaustible, unplumbed country. These were the places I loved to sink into, away from the noise and business of the house and garden. I dawdled in the wood, under the dark of the leaves; when scarcely a hundredth of the light in the air outside penetrated to the wood floor, the whole place was as cool as a church. The air in springtime by the streams was thick with wild garlic, and later with the sweeter, gentler smell of the bluebells. The swallows and house martins dipped on to the lake and the woodpeckers yaffled in the distant trees. The grassy banks on the field edges were dense with archangel, red campion, and stitchwort, before the brambles and the nettles, always the winners in this annual race, strangled and overwhelmed them. All of these were the deep constituents of home. For days at a time, I circled the house and garden, all the public places at Sissinghurst, through this other hidden world, and never, or so it felt, emerged into view. It was as if out here, concealed from the public, the real thing existed, and that other place, over there, was an ersatz version of it, prepared for public view, with public, adult concerns dominating it in a way they wouldn't or couldn't in a distant field or wood.

Late 1950s: *Sissinghurst from the east.*
Apple orchard in Lower Horse Race at top right.

The only person I ever met in the wood was the woodman. I never knew his name; neither he nor I was exactly adept at conversation, but I liked his thin, silent, pensive presence, as narrow as a rolled cigarette, intensely solitary, shy, turning away from any question to bend over his work. Every year in the winter he would buy the growing timber on an acre or two of wood, an area Kentish men have always called a "cant." In a system of management at least as old as the Stone Age, a broadleaf tree if cut (or "coppiced," the Norman-French word) would sprout again from the stump or stool. Within ten or twelve years, the new shoots would grow thick enough to be usable for firewood or fencing and could be cut again. In this way the wood yielded up a steady harvest, cant by cant, twelve years by twelve years, and each part of the wood was at a different stage in the cycle: the tall smooth poles ready for cutting, the dense scrubby younger growth, or the cant just cut, shorn and freshened, like a stubble field after the harvest.

Each year the woodman bought his cant, and alone, with his rough shed made from spare poles and a tarpaulin strung across them, he would fell the chestnuts, cut the trees to length, split them, and peel them, so that by the end of the winter huge piles of clean, shaved lengths and gray shaved bark came to lie around his shelter. The waste he would burn in big fires whose smoke trailed out over the heads of the trees like a picture, it always seemed to me, of medieval England. You could have stood in the field outside the wood five hundred or even a thousand years ago and seen precisely that, even heard—if you edited out for a minute the repeated whining and relaxing of the chain saw—the same sharp-heavy falling of billhook on wood stem, a clunk-cut, half heard across the distance, the same sudden crackle of a flame as it caught.

Then one day late in the winter, he would be gone, sometimes leaving his tractor there, wrapped up in tarpaulins, the rubbed places and hollows still worn around his shed where he had been working, but the chestnut poles gone, leaving only the clean faces of the cut stools.

As the spring returned, the anemones flowered in the cleared wood and those coppice stools began to sprout again for their next cycle. Above them, the trunks of the oaks stood out in the air for the first time in years. And in the new openness of the cleared cant, the emergent dagger leaves of the bluebells pushed through the leaf litter as if from individual silos. That sense of purpose was everywhere: the primrose leaves crinkled like a Savoy cabbage, with the flowers just then unfolding; the cow parsley in low soft-edged pouffes about the size of a dinner plate at the foot of the hedges; dog's mercury everywhere in the woods, as well as lords and ladies above the brown wood floor like the blades of green, soft-bodied spears.

Following that, in the great annual unfolding, the nightingales arrived and sang, as they do now, in two patches of thickety wood, one in an abandoned loop of the river, toward Bettenham, another a third of a mile to the south where the Hammer Brook is joined by the boat-race stream coming down through the Sissinghurst woods. The nightingales sing so loudly that you can hear them half a mile away in the garden by the moat, but faintly, like the weakest of signals picked up by the most sensitive of antennae. I remember that as a teenager once, on a warm night, after dinner, with half a moon shining, when everyone else had gone to bed, I went out toward them, walking and stumbling across the fields to where they were singing in their little moonlit thickets, bubbling and trilling, a song interrupted now and then by long, ecstatic, deep-throated slides into the bass register, which seemed to come from somewhere deeper within a body than any bird could manage. Those notes sounded as if the ground itself were singing. I lay down on the warm earth next to the thicket, in the field by the trees, and listened to one on my left, unseen in the bushes, and the other answering him six hundred yards away up the little valley, first one and then the other, a duet or duel, I couldn't tell. Like most birds, it is the males who do the singing, and they sit on the ground inside their protective thickets. That is scarcely what it sounded like then: men, for sure, but more like the lords of two manors, shouting from their tower tops, each proclaiming the virtues of their wives and lands, their need for dominance and love of possession, the deliciousness of this thicket, the ridiculousness of the other, the hilarious beauty of this life, all its sorrows and all its wonders. I fell asleep and woke an hour later, with the stars turned in the sky above me, and the two of them still singing away, blow for blow, note for note, their sliding gurgle-ecstasies exchanged across the moonlight, and I left them there, walking back through the bright blue fields, listening to the sound of the birds slowly weakening in my ear.

Sissinghurst then, in the 1960s, as well as a house, a family home, and a garden open to the public, was a fully working farm. James Stearns, the farmer, a big, tall young man, with enormous hands and a way of looking down at you from a vast height, lived with his wife, Pat, in the Victorian farmhouse. Seven or eight men worked under him, milking a Guernsey herd, keeping chickens and sheep, growing hops, wheat, barley, and oats, with orchards, one of Worcesters, one of Bramleys. They made hay, still cut faggots from the wood, and carted enormous quantities of farmyard manure out onto the fields at the end of every winter. Year after year, plowing, rolling, harrowing, pruning, hedging, woodcutting, sowing, hop-stringing, sheep-dipping and -shearing, mowing, haymaking, baling, clearing the streams, harvesting the cereals, picking the apples and then the hops—year after year, the farm was an intensely worked and busy place.

As a boy, I felt this was only how things should be. The cattle pushing into the yard to be milked, their dung flopping out on the concrete, their sweet, milky breath, the massive stodge of mud and straw they made in their winter housing down by the big Elizabethan barn, the sound in the summer fields of their teeth tearing at the grass, the rough sandpaper lick of their tongues through the bars of a gate, the feeling that they might eat you if they could; the pigs and their own version of stodged-up chaos in the shed where the National Trust shop now is, and Copper, the chauffeur-handyman, telling me that they were the cleanest and neatest of animals; the chickens pecking their way around the pats in the Cow Field; the flock of Jacob sheep that lived in the field by the lake and were always, it seemed, afflicted with foot rot; the harvest moment in the summer when the tall-laden carts came back up to the barns from Frogmead and Lodge Field, piled high with straw bales, the men who had been stacking them riding on top, ducking under the branches of the oaks where they came past the moat; the hay harvest in the park, where the lines of cut hay swerved to avoid the ancient trees, leaving eye-shaped lozenges of uncut grass around each trunk, as though the trunks were the pupils of those eyes; the white clouds of blossom in the pear and apple orchards and then the autumn smell of the apples coming wafting to the house on the wind: these were the ingredients of the world as it was meant to be.

Down in the southern end of Frogmead, there was a hop garden. It was only ten acres but seemed huge then, the hops growing in towering alleys stretching miles away into the dark, as if they were the creepers of some Amazonian forest. I scarcely dared go in. But in September, when the hops were ready, they were harvested, the bines cut from the network of wires and string, loaded into trailers, which were then hauled up the track to the oast houses for drying. I used to bike up behind them, pulled along by a smell that once smelled could never be forgotten: sweet, acrid, vegetable, mineral, woody, flowery, odd, heavy, heady, druggy, earthy, and sharp, a taste more than a smell, its acidy resins catching at the back of the throat. I can taste these hops as I remember them now. As the trailers bumped along the track, bruised bodies of individual hops were left lying behind them like little green birds. As I rode over them the air turned green. There is something alien to the smell, not what you might expect from a plant that is native to England. It is more outlandish than that. Hops are a relative of cannabis, one of the Cannabaceae, and the air that hangs about them is smokily dopy in the same way, a subtle and combined smell, a blended soporific that would be more at home away on the other side of the Mediterranean, hidden in the souks of Aleppo or Isfahan.

The tractors came up to the oast house, where gangs of men and women dragged the bines off the back and pushed them into the stripping machines on the ground floor, jiggering and sifting the cones from the leaves and string and stalks, and then feeding them through to the gantry, where they were taken to the kilns.

From below, for eight hours or so, giant diesel boilers dried the hops, which were stacked a yard deep above the slatted floor in the big round oasts. When dry, they were shoveled out onto the upper story, the hop loft, which was sheeny with a century of resin gelled into place, burnished and sticky with it. Hop lofts are always dark, with small windows, because light degrades a hop, and the only illumination comes sharply in at one side, from the open doorway, as if from the wings. It was a beautiful scene: the walls and beams whitewashed, the fresh hops going into the kilns lime green, the dried hops transformed, their color, as my grandmother once described them in this same loft, "a cross between ash and gold, the color of dust motes, of corn in moonlight." In the worn and darkened wood of the room, the men brushed the dried hops into piles with birch brooms before pushing them with canvas shovels called scuppers toward a hole in the floor. A giant press stood over the hole, and underneath it, on the floor below, a giant sack, called a pocket, was hung from the beams. Into it the hops were first deftly shoveled, and then, as a man turned the giant iron wheel on the press, a weight dropped into the pocket and pressed the hops into their bag. So tight were they in a full pocket that the two top corners of the sack, where it was tied, stuck out like bullocks' ears. Each pocket had stenciled on it the horse of Kent, the county's Invicta motto, the name of the farm and of the farmer, still here called A. O. R. Beale, James Stearns's grandfather. At the end of the season, the number of pockets achieved that year was painted on the whitewashed beams above our heads.

1930s: *In the Sissinghurst oast house, shoveling hops into a pocket.*

I loved the farm as it was then. I loved its detail and business, the sheer fullness of what happened there, the way the young men in the summer with their shirts off would chuck the tractors down the lanes between the buildings, throttle open, work to be done; or the shoving and jostling of the cattle, the business in the hop gardens, the orchards and the arable fields, the way that the men with their Jack Russells would stand around at the door of the barn, sticks in hand, smoking and laughing, waiting for the rats to run, the quivering dogs on the edge of the group, suddenly jumping for the rat in the dust and the loose corn, gripping it by the neck and shaking the body to death, while the men joked and rolled another.

I loved the roughness of that world, the thorns and elders pushed up against the side of the buildings, the way that tractors would be left parked at loose and unconsidered angles by the garages, the nettles behind the pig shed, the stacks of logs in from the wood, waiting to be sawn in the saw shed next to the piggery, the sense of unregulated space and the freedom that came with that. This was not somewhere that was made for show, but had evolved this way because of what it did. All parts of the wider Weald that I was coming to know on my bicycle—the streams and the wood, the huge beech trees whose outer tips would come down so near to the wood floor that you could climb onto them and walk all the way up to the main trunk, the variety, multifariousness, and vitality of this world on my doorstep—all of that was at the root of what seemed good here.

Summer 1965: *The southern end of the front range, just after it had been converted from two cottages into a family house.*

In the middle of it all was the house and garden, where we lived. Sissinghurst had reached its apogee in the sixteenth century when an ambitious young man had built a giant, multi-courtyarded palace in which he could entertain Queen Elizabeth. That great building had fallen apart over the following centuries so that by 1930, when my grandmother, Vita Sackville-West, bought it, only fragments remained. The broken romanticism of its condition was one of the things that drew her here. She and her husband, Harold Nicolson, had slept in the only remaining part of the main courtyard, a fragment called the South Cottage. She had worked in the great Elizabethan Tower, their dining room and kitchen was in a small Elizabethan banqueting house on the northern edge of the garden, known as the Priest's House, while their (largely unused) library-cum-sitting-room, called the Big Room, was made in the old stables, part of a long front range. Their sons' rooms were on the floor above it. The southern end of that range was divided into two dwellings, one for Mrs. Staples, the cook, the other for the chauffeur-handyman, Jack Copper.

In the early 1960s, after Vita had died and my father moved us back here from London, my parents converted those two dwellings into a single-family house, and that is where we now lived. Jack Copper and Mrs. Staples had moved to new flats in the other half of that range above the Big Room. In our part, my mother had installed a new, clean pine kitchen, with dark blue Formica surfaces and a big six-burner gas stove in the center of it. Mousse-molds in the shape of curved fish hung from the wooden ends of the shelves, and there she cooked warm and delicious food, enormous cartwheels of mushroom quiche, sole in creamy sauces, giant pieces of roast beef, and roast potatoes that she fried to make crisp. One summer, when some people we hardly knew came to lunch, they said to her how delicious peas were when they came straight out of the garden. She and I knew they were frozen, Birds Eye, from the village shop. I had opened the bag earlier for her and poured them rattling into the pan. She thanked our stranger guests, agreed with them, and then looked at me and smiled. I see the smile now, her crinkled laughing eyes, our precious secrecy.

That dining room was lit with silver sconces that Vita had brought from Knole, the great Sackville house in which she had grown up, twenty-five miles from Sissinghurst but still in the Weald. The sconces were fixed to the umber hessian of the walls, and between them hung a large portrait of a Sackville ancestor, the puritan first earl of Dorset, who had been chosen by Queen Elizabeth to give Mary Queen of Scots the news of her impending execution. His rheumy, pink-edged eyes followed me around the room. Beside him were two pictures by John Piper—of Knole in a rainstorm, and a snake strangling a horse, somehow made out of sand. There was a large carved chest, inlaid with mother-of-pearl, which I think may have been Spanish, to hold the glasses, and one or two odd framed things: a drawing on a menu from a London restaurant in 1919, which was Edwin Lutyens's first sketch of the Cenotaph, made for Vita over lunch; a poem of Verlaine's written in high calligraphy on vellum, *"Je suis venu, calme orphelin,"* an offering to Vita from one of her lovers;

June 1962: *Juliet, Philippa, me, Nigel, and Harold Nicolson, in the garden at Sissinghurst in the days after Vita's death.*

and a battered medieval wooden Spanish saint called Barbara, Harold's first present to her when first in love. The place was full of memorabilia, fragments salvaged from earlier lives.

For all that, there was no heaviness about it, nor any atmosphere of gloom or ancestor worship. The very opposite: noisy, talky, warm, engaged, alive, nothing formal. I remember as a boy sitting at the long oak table, my back to the frightening earl, on the tall 1890s faux-Jacobean chairs, with flat wine-red velvet cushions on the cane seats, my father at one end, my mother at the other, my two sisters, our nanny Shirley Punnett and I along the sides, feeling in one of those rare moments when, however fleetingly, you imagine you see your life as it is, in its present form, exactly how it is, with all its parts combining and colluding, that here, at this table, with these people, in this house, with the farm beyond it and beyond that the woods and lanes of Kent—the onion skins of my world—I was happy and even blessed that no one could properly ask for anything that I had not been given.

Summer 1967: *Nigel and Harold Nicolson.*

Across the other side of the garden, in the South Cottage, my grandfather lived alone, or with the series of young male nurses who looked after him. He had lived there ever since he and Vita had come to live at Sissinghurst in 1932. By the mid-1960s, when he was almost eighty, he was in a sad and pitiable state, broken by a series of strokes and by his grief after Vita's death in 1962. I remember nothing of her. Or what I do remember has been overlaid by books, films, and photographs, so that I can no longer distinguish what I remember from what I know. Of him, I knew only his fragility, his canes, his slow, shuffling progress down the garden paths, his weeping silently as he sat at the end of the lunch table, his gobbling of his food so that he had finished before my mother sat down, his strange clothes, left over from an earlier age— huge white or cream summer trousers with turn-ups, the broad-brimmed hats he always wore, plimsolls looking too small below those trousers, always a tie, however ragged. When he looked at us, it was with an un-bridgeable distance in his eyes, as if we were scarcely there. In private and occasionally, he had moments of lucidity, particularly with my mother, in which he told her how much he hated the humiliations of his condition, how much he wanted to die, how much he missed Vita. With us, though, he seemed to be looking through a screen.

Although the garden had been open to the public since 1938, it wasn't treated with the sense of exquisite preciousness it is today. My friends and I used to bike around it and invent racetracks through it. The start was at the front of the house, between the nineteenth-century bronze urns and the floppy arms of the old rosemary bushes: down through the medieval gateway into the Upper Courtyard, sharp right in front of the pink brick Elizabethan Tower swathed in clematis, across the lawn and through the narrow gateway into the Rose Garden—a terrifyingly spiny acanthus bush on the corner there—a zigzag through the alliums and the mounds of old roses before hitting the fast-est of all straights through the Lime Walk and under the branching hazels of the Nuttery, where I would finally skid to a halt outside the Herb Garden. The whole thing, which is slightly downhill, could be done in just under a minute. If you had left the gate open there, you could cut through it, along the far side of the moat, up the tail end of the Bettenham track, and back to the front of the house to complete the lap: three minutes if you were on form.

There were no exclusions. Our dog, Rip, a terrier, chased cats down the Yew Walk and through the Rose Garden. In the evenings my father used to stand on the lawns with a tennis racket and hit a ball as high as he could, sixty, eighty, one hundred feet in the air, and ask one or another of us to catch it as it came down, stinging our fingers or smacking our palms, all for increasing double-or-quits money, starting with sixpence, going up sometimes to the heights of thirty-two shillings, sixty-four shillings, before crashing to zero when you dropped one. We did three-legged races from one end of the courtyards to another. And it wasn't only us: children from the village used to come and play hide-and-seek in the garden. All the gates were always open. There was scarcely a lock on the place. I had a friend, Simon Medhurst, the son of a skilled mechanic and blacksmith who lived in a cottage on the farm, and together we used to make bases for ourselves in the attics of the long range and in the ratty barns. One day we found a pink cardboard box, filled with lead knights and their horses, both men and horses armored, and plumes on their heads. They had been Vita's toys from the 1890s. Simon, his sister Alison, Juliet, and I played in the hay barns, making terrifying tunnels through the bales, filled with the threat of collapse and suffocation. There was a frighteningly dark air-raid shelter in the orchard where we all played naughty games of show and tell. More politely and more publicly we had a gypsy caravan where Juliet played at tea parties for our parents and their friends. Or we used to stand all morning in the fruit cage, eating the red and green gooseberries from the bushes and pulling the raspberries from the canes. Above the piggery, Simon and I made a den that no one guessed was there. We dragged chairs up the ladder and made a table from boxes. From there, through the warped gaps in the weatherboarding, we could spy on the world outside.

1996: *Tug-of-war in the orchard.*

All of this looks in retrospect as if it might have been a dream of happiness and integration. It wasn't entirely. Inside this beautiful outer shell was a pool of unhappiness. Harold's grief was explicit, but at least that was a symptom of his love for Vita. Between my own parents there was no longer any love. My father no longer slept in the same room as my mother. Very occasionally, their mutual frustrations burst out into the open. I remember one evening at the table in the kitchen, with all of us, as well as my nanny Shirley Punnett, who had been born in the village, sitting around the scrubbed deal, when the two of them began to shout at each other, from one end of the room to the other, a terrifying, exchanging, shouting barrage in the air above us, as if shells were exploding inside the room, and we ran away upstairs to our own rooms in tears. At another time my mother threw precious plates the length of that table, beautiful nineteenth-century plates on which early balloons were painted—they had belonged to Vita—while my father stood there fielding them as if at cricket.

She couldn't bear to be alone with him, and, inevitably, another man fell in love with her. She was sad, beautiful, in her late thirties, and looking for someone who would give her a warmer and more comfortable life than the distant, unsexual, and reproachful supervision that was all my father could offer. She left in April 1969, when I was twelve, and went to live in a flat in London while my father continued to live alone at Sissinghurst.

The warmth left Sissinghurst that day. The warmth left with her. The kitchen there never smelled good or right again. It became cold and inert. My father replaced the old double gas stove with a cheap upright electric thing and had the gap filled in with the wrong-colored Formica. The house was never warm again. My father shrank into a feeling of hopelessness and despair. He heated the room he worked in with an electric blower, and the room with a television at the far end of the house with another. The rest of the house remained fridge cold. The cold clung in the walls. Cold seemed to hang behind the curtains and seep up from the floor. If the heating was ever turned on, it would take days for the warmth to penetrate the depths of the house. Getting into bed was like getting into a sea.

My mother had removed some furniture and my father rearranged what was left to fill in the gaps. He made himself instant meals and boil-in-the-bag kippers. Entire weeks went by in which he ate nothing but bananas and cream, occasionally relieved with a Findus fish pie. If any-one came to lunch, he would get the caterers in. One Christmas, when I was there with him alone, as I had asked to be, we exchanged our pres-ents at breakfast and he went up to his room to work. I spent the morn-ing picking books from the shelves and reading a page or two before returning them to their places. At lunch we had half a pound of sausages each and half each of a side of smoked salmon someone had given him for Christmas. Then we watched television and scarcely spoke. A few years later, when my sisters all came to warm up another Christmas, he went to bed on Christmas Eve and stayed there until we left a week later, his meals being brought to him on trays and a few muffled remarks passed through the door. He could not live with the reality of human engage-ment. It was as if his need for love, real enough, had never been quite unlocked. I did not know it at the time, but he felt he had failed. Any confidence he had once enjoyed now drained out of him.

He worked in the meanest and pokiest room in the house, with no view from the windows, using a varnished modern table from a shop in Tunbridge Wells, sitting on an old and dirty chair. He rarely turned the hot water on. Was it somehow gratifying to combine this private despair with his charming life outside? I doubt it. His repeated nightmare, when he was about eleven, was standing on the stage at school while the audi-ence and the rest of the cast waited for him to speak his lines, but no words came and he was left standing there, his mouth silently opening and closing as if he were a fish.

Just at this moment, in June 1976, Jim Lees-Milne wrote about him in his diary, and in what Jim wrote I suddenly see my father not in the clawing, anxious way that children attempt to understand their parents, but from the outside, and through the eyes of an acute and informed observer. "What an odd man Nigel is," Lees-Milne wrote:

> Affectionate, fair, honourable, just, dutiful, hardworking, a first-class writer, an exemplary parent, an aesthete, exceedingly clever yet modest. At the same time, is he quite human? He speaks didactically, in a precise, academic manner. He is a cold man who wants to be warm, and cannot be. He has humour and understanding, being totally without prejudices. Discusses his parents' love lives as though they were strangers. Asked me whether Harold picked up young men of the working classes. No, I was able to tell him. Asked me if I had an affair with Harold. Yes, I replied, but he did not fall in love with me for longer than three months. Nigel told me he was in love with James [Pope-Hennessy] at the same time as his father was and had an affair with him. I know more about this incident than he thinks. For Jamesey told me he was in love with Nigel and used to lie with him without touching. That has always been Nigel's failing, the inability to make close contact. I expect he regrets it in middle age.

That is not the sort of thing anyone tells their teenage children, and so my sisters and I orbited around the sad and central absence of our father, his regret-filled cold, without ever quite seeing it for what it was, and all of us saddened and angered by it in our turn.

More than anyone I have ever known, he came to polarize the good and the bad in his life: social, warm, delighted, graceful, generous, successful, and hospitable summer openness; solitary, unseen, parsimonious, gloom-ridden, cold, unwelcoming winter despair. If we came to stay, he would long for us to leave. I said to him once that he treated his books and everything he wrote in the way that most people treated their children, with endless, careful nurture; and his children in the way most people would treat a book—look into it, see what it has to say, and put it back on the shelf. Sometimes, he seemed like the enemy. In his files, he kept the letter from the headmaster of my boarding school, saying that I was the most neglected boy the school had ever had. Did he not realize that boys needed visiting from time to time?

He certainly wrote, wonderful letters, which made me cry with longing for home. Only many years later would I come to distrust them, and through them everything about our family's word obsession. Sissinghurst floats on a sea of words. Shelf after shelf in our house was filled with the millions of words a family of writers has produced over three or four generations. Filing cabinets stood around in our corridors and our landings of my grandfather's letters to my father and to his brother Ben, my father's and Ben's letters to their father, my father's letters to me and to my sisters, and all of ours to him. There were hundreds of my father's letters to my mother, if few from her to him, not to speak of the thousands of letters from Harold to Vita and her to him. Harold's diaries and my father's diaries occupied complete cabinets of their own. Yards of shelf were filled with the books they had all written. Tin boxes stood stacked in the corner full of Vita's letters to her mother and her mother's in return. And so there was another landscape here, written and rewritten, sheet after sheet, a whispering gallery of family meanings, lasting more than a century, from my great-grandparents to us, a layered tissue of communication. You could make a mattress of those papers, lie back on it, and feel the past seeping up into your flesh like a kind of damp.

But for all the volume, all the drawers and files, there seemed to be something lacking. So much was written but so little seemed to have been said. If I think of those filing cabinets standing there in the corridors, what I see is a world that is said to be private and intimate but is in fact colored with performance and display, a show of bravado and communication laid over the anxiety and apprehension underneath. How much of it was real? Was this world of written intimacy and posted emotion, of long-distance paternal and filial love, in fact a simulacrum of the real thing? A substitute for it? Nicolson closeness had been a written performance for a hundred years. And that unbroken fluency in the written word made me think that it concealed some lack. If closeness were the reality, would it need to be so often declared?

My father's social life consisted not of a steady stream of friends and visitors but bursts of smart sociability in the summer, what he called The Season. I remember one lunch party he held at which everyone had a title. I looked at it all in the unworldly, unforgiving way of adolescence and as I remember it now I can feel the chill of my own regard. Without pause, for what seemed like weeks at a time, they would discuss the Bloomsbury Group. I deliberately learned nothing about it. There were waitresses and cooks, bottles of Riesling, conversational sallies. In each of the guests' bedrooms my father would provide short, semi-complimentary resumés of the other guests. Only once, thankfully, did he put the wrong list in the wrong room so that one man found himself described as "past his best," another as "patronizing." I looked at my father and thought he was living each day for the account he could write of it the following morning in his diary. After that summer show, he retreated to boil-in-the-bag TV dinners, a sense of diminution and failure. This polarized spectacle, the deep disconnection in him, troubled me then as it does now. I remember accusing him once of "dishonesty"—the only word I could bring to address this troubled core of unhappiness—and he of course asked me, cold, angry, and forensic, for examples, of which, in fear, I could provide none.

As a teenager, I remained both devoted to him and angry for what I thought of as his selfishness, his hiding of the truth, his weakness, his lack of practical love, the theatricality of his life, the way in which he would do little or nothing for us and demonstrate so much vivacity, charm, and engagement to those people who hardly knew him and who can have meant little to him. His love of America was the encapsulation of all that: visit after visit, in which he would act "Nigel Nicolson" in front of adoring audiences to whom the edited version could be presented, before returning to the cold of Sissinghurst, to be that other, self-despising person, living, as he put in his private memoir written in 1985, in "the morass of self-reproach I feel."

In that memoir, written when he was sixty-eight, he summed himself up:

> The two great deficiencies in my make-up are lack of judgement, and an incapacity to feel deeply, in anger or in love. A mushiness of temperament, a short-cut mind, indolence, no power to execute, a copy-cat mind, poverty of intellect and spirit, constantly wishing myself more rich in scope, self indulgent, and selfish were it not that I take pains not to appear so, my generosity fake, my gentleness an excuse for lack of vigour. It's not a pretty self-portrait.

He was so lonely that he could feel comfortable only with people who scarcely knew him. Anyone who came at all close was, to use the word he used in his own memoir, "menacing." Intimacy itself was menacing.

He and I were always different. I liked roughness and incompleteness, the wrinkled suggestion of things, Romanticism, the seventeenth century, and authenticity. He liked Palladianism and neatness, the Augustan vision, Chippendale not oak, Jane Austen not Shakespeare, tidiness and the effective display. He couldn't contemplate the idea of religion or psychology; he developed an overt distaste for sex or even any talk of it. I played Bob Dylan loud on the record player but he was unable to listen to music, thinking instead that he should read a book about the workings of the orchestra. He once said to me that if anyone was ever moved by music, it was a symptom of sentimentality.

All he wanted was clarification and tidiness. He was in many ways disgusted by mess and increasingly fearful of the anarchic or the spontaneous. But it is one of the consolations of age that the anger and incomprehension of the adolescent can turn to sympathy and love. I feel toward him now as a father might feel toward a son who seems curiously stuck in his relation to the world, who has not let himself emerge, who has not in some ways let himself *be*, to be the immediate creation of flesh and appetite he, at least in part, might have discovered. It is as if my father spent his life not existing but making himself up, endlessly fashioning a papier-mâché skin to cover the hollow he both knew and dreaded beneath it.

In his later years he cleared, ordered, and sorted Sissinghurst. Everything found its place. No letter was written without a copy being kept, none received without being filed. He burned a great deal of the lumber in the attics. All our childhood toys were thrown away. I didn't see any of this for what it was at the time. I was away at school, university, and work. I didn't realize that this process of clearing up, of cleaning, sorting, and clarifying, not only represented my father's attempt in the outer world to cure the sense of worthlessness and dirtiness within him, it also coincided with some kind of ending of the world I had known as a boy.

In June 1962, when I was four, a week after Vita died, I sat with my father and grandfather on the Lutyens bench in the garden. A quarter of a century later we did it again, this time one chair up, with my eldest son, Tom, who was two, in the newcomer's seat.

Of course, other factors were in play. The landscape historian Oliver Rackham has called the central decades of the twentieth century "the locust years." It was the period when a hungry and powerful simplicity, a rationalist clearing away of the mess, was imposed on the world, when *logos* was substituted for *mythos*, the rational fact for the imaginative idea, something rather blank and reasonable for the complex and wavering story. In the outer world, the demands of modern agricultural systems meant that the same simplifying, tidying up, and "making efficient" was occurring across the entire farmed landscape of England. Mixed farms were giving way to more profitable monocultural systems.

Sissinghurst had been open to the public since the late 1930s, and for us the visitors had always been as much part of the place as customers in a shop. A Sissinghurst without visitors would have felt odd and incomplete, as if a play were being performed to an empty house. But in the 1960s and '70s, as Sissinghurst became more famous, the ever-growing numbers of visitors had to be accommodated in new ways. So the hops went, as their market collapsed, and the hop gardens were taken out. The oast houses went silent, to become first a tea room and then an exhibition space. The black tin hop pickers' sheds, whose pale, light blue interiors were like the miniature parlors of London houses, were demolished. The orchards were grubbed up and grants were given to bring that about. I still remember the lopped branches of the trees lying on the autumn grass and the stubs of the trunks standing there in their orderly rows like an abandoned cemetery. The cattle went and then the farmhands. The tractors went: there was no more of that familiar open-throttle chucking of the tractor through the gap between the pig shed and the garden fence. Then the pigs went and their place became a series of carports of which my father was particularly proud. The Jacob sheep's foot rot became worse than ever and they went. The chickens went. The hay was no longer stored in the brick barn and the old Dutch barn outside it was demolished. The woodshed and the pig shed became a shop. The old granary, where the wood of the partitions was worn by the heavy usage of filled sacks, men, and labor over three hundred years, so that the wood inside looked as if it had come from the groynes on a beach: all of that was taken out and converted into part of the Granary Restaurant.

Jack Copper died, his garage was taken down, and a smooth mown piece of grass with elegant parkland trees replaced it as though a slice of an American campus had taken up residence in the farmyard. My father had the rough, shedlike buildings removed from around the perfect arch of the sixteenth-century barn. The thorn trees and most of the elders that grew next to the oasts were removed, so that their uninterrupted forms could be seen clearly, out and in the open. The cart shed became a ticket office, the dairy and bullpen a coffee shop and plant shop. The stony track was tarred and smoothed. Neatness, efficiency, modern systems, and a certain absence and emptiness replaced what had been the lifeblood of a lived place.

No longer was any dung carried out to any field. Dung in fact entirely disappeared from Sissinghurst. No produce from the fields returned to any of the buildings. No animals lived here. No one worked on the farm full-time. "I look at this farm now," Mary Stearns, James's mother, said to me one day, "think what it once was, and almost weep." The old veins and arteries of the place, the routes going out into the land from the cluster of buildings at its heart, were not used anymore except for ladies taking their dogs for a walk. Only the widened busy arterial lane that is Sissinghurst's umbilicus to the outside world remained an active, living route. Along it came the hundreds of thousands of visitors, all supplies, all the food for the restaurant, and all the oil for the central heating. Back along it, all the visitors left and all the rubbish with them.

I scarcely saw this change for what it was, but that is how the real losses occur: invisibly, cumulatively, in a way one cannot grasp or measure. Only afterward you see that the snow has melted, that autumn has somehow become winter, that the evening or the past is over.

1965: *Sissinghurst, east front of south range.*

When my father was ill in 2004, we came back to live at Sissinghurst. When I was a teenager, I had left for university and then lived in
London and other places. Since 1994 my wife, Sarah, and I had been
living, with our two daughters, on a small farm about twenty-five minutes away, just over the county border in Sussex. Now my father, who
was eighty-seven, was fading, but outside Sissinghurst was throbbing
with its new life. It had become one of the most successful "visitor attractions" in the southeast of England (180,000 visitors a year, turning
over £2 million), and in doing that had slowly and invisibly lost its soul.
Remembering what had been here, I came to realize what had gone: the
sense that the landscape around the house and garden was itself a rich
and living organism. By 2004, all that had been rubbed away. An efficiently driven tourist business, with an exquisite garden at its center,
was now set in the frame of a rather toughened and empty landscape. It
sometimes seemed as if Sissinghurst had become something like a
Titian in a car park.

I walked a lot around Sissinghurst, its woods and fields. Sometimes it filled me with despair. It seemed as if the country was over. It had become a bogus version of itself: thin city, tied together by cars. Get up in the morning at Sissinghurst and you heard the pulse of rural England: not wonderful, variegated birdsong, but traffic—the seamless, unitonal, flat, and flattening noise of tires on tarmac. This ubiquitous presence of traffic in the morning was for me a sudden and terrible measure of what had happened in the twenty-five years I had been away. The traffic laid a lid of sound on everything else. Sissinghurst on those exquisite mornings would be beautiful only if you were deaf.

As I took the dogs for a walk in the wood, the mist lay along the stream in the valley, threading itself in and out between the alders that grow there in a woody marsh. The early sun was pouring honey on the trees and over the fields of the Weald beyond them. Between them, just appearing over the wooded shaws, the tile-hung farmhouses and the white cowls of the oast houses looked, as my father always used to say, as if nothing had happened here since the first maps were made at the end of the eighteenth century. The dogs sniffed for nothing in the grasses. But behind and over it all, the traffic roared, and the traffic was the new reality.

The sound of traffic is the great eroder, the dominant signal that although, in some aesthetic way, little may have changed, in reality everything has. The planning system might have guaranteed that farmers have not sold off garden-sized plots for bungalows. No motorway has been cut through here. But that noise means the old meanings have gone. Was I sentimentalizing this? Was it ever different? I feel sure it was. I can remember hearing, as a specific instance, the sound of motorcycles burning up the road that runs along the ridge above the wood, like a slice cut through the air. That can only mean that the air itself was silent, or near silent. Now it was filled with this aural otherness, a thick substance of the not-here laid all over the here, like a heavy replastering of the walls in an old room you have always loved.

There was nothing now to be done about that. Nevertheless, I knew in my heart that to look across this landscape now was to see something that was not as it should be. The house and garden were no longer connected to a working landscape. There were no animals here, no farmer who considered this farm his own, no farm building used for farm purposes, no sense that this place was generating its own meaning or its own energies. The fields were inert, with no movement or life in them.

And so, on these morning walks, while my father lay in bed, asking about the garden, the flowers, I could see only a kind of voltage gap: between everything I had emotionally invested in this place, inadvertently or not, and the lifeless collection of fields and buildings on which my eyes fell. It looked like façadism to me, an eviscerated pretense, not really a farm anymore, scarcely even a place anymore: just a beautifully maintained garden dropped between a café and a shop, with some fields somewhere in the background. Is there any atmosphere sadder than an empty, dead barn? Or a field that used to glow with health now simply the sterile medium in which highly chemicalized and industrialized crops could be produced? Christopher Lloyd used to say that there was nothing sadder than a garden path that was not used. But here I saw something sadder still: something which for perhaps forty or fifty generations had been fully alive, now maintained in a condition of stilled perfection. There was no longer any relation of life to place.

THE AFTERNOON OF THE DAY MY FATHER DIED, late in September 2004, I went up to a hill on the edge of the land that surrounds and belongs to Sissinghurst, and for the first time in ten years, and for the only time since, smoked some cigarettes. They were delicious. The burnt matches smelled sweet and woody in the sunshine and the smoke filled my throat and lungs like a drug. It was settling, being there and doing that. I smoked and looked, picking the tobacco from my lips, as nothing much happened in the five hundred acres of wood and farm in front of me, the trees dark blue, the stubble pale with age, a kestrel hanging and then falling into a long curving cruise above the grasses on the edge of the fields.

2000: *Nigel Nicolson in the Bishops' Gate outside the White Garden at Sissinghurst.*

The top of that hill, only half a mile away from the house and garden that five million people have visited in the last thirty or forty years, is almost private. From there a track drops down the field to the Hammer Brook and then across the wheat fields before making its way through a pair of hedges, one old, one new, to the moat, buildings, and lawns of Sissinghurst itself. From time to time a man and his dog came past. There was a woman on a gray horse. And a polite couple in green anoraks. A wind from the northwest was blowing across us all, as it would for the next few days, and the flag on the Tower, at half-mast, stood out like a noticeboard of my father's death. The kestrel, now over the alders by the stream, hung and flickered, that steady eye, slid away ten or twenty yards, and hung again. Pigeons flustered out of the big wood to the south and flogged their way across the open ground.

Death itself is more than welcome after the strain of dying, and the air that afternoon felt light and heady, as if a clamp had been released. I looked across the fields and felt I could breathe at last, not because my father had died—not at all: I had come to love him—but because the many months of his lying in bed, gradually thinning under his bed-clothes, the sheets becoming tents across his bones, as he made inordinate efforts to be polite for his visitors, even for us his children, leaving him slumped and exhausted afterward, alone with the humiliations of age, the shame you could see every day in his eyes—at last all of that was over.

For all the sense of relief, even if you are in your forties, the death of a father leaves a feeling of orphanage in its wake. A fixed point in the landscape had been removed and the flag flying from the Tower, and extraordinarily bright in the sunshine, was all that remained. I was suddenly responsible for my life in a way I had never been before. I was dislocated, both free and loose, as if a limb, the limb of my own life, had come out of its socket.

When he died, early that morning, very calmly, his nurse, my two sisters, Sarah, and I were all with him and it was, in the end, the steadi-

est and gentlest of moments. It felt simply, in the quietness of his breath-
ing having stopped, as if the race was over. Only the week before,
typically of him, he had given me the *Oxford Book of Death* to read. He
had reviewed it when it came out in the 1980s—slightly offended that
the literary editor of the *Spectator* had considered him a suitably aged
candidate to be its reviewer—and had quoted in the review Henry
James's words as he felt death approaching: "Ah," the novelist had mur-
mured, "the distinguished thing." That is what it felt like the morning
of my father's death.

My elder sister Juliet said we should pick some flowers for him: three
of the late "Iceberg" roses from the White Garden, their second flush of
the year. We cut them with scissors and put them on his chest as he lay
in his narrow, single bed, with the nineteenth-century drawings of Ath-
ens given him by his mother when he was a boy on the wall beside him,
a photograph of his brother Ben on the bookshelf, next to a jacket of a
new edition of his father's diaries, the window open and the cold September sun coming past the magnolia outside. The doctor arrived and
then the undertakers. They carried his body downstairs on a stretcher
from which a set of wheels could come down, turning it into a trolley.
They wheeled him along the stone path in the Upper Courtyard and
out through the entrance arch. They had brought a blanket and put it
over his body and face, but you could see the outline of a person beneath it. The hearse—not a hearse but a white Volvo—was parked by
the entrance. It was a Thursday and the garden was closed, as it usually
is in the middle of the week, with little chains strung between posts. As
I was unhooking them to allow the undertakers to put him in the car,
an Italian came up to me, tall, a little agitated. "Is the garden closed?"
Yes, I am afraid it is today. "But we have come from Italy." Yes, I'm sorry,
it is always closed on Wednesday and Thursday. "Why is it closed today?" Because it needs a rest every now and then.

The undertakers had opened the trunk of the car and were maneuvering my father into it. "But we have come from Milan. Could we not

just for a few minutes . . . ?" His body was in and the trunk lid down. The Italian seemed not to have noticed what was happening. I am so sorry, I said, there are one or two things going on here today. "Just ten minutes?" No, I'm sorry, no. The undertakers got into their car, saying they would be in touch later, and drove quite slowly away. "Five minutes?" asked the Italian, now with his wife smiling kindly beside him.

No, I said, not today.

I thought about my father as I looked at Sissinghurst. All I could feel then was gratitude for his love and affection, for the way, out of his own fragility, he had loved us. Fathers inevitably forget the most important moments in their relationships with their children. There were many, but I remembered one in particular. I talked to him about it one day when he was ill in bed, and of course he had forgotten. I was small. I must have been about seven. We were at home, looking out at the grass on one of the lawns at Sissinghurst where a mulberry tree used to grow. Gordon Farris, the gardener, was hoeing the beds under the lime trees, and my father described to me the difference between Gordon's work and the work of what he then used to call a "city slicker," and the contrary difference in what they earned, and their status in the world because of it. In that tiny parable was bundled up an entire universe of liberal political and social ideas, a kind of moral baseline, a yardstick against which the acreages of life could be measured. There were many other things—more than he knew: the importance of love and work, of treating people properly, of not giving up, not cheating, of friendship, efficiency, and honesty; of the love of nature and the landscape; of buildings, history, and archaeology; and above all, as the defining frame for all these things, a love of and attachment to Sissinghurst.

I was thinking of this, this gift of a place, with all that word means, as I sat and smoked that long afternoon, looking across a piece of England, of Kent, the Kentish Weald, which I knew better than anywhere on earth. I listened to the traffic booming on the road to the south and looked at the bobbled roof of the woods, on which the sun was just laying its coat of afternoon light, the scoop of hedged fields between them, the shadows of the trees drawn out across the stubble, almost from one hedge to another, the dust lying in pools on the track at my feet. Was Sissinghurst, this picture of rooted and inherited stability, to be the frame for the remaining half of my life? That afternoon I thought so, and felt its arms closing around me.

I went down to the Hammer Brook. It was a quiet and windless afternoon. The stream, at the end of summer, was low and the feet of the alders exposed, but here and there along its length, over some of its darkest pools, so deep that there is no telling where the bottom lies, the big old oaks were standing on the banks and stretching their arms out across the river to the other side. One by one, quite regularly, every now and then, the acorns fell from the trees into the river, a slow, intermittent dropping, occasionally hitting a branch on the way down and ricocheting through the tree, but more often a steady, damp, percussive music: a plumlike plop, a silence, and then another, *glop*. The acorns didn't float, but sank into the depths of the pool to join the piky darkness of the riverbed.

When there was a gust of wind, some of the leaves came floating and zigzagging down to the water, where they landed on the surface as curled boats, to be carried away downstream, or more often caught in the banks, or on the logs and branches that stuck out from them, where in the damp they started to rot, already becoming humus, returning nutrients to the soil from which they had sprung. Meanwhile the soft, slow oak-rain continued, a glugging, swallowing cluck or two each minute, the dropping sound of history and time, mesmeric as I listened to it, the twin and opposite of fish rising, the gulp of a river swallowing seed.

"The past is never behind," John Berger wrote in *Pig Earth*, his great collection of tales and meditations on life in a small village in the French Alps. "It is always to the side. You come down from the forest at dusk and a dog is barking in a hamlet. A century ago in the same spot at the same time of day, a dog, when it heard a man coming down through the forest, was barking, and the interval between the two occasions is no more than a pause in the barking." That is what I have come to understand about the acorns dropping into the Hammer Brook. Nothing is intelligible without the past, not because it is the past but because it is the missing body of the present. The bed of the Hammer Brook has always seemed to me like an ancient place, where without effort one can see and feel what it was like here in the distant past, but Berger's point is more than that. In places like this, at this level, time has not passed at all. The dropping of the acorns is how things are.

I CAME TO REALIZE what I was hungry for, not that afternoon, but in the weeks and months that followed. It was to revive a landscape that had been allowed to forget its past. That desire, my attempt to make it a reality, and a belief that it was something that had significance beyond Sissinghurst, is what this book is about. I knew that to understand it I first had to go back to some roots and sources, to the beginnings of this place, to establish some of the foundations, to understand what the historical beginnings of Sissinghurst had been, to discover its hidden meanings. But even as I began to think about them, I understood that the place I remembered, with all its multifarious life, was the last of the great continuities that stretched back from here deep into the past. By chance, just at the moment it was coming under the knife, I had been allowed to see it, before the locust years ate away at its body. In the light of that, those years, the years of "modernity," seemed now to have been an aberration. The lasting fact was the system as it had been. The new sanitized monoculture was a short wrong turning. All I wanted was to rejoin the main path.

How to make these landscapes live again? How to sew back together the very things that modern life seemed to have severed: people and place, good food and good environments, what was done now and what had been done here before? How to reconnect? That was the all-important question: how to reconnect the deeper meaning of the place with the way it existed today. That need for connectedness became the driving motive for me. If I could help steer Sissinghurst toward a richer condition, that would be a form of reclaiming it, of moving it on to another stage in its existence. Sissinghurst had to be restored to a fullness of life, but how to do it? That was the task and the question.

1960s: *View of the farm buildings and the Weald beyond them.*

CHAPTER 2

Inheritance

SISSINGHURST BELONGS TO THE NATIONAL TRUST. In a cabinet on the second-floor landing, my father had left a file for me. All the relevant papers, carefully arranged in chronological order, some of them marked with Post-its, told the story of how and why he had given Sissinghurst to the Trust in the 1960s. Soon after he died, and after I had replied to the five hundred condolence letters we had received, I sat at his desk and read through the file. I knew that if I was going to do anything for Sissinghurst I had to understand the relationship with the Trust in detail. Nothing would happen here unless the Trust came to share the ideal.

By June 1962, when Vita died, the Trust had already become a complex organism, well into its middle age. It is a profoundly English institution, in love with the past and with the natural world, polite in its ideals and civilizing in its aims. As David Cannadine has written, it had its beginnings in a period at the end of the nineteenth century when, along with "royal ceremonial, the old school tie, Sherlock Holmes, Gilbert and Sullivan, test match cricket and bacon and eggs," a whole clutch of institutions was established that have survived and have come to define a certain kind of Englishness. The Society for the Protection of Ancient Buildings (1877), the *Dictionary of National Biography* (1885), the Royal Society for the Protection of Birds (1889), and *Country Life* (1897) are all the National Trust's contemporaries. It had begun in 1895 as an entirely private charitable project. The motive behind it was a high-minded, liberal, philanthropic desire to bring the solace of the untouched natural landscapes of England and Wales to the multitudes of Britain's industrial cities. The properties it owned—largely pieces of beautiful landscape—were to be "open air sitting rooms for the poor." After 1918, that liberalism morphed into its conservative cousin, a Stanley Baldwinesque longing for the perfections of a forgotten age. In the late thirties and even more after 1945, that reactionary glow to the Trust deepened once again into the phase that still marks it in the minds of many. With a helping hand from the old Etonian Labour chancellor Hugh Dalton, the Trust was able to acquire a string of country houses and their estates. Dalton's scheme was to encourage large landed families, many of them faced with enormous death duties, to transfer the ownership of their properties to the government, which would then hand them on to the Trust. The value of the properties would be set against the amount of tax that was owed. Many great country houses were in this way saved for the nation. Dalton thought of them, collectively, as a magnificent memorial to the dead of the Second World War. In return for giving their inheritance to the nation, the donor families, as they were called, were allowed and encouraged to remain in the houses that they no longer owned.

Some families, like the Sackvilles at Knole, which was transferred in 1948, were given a two-hundred-year lease. Others were granted the right to stay there forever. It may seem in retrospect like a slightly strange deal to have been struck by the government. Why, if it was accepting these properties instead of tax, should the ex-owners have any rights there at all? The answer lay in the nature and beliefs of the National Trust at the time. Presided over by the spirit of the charming, archconservative, gentry-loving Jim Lees-Milne—one of my grandfather's most devoted lovers—the Trust was an elite oasis in which a version of old

England was able to survive. It was, until the mid-1960s, a club for aesthetically inclined grandees. Its all-important Historic Buildings Committee was made up almost entirely of peers. When a man called John Smith was proposed as a member, the chairman, Viscount Esher, said, "I suppose it is a good thing to have a proletarian name on the Committee—anybody know him?" "Yes," said the earl of Euston, "he is my brother-in-law." This was the organization that persuaded the government that donor families should be allowed to stay put, some forever.

The curators and designers who formed a (largely gay) coterie at the center referred to the muddy-booted agents and land managers in the regions as the "mangel-wurzels." There was little concern for the realities and subtleties of landscape ecology. What mattered was the elegant view and the general sense that here at least the inroads of the vulgarizing masses had been resisted. Enormous liberties were taken not only with historic interiors (where the favored decorator, John Fowler, devised a kind of all-purpose National Trusty loveliness) but with historic gardens (Hidcote had its authentically vulgar cherry trees removed) and important landscapes (the great if battered avenue at Wimpole in Cambridgeshire was needlessly cut down and many of the Trust's ancient woods were planted with conifers). Angry reports by the conservationists springing up in the 1960s regularly condemned the organization for an indifference to the things that really mattered.

The 1960s saw the beginning of a fourth phase: more efficient, less introspective, more commercial, pushing for large-scale membership and large-scale visiting, publishing more, opening up the previously hidden parts of their properties, getting serious about nature conservation. This was just the moment Sissinghurst engaged with the Trust. It had become a classic English organization, riddled with tensions: money-making against high-level aesthetic appreciation; wide-scale access against conserving the fragile and the delicate; purity against populism; a grandee vision against popular need.

Both Vita and Harold had a long relationship with the Trust, serving on its committees and writing its guidebooks, even in Vita's case the guidebook to her beloved Knole after the Trust had taken it over in 1948. Harold had eventually become vice chairman of the governing council. Sissinghurst and the Trust were always in each other's orbit, even if, for Vita in particular, its value was ambivalent. It represented for her both the preservation of what was precious and the very forces of bureaucratization and mediocrity against which the precious needed to be preserved. When in 1954 my father, rather bravely, first mentioned to her that he thought the Trust might be the ideal owners and managers of Sissinghurst, it did not go well. "Never, never, never," she wrote in her diary that evening.

> Au grand jamais, jamais. Never, never, never. Not that hard little plate at my door. Nigel can do what he likes when I am dead, but as long as I live no Nat. Trust or any other foreign body shall have my darling. Over my corpse or my ashes; not otherwise. It is bad enough to have lost my Knole, but they shan't take S/hurst from me. That, at least, is my own. Il ya des choses qu'on ne peut pas supporter. They shan't; they shan't; I won't; they can't make me; I won't; they can't make me. I never would.

About ten days after Vita died in June 1962 my father met the Trust's secretary, Jack Rathbone, "all casual like," for a drink in the Travellers' Club in Pall Mall. Would they be interested in taking Sissinghurst on? Vita's estate was worth about £100,000, on which there was £38,000 of inheritance tax to pay and hardly any cash to pay it with. Harold was chronically in debt and Vita had spent almost everything she had on the garden and buildings. My father's only options were to sell the whole thing, sell everything else he had, or give Sissinghurst to the Trust. Only by giving it to them could he guarantee that his parents' life work, far more lasting than anything either of them had written, would have a chance of surviving. Rathbone agreed to a visit.

He and Sir George Taylor, the head of Kew, came down by train on July 5, 1962. My father was with them, at his most Tory MP charming. He gave them copies of the Sissinghurst accounts. It all looked neat, the books balancing satisfactorily year on year. Money from the garden visitors, farm rents, timber sales, and the sale of plants just about covered the costs of the six gardeners, the secretary, the chauffeur-handyman, the cook, and Mrs. Honeysett, the daily. Rathbone and Sir George— described by my father in his diary as "a big bluff man, rather like an Australian who has discovered an unknown gentian in the Andes"— arrived at Staplehurst station in a good mood. There they were met by Jack Copper, the chauffeur-handyman, famous at Sissinghurst for two things: the homemade hand grenades he had prepared during the war in case the Germans arrived, and the cider press he kept at the back of the garage for a swift one whenever any of the gardeners or farmhands felt a thirst coming on, as they did most afternoons. A famous incident involved Vita walking out of the garden and down to the garage, to find George Taylor, one of the gardeners, coming toward her.

"Drunk again, George," Vita said.

"Are you, madam?" George said. "That's funny, so am I."

A companion story, which has lurked for years in the Sissinghurst undergrowth, never mentioned by my father, tells of Vita, after a glass or two of sherry in the Tower, being taken by the gardeners in a wheelbarrow to her bed in the South Cottage.

Here, immediately, was a signal of that other Sissinghurst world: rough around the edges, idiosyncratic, authentically itself, not smoothed or sheened, not tightly controlled but a little improper, alcoholic, not quite respectable. That morning, the grandees from the Trust wanted to see something of the estate, and so my father told Copper to drive round by Bettenham. Leafy lanes, lovely views, everything going very well until Copper pulled over. He had got himself lost in the four miles between Staplehurst and Sissinghurst. I can imagine my father's clearing of the throat. "We'll have to go round by Horse Race." Eventually they arrived, having lost the way again, coming in over the "smooth shorn grass between the orchards" to find the secretary, Ursula Codrington, who had some thwarted dramatic ambitions, coming out of the entrance arch "looking like an Andalusian peasant with a striped apron." She was followed by the two head gardeners, Pam Schwerdt and Sibylle Kreutzberger—both impeccably and utterly English despite their names—who were desperately anxious at the threat of a dead managerial hand being applied to the place they loved. They had been getting ready for a fortnight, sweeping and preening the place so that it looked as perfect as they could make it. Nervous introductions, then the slow walk round: Upper Courtyard grass and the purple border, the Tower lawn with pink and lemon-yellow roses trained against the walls, the Rose Garden, in which the ancient damasks and gallicas were erupting in slow vegetable fountains, the Lime Walk and the Moat Walk, the Herb Garden with its view out to the wood, the Orchard, the White Garden, the stony half-Mediterranean Delos, the greenhouses, the vegetable garden, while the two great men tested the competence of the gardeners at every turn.

Then a pause, and the secretary of the National Trust turned to Nigel and said, "Do you know the thing I like most at Sissinghurst?"

"No," said Nigel, looking anxiously at Pam and Sibylle.

"I just love the fact that it is quite so untidy."

"Untidy?"

"Well, you know, that relaxed look, as if no one has bothered to tidy up."

Nigel rushed them all up the Tower. "The whole Weald was bathed in sunshine," he wrote to my mother in London that evening. "I have never seen it so clear. I pointed out the boundaries of the estate. The clock struck one. It was at that moment I think that the fate of Sissinghurst was decided. It will pass into the hands of the National Trust."

Or so he hoped. Rathbone and Taylor recommended acceptance of Sissinghurst, but only "subject to finance." Their previous acceptance of houses and gardens without thinking hard enough about the money had landed them in trouble. Nigel's first breezy suggestion was to give the house and garden to the Trust, sell most of the farmland to raise an endowment, and keep the nearest fields and woods for himself. To this Rathbone replied that Sissinghurst represented "a very difficult finan-cial problem." In October 1962, he warned Nigel that "this is likely to be a long business." My father wouldn't have that. In December 1962 he was tugging at Rathbone like a terrier. "Don't you think we should take this a stage further. It would be nice if we could have the thing agreed before the opening of the garden in April [1963]." Rathbone: "It may take a little longer than that."

By January 1963, my father had refined his proposal: house and garden to the NT, plus some surrounding farmland, most of the rest sold off to raise cash with which to endow the property with £15,000 and a couple of fields kept for himself. He and "any descendants of mine" would have the right to live there for free. He would act as the Trust's unpaid manager and have the right to be consulted over any decision affecting Sissinghurst. Any income at Sissinghurst would remain at Sissinghurst. Its coffers would never be drained for general National Trust purposes—this profoundly valuable clause made at the suggestion of the National Trust itself.

The proposals were to come up before the NT finance committee that July. They looked at Nigel's figures for income and expenses and reached a set of gloomy verdicts. After Vita's death, they were sure that visitors would fall away. They had no inkling of what would actually happen: that Vita's Sissinghurst, which seemed a little out of date in the early sixties, would come to represent for hundreds of thousands of peo-ple a lost world of romance and beauty. It is as if the Trust in the early sixties was not quite aware of the hunger for the past that would build so powerfully over the next thirty years. Kipling's house at Bateman's in

Sussex, which the Trust had owned since the 1930s, had never been popular with visitors. Why should anyone be interested in the garden of a minor poet, long since unfashionable and "back-number," as Harold had called it? The Trust also thought that the beauty of the garden itself would slowly and inevitably diminish as Vita's inspiration sank into the past. It was, anyway, going to be increasingly expensive to keep the buildings going.

The arrangement with the donor family was that the Trust would pay for virtually everything—building and garden maintenance, wages, farm and estate costs—and would receive all income from visitors and farm rents. The family itself would pay for the decoration and furnishing of the parts of the house it lived in, and for its own domestic costs. But there were problems. The Trust, as a public body charged with looking after its properties "in perpetuity," had standards of maintenance that were higher than a private individual's. Besides, Vita had been underpaying her garden staff, and wages would now have to rise. There had to be allowances made for disasters and contingencies. There were management costs. The Trust had accepted responsibility for Knole without an adequate endowment and now they were suffering an intolerable financial burden there. Their "realistic forecast for the future" at Sissinghurst saw a heavy ongoing annual deficit of £3,625. If the Trust were to take Sissinghurst, Nigel would have to provide an endowment big enough to make up that annual shortfall. On top of that, he would have to pay a market rent for his part of the house if he was not to fall foul of the Inland Revenue. As it stood, there was no way the Trust could accept my father's offer.

Nigel wrote to Ivan Hills, the Trust's area agent:

Your draft budget is appalling. If the logical consequence is that the Trust could not take Sissinghurst without an endowment of something like £90,000 [the amount required to generate £3,625 a year; about £1.5 million in 2008 terms] then very regretfully we would have to abandon the idea, for I haven't anything like that amount of money in the world. I haven't any idea where this amount of money is to come from. Annual repairs, contingencies, £800 a year for a management fee, a gardens advisor. . . . And now you tell me that, in addition to that, I shall be expected to pay a rent. Really I can't do this.

Three-way negotiations between my father, the Trust, and the Treasury dragged on through 1963 and 1964. Nigel remained convinced that the Trust had overestimated costs and underestimated income. He wrote to my mother, "It is difficult to see why they need £3000 more than we have ever spent on it ourselves. 'Oh,' says Jack Rathbone, 'the Tower might fall down.' 'Well,' I say, 'it won't fall down every year.'" Negotiations were opened with other government departments, and by January 1965 the Trust had managed to extract from the Ministry of Works the promise of an annual grant to cover the expected shortfall. With that in their pocket, the Trust decided to accept Sissinghurst if Nigel could provide a £15,000 endowment. He was earning £3,000 a year at the time, but the sale of Bettenham and Brissenden farms could raise the cash.

Rather gallantly, at the same time he had embarked on a new conversion project for turning the southern end of the front range into a single-family house. Neither he nor my mother wanted to spend their lives, as his parents had done, traipsing between bedrooms in the South Cottage, sitting room in the old stables, dining room in the Priest's House, workroom in the Tower, children's rooms in the brewhouse. It was to be one warm, centrally heated, hot-watered house for a single happy family. By 1965, he had spent £17,000 on that, inserting a beautiful new oak staircase, my mother's modern kitchen, a big sitting room, and eight bedrooms into what had been the two cottages occupied by Mrs. Staples and the Coppers. I remember moving in that summer, the physical pleasure of the big new oak doors, my bedroom up in the attic, one dormer window looking out to the poplars at the front, the other to the Tower and the wood, my mother at home in the kitchen, and the dreadful leaving of it that September as I went away for the first time to boarding school in Oxford.

Summer 1965: *The sitting room in the southern end of the front range.*

He loved Sissinghurst more than anything in the world. He adored his father and in a more distant way admired his mother. The remaking of Sissinghurst was the best thing they had done, they had done it together, and its preservation was, for my father, an act of intense filial duty and care. Sissinghurst was them. He could never have let it go or cashed it in and still looked at himself in the mirror in the morning. He needed to preserve Sissinghurst, he wanted for me not to have to sell it, and by the autumn he had become desperate. He offered the Trust everything he owned: all books, pictures, silver, the small islands he owned in Scotland, if only they would take Sissinghurst off his hands.

Sissinghurst is somehow kept going while my resources are running out. Everyone here is gradually losing faith in the deal coming off at all. Meanwhile our finances are very delicately balanced and there are almost no reserves. The weekly wage bill is large for a private house. There is no income from the garden throughout the winter months. I am taxed on the income I get and the rents. I pay interest to the Treasury. All this is draining what little I have left. I shall simply not know what to do if the negotiations are not completed soon.

Faintly, in my memory, looking now at these blurred carbon copies of his letters, I see myself then, aged eight, that Christmas, putting my head around the corner of the door into his workroom, his Anglepoise light down low over the surface of the table, smoke from his cigarette curling up into its beam, a yellow ballpoint in one hand, and the fingers of the other pushing back over his scalp through his hair. Briefly he looks up at me and smiles.

The uncertainty dragged on for the best part of another year. Treasury officials did not respond to letters for months. Civil servants moved jobs and the details of the case were forgotten or pushed to the back. My father's attempts at a viable budget became ever more agonized until, at last, in August 1966, a breakthrough, a very English solution. He realized there were strings to be pulled: he had been at Balliol with Niall MacDermot, the financial secretary to the Treasury. Nigel wrote to him: "My dear Niall." Surely he could get something moving on this? Within a month the juices started to flow and the Treasury accepted the offer of house, garden, and farm. The sale of Bettenham and Brissenden raised quite enough money for an endowment. There was no talk of a rent. Nigel would not have to give the Trust everything he owned. The Ministry of Works would give an annual grant for five years to cover the expected deficit. By Christmas 1966, it was settled. A solution that had seemed inadequate for years now for some reason seemed to be perfectly fine.

On April 6, 1967, the metal plate saying "National Trust Sissinghurst Castle" arrived from the Royal Label Factory. On April 12, my father wrote to the new secretary of the Trust, Jack Boles:

> *My dear Jack,*
>
> *This is just a note of thanks from your newly adopted child. I heard today that everything was completed according to plan and the announcement will be made this afternoon.*
>
> *So ends happily negotiations which have lasted almost five years. I have a real affection for the Trust, deepened by this experience, and to me it will cause no pang when I raise your metal plate this evening at our gate. I feel only gratitude and thankfulness that Sissinghurst will thus be preserved for ever.*

Juliet and I went up with him to the top of the lane that evening to see the new plate on its new oak post, which Jack Copper had set up that afternoon. It meant nothing to me then, but everything to him. He felt, I think, that he had done his duty to this place, that he hadn't wrecked it, or simply disposed of it, or betrayed his inheritance. The National Trust was a resting place, a cradle from which threat could be warded off and change kept at bay. It had come at some emotional cost. That April, my mother wrote to him:

> *It's time you left this place for a while. It's wrong for you to stay here all the time. You become confused and muddled as to how you and I should regard Sissinghurst. Finally, now you've achieved the assurance of its protection, you may have to worry a bit how you care for and protect your family. But away from us all you may be able to consider this rationally.*

A few days later he set off for a four-month tour of Europe, writing a book about great houses of the Western world.

My father had saved Sissinghurst. He had bound together house, garden, and most of the farm in a single quasi-public ownership. By doing that he had made it inviolable and established our own family's presence here forever, at least in theory. And the process of how he did it was at least in part a model for me, forty years and a generation on: engage with the world as it is; keep pushing; don't be put off by the sluggards; keep your sense of humor; don't be afraid to show your teeth now and then, but don't hold grudges; be generous and grateful; always have the goal in mind, but remember too that Sissinghurst isn't everything. He had done it well, with all the qualities required: doggedness in a corner, love of Sissinghurst, acumen, persistence. The National Trust had shown itself too: as a rational operator, prepared to be patient, in for the long term—it was to own Sissinghurst "in perpetuity"—financially cautious, dedicated to an ideal of beauty, not afraid to say no, and not to be swayed by emotion or romance.

I HAD NEVER BEFORE EMBARKED on any enterprise that involved steering a large corporate body into a new direction. I had worked for newspapers, broadcasters, and publishers; I had founded and run with my cousin Robert Sackville-West a small publishing company. But each of those involved making something new and self-contained. This would be different: a change in ideals and practices for something that already felt it was doing fine. The systems at Sissinghurst were heavily dug in and highly evolved. They would have bucketfuls of answers to any proposal I might make. It would be a case of uncorporate man meeting corporate life, and both, inevitably, being changed in the process.

I realized that if I was going to propose something to the Trust I had to know in some detail what had happened on the farm here in the past. In 2005, there was no farmer at Sissinghurst. The land was let out to four separate farmers who had the bulk of their businesses elsewhere.

It was a place that had been cut in four, the landscape equivalent of low-maintenance gardening.

From the 1920s until 1999, the very opposite had been true. A dynasty of outstanding men, with their wives, sons, and daughters, had been the farmers both on Sissinghurst Castle Farm and at Bettenham, its neighbor. Their latest representative, James Stearns, who had the farm until his retirement in 1999, still lived in the big Victorian farmhouse, which he and his wife, Pat, ran as a bed-and-breakfast. I knew that in them was a deep reservoir of understanding about how this place might work as a single integrated farm again. So one morning early in 2005, James walked me round the fields. All the generalized nonsense that people talk about landscape fell away with the farmer's eye, with James's big bass voice and his gentle, half-hesitant, half-adamant air. The engine room of the farm, as he called it, was in the northern half, the big arable fields called Lodge, Large, Frogmead, and Eight Acres. "You could get four and a half tons an acre of wheat off all of them in a good year," he told me, looking at me with his huge bloodhound eyes. Some of Frogmead lay a little frosty, and so "you would need to be careful if you were thinking of putting fruit in there." In other words, don't. The hops did well in Frogmead, but only a madman would consider setting up a hop garden nowadays. The economics of hops were in tatters, destroyed by a combination of lager (which needs no hops) and chemical substitutes, which were said to flavor the beer just as well.

1940s: *The Stearns family at Bettenham.*

The whole of the rest of the farm was, in James's view, rather subsidiary to that northern arable block. He had never been a great man for animals, and all the photographs his mother showed me of him when he was young had him sitting on a tractor, plowing or bringing in the harvest. The belt of grazing around the Castle and garden, the four wet fields, known as the Well Fields, in the far southwestern corner of the farm, and the very rabbity Horse Race and Nine Acres, all varied in his mind from "too small" to "clogged" and merely "rubbish." Only the Park and the Cow Field next to the old dairy survived James's general verdict that the arable engine room was what counted. What was so good about the Park? It made "beautiful blue soft hay," especially at the far end. And the Cow Field? "It's the best bit of dirt on the farm. The cows were always turned out onto it and it would grow anything now. It's wet along the southern edge and up in the northern corner. I think there might be a broken drain there. But the rest of it, you couldn't look for anything better."

I had never heard anyone talk about Sissinghurst like this before. No one here had ever talked to me about dirt as a lovely thing. It was as if James was a voice from the past, from a time that understood the reality of something I only half remembered, a reality beyond the reduced condition of the modern world. I loved talking to him, and I could see he loved talking to me. I don't think anybody had talked to him like this for years.

Even so, I knew this emphasis on heavy arable cropping was not quite the whole picture, or at least it was a picture that had already come down from the high point it had achieved a little earlier under his grandfather. I went to the National Archives in Kew in southwest London. During the war, confidential reports were made to the government about the state of every farm in the country. I looked up the Farm Survey Record made at Sissinghurst and Bettenham on June 4, 1941. The two farms were being run in tandem and the farmer was listed as Captain A. O. Beale, James Stearns's grandfather. Here at last, in all the sterility

1930s: *Threshing the wheat.*

of a ministry form, was the picture I had been looking for, the concentrated meaning of a place complete in itself, quite straightforwardly
listed in the printed boxes and dotted lines of an airmail-thin, sky-blue
government form.

The mixed and variegated fields were laid out in front of me: ninety-
three acres of wheat, seven of barley, eleven of oats, one of rye, five of
mixed grains, and twenty-three acres of beans, into which the animals
could be turned at the end of the year. There were three acres of first
early potatoes and five of maincrop. (These the Beales used to sell to
local schools and individuals, bag by bag.) There was kale, a little rape-
seed, an acre of turnips, and two and a quarter of mangolds or chard.
There were ten and a half acres of hops in Frogmead and forty-six acres
of orchard with grazing below the trees. The fifteen acres of peas were
to go for canning. Fifty acres of meadow were to be made into hay and
one hundred and forty-four acres of grass to be grazed by forty-five head
of cattle and six-hundred-odd sheep, ewes, and lambs. There were
twelve pigs and twenty-seven piglets, one hundred and ten chickens,
four horses, and twenty-one people, men and women, boys and girls,
working here.

It was no fantasy, then: here at one level farther down than James's memories was his grandfather's farm at full stretch at the height of the war. All of it, according to the report, was in a near-perfect condition: rich, busy, and complex, with piped water to the farmhouse, fields, and buildings, all fences, ditches, drains, eight farm cottages, and the farmhouse itself in good repair, with no infestation of rabbits or moles, rats or mice, rooks or wood pigeons, and with no derelict fields. Two twenty-two-horsepower Fordson tractors as well as five fixed engines powered

The front range of Sissinghurst during the war.

the work on the four hundred and fifty acres Captain Beale rented from Vita. Messrs. S. J. Day and L. Holland, who compiled the report, wrote, "This farm is being farmed to full capacity in a most excellent manner. The present arable crops being especially good."

I looked through the neighboring farms. There was no scrimping of criticism there. Captain Beale's neighbors would have been crushed to read the verdicts written on them and their farms: lack of energy, insufficient attention, no good with hedging and ditching, illness, igno-rance, lack of experience and ambition, lack of modern knowledge, "not enough pains being taken with the arable," "I do not think the occupier has much idea of how to manage land," poor plowing techniques, their farms infested with magpies, anthills, charlock, docks, and thistles, their ditches clogged, their fields too small, their drainage hopeless, their houses reliant on wells and without electricity. Almost alone in the en-tire parish, Bettenham and Sissinghurst Castle Farm stood out as a joint model of completeness.

"The Hon Mrs VM Nicolson" filled in her own form, listing her half-acre of maincrop potatoes, six acres of orchard and grass, one acre of vegetables for humans, her three cows, eighteen ewes, forty-two chick-ens, "1 motor mower for lawns (not used yet this year)," and "1 engine to drive circular saw for wood." I knew that engine, still there when I was a boy, connected with a long wobbling belt to the naked saw-wheel that would spin to a blur when Copper started it up with the crank and make its own repeated animal whine as he pushed one log after another past its revolving teeth. Vita could not "give the best estimate you can of the annual rental value" because "much of it is a pleasure garden."

There are moments when you realize that what you had only been sleepwalking toward has suddenly acquired a substance and a material-ity. That is what it felt like at the varnished beech desk in the National Archives, looking at these forms, which I am sure no one had looked at since the 1940s. I do not need to have the fields at Sissinghurst in front of my eyes to see them in every detail, but that morning I saw them as I knew I wanted them to be.

Linda Clifford, James Stearns's sister, gave me something even bet-ter: her grandfather's farm diary for 1954. Here, thirteen years later, in the peak of the 1950s boom, were the same pair of farms still pursuing the same wonderful, variegated, polycultural ends. Captain Beale, now in partnership with Stanley Stearns, still had seven men working for him, not to speak of the thirty or forty hop pickers who came down from London in the autumn and stayed in the sheds beside the Hammer Brook, where their foundations and bits of corrugated-iron roof are still to be found in among the brambles. There was a herd of dairy short-horns at the Castle, and another of Guernseys at Bettenham. There were pigs and sheep, all the same cereals, as well as plums, pears, and two sorts of apples. The breathtaking part of it was the work program for the year. I made an abstract of the year's tasks:

Plowing (Jan. 20; July 23 Tassells; Oct. 4)

Defrosting pipes (Feb. 1)

Littering yards (Feb. 1, 2, 11)

Snow clearing with dung lifts (Feb. 2)

Sawing (Feb. 5)

Shooting foxes (Feb. 8)

Hedging (Feb. 9)

Pruning (Feb. 9, Nov. 5)

Woodcutting (Feb. 9)

Sowing (Peas March 12; Barley March 13; Wheat March 15;
    Clover under barley April 13; Kale July 30 (Bettenham);
    Oats Oct. 6; Wheat in Banky Nov. 3)

Hop dressing (March 15)

Moving poles in hop garden (March 28)

Rolling (April 9, 13)

Harrowing (April 13)

Hop stringing (April 14, May 17, 29, June 1)

Sheep dipping (April 14)

Faggot carting (April 30, May 17)

Weeding (April 30)

Turning out heifers (April 30)

Gang mowing in orchards (May 15, 18, 29, June 1, 5, 22, 24)

Hop earthing up (June 1, 24)

Mowing (Park June 8)

Hoeing (Kale June 22)

Haymaking and baling (June 23, 24, July 7, 8, 9, 12, 13, 15,
    20, 21, 29, August 3, last bale made August 4)

Silage making (Hoppers Hut July 2, August 11; Horse Race
    August 13, 14, 17)

Cutting clover (August 11)

Combining barley (August 11, 13–14)

Apple picking (August 12, September 2, Oct. 4, 27, 28)

Combining oats in Birches (August 14, 15, 16)

Baling straw (August 16, 17, 19, 21)

Cutting peas (in Banky August 16, 17, 18, 21; in Frogmead,
    Hop Garden August 28)

Combining wheat in Large (August 20, 21, 22, 23, 25, 26)

Combining clover in Lodge (August 23)

Hop picking (Sept. 6–30)

Combining barley in 8 acres (Sept. 13–17)

Combining peas (in Hop Garden Sept. 19, 20, 21; Banky
    Sept. 23, 29, Oct. 4–8)

On top of all this was the pharmacopeia of treatments to which
the crops and fields were subject. Although monumental quantities of
farmyard manure were being carted out onto the fields from the cattle's
winter housing, any thought that fifty years ago this was an organic
farm, as I had fondly imagined, soon disappeared under Captain Beale's
busy, often slightly scrawled diary jottings. Chemical imbalances, fertility deficiencies, fungal and pest attacks: the tractors were out almost
daily applying one potion or stimulus after another. Nitrate chalk, potash and superpotash, Epsom salts and "Copper colloidal" for the peas,
metaldehyde on the wheat, slag on the orchards, Arcolin on the kale,
the kale sprayed for flea-beetle, and the full battery of sulfate of ammo-
nia, Pestox, Blitox, sulfur, copper sulfate, and Boclear all applied to the
labor- and capital-intensive hop garden.

All this was clear enough. There had not been a moment when the guillotine had come down. Here was the farm in transition from its old to its modern state. The large workforce, the integration of the dairy herds with the pastures and arable fields, providing their dung and requiring their fodder, was still the old world going at full tilt. Alongside it were all these "artificials," these answers in a bag. By the end of the decade, Stanley Stearns had bought a hop-processing machine that made the forty hop pickers unnecessary. By 1968, the hops, which had caught "wilt," a fungal disease, were no longer worth going in for. The cattle finally went in 1980. Any idea of rotation went with them. There was no longer any need to interrupt the growing of arable crops with a fertility-building clover and grass ley if you could simply apply fertility brought in by a lorry. Artificial fertilizers made mixed farms inefficient. If you could grow four and a half tons an acre of wheat on a field year in, year out, then that was the way to go. Sissinghurst became a mainly arable farm, with some field-scale lettuces and Brussels sprouts grown on the side. It made some money—just—but its 259 acres were too small to compete with the East Anglian cereal barons, let alone America or the Ukraine. The industrial processes that made chemical farming possible had not only removed from this landscape almost everything that I loved about it, by the 1990s, they had also made Sissinghurst unviable as a farm.

Given these economic and technological conditions, was there any way of recovering the enriched landscape? Was Sissinghurst caught in a kind of historical bind? Or was there a route out of this, based not on competing in world markets but by satisfying the modern appetite for "real food"? Could Sissinghurst become, in effect, a retail farm? Could a new version of the high, expert agriculture that Captain Beale, in his tweed jacket and tie, his pipe in one hand, the other in a jacket pocket, had performed so expertly, could that be practiced here again?

CHAPTER *3*

The Idea

I N THE WINTER AFTER MY FATHER'S DEATH I started to feel my way toward a new, or at least a new-old, understanding of how Sissinghurst might be. I wrote to Fiona Reynolds, the director-general of the National Trust, who I knew slightly, to thank her for coming down to his funeral and to float past her a rather public version of the ideas that were on my mind.

There is only one thing at Sissinghurst I would love to see different—which is the farm not producing commodity cereals in a contractorised and heartless way, as it does now, but becoming a model of polycultural richness as it was 40 years ago: hops, fruit and dairy, to all of which it is well suited, and all of which could become the basis of a rampantly successful Sissinghurst brand of jams and beers and cheeses and all the rest of it. You would have to go a long way to find as good a ready-made brand as Sissing-hurst waiting on the shelf. And it would employ people on the place! I am sure I have heard you talk often about a people-rich countryside, labour-intensive and high-value-added agriculture and so on. The country needs it and this could be such a good and profitable working model for that idea. That is a long-term dream of mine, but it is one I feel in my gut you might share.

She replied nicely but uncommittedly. "Long-term" was probably the phrase. Anyway, the idea of the "Sissinghurst brand" is something that would come to seem too thin and wrong. The whole notion of a brand, even if the brand was meant to embody authenticity and richness, contradicted the very qualities it was meant to convey. The idea I had of Sissinghurst was something that was too much to be encapsulated in anything resembling a brand. I wanted to rekindle the sense of this place as a fully working and integrated whole. To do that, we had to sell something from it. We even had to sell the idea of "wholeness." But that didn't mean the brand was the destination. The brand was an instrument, not the goal. I wanted a sense here of overwhelming well-being, which could be interpreted, I suppose, as a kind of brand but could scarcely be achieved if thought of as one. That was the paradox: a brand whose brand identity was its brandlessness.

Perhaps Sissinghurst could be considered a product, and like all products it needed to renew itself, to sew together its old self, its particular qualities, with a new kind of response to an evolving world. And perhaps, now I look back on it, that is what I was engaged in: a rebranding exercise. What, in the most brutal, modern commercial language, was the business here? Heritage horticulture with a lesbian-aristocratic gloss, allied to a tranquillity destination with café and gift shop attached. That was the old proposition. My ideas, equally brutally seen, were to bump that into another market niche by laying over it a holistic real-food agenda that would appeal to the urban middle classes, precisely the kind of moneyed market the National Trust needed to court. I can write that now, three years later; it was certainly not how I was thinking at the time.

Meanwhile, Sarah and I tried to settle into Sissinghurst with our two daughters and my three sons, who were mostly away at school and university. It was a slightly strange experience. The house was overwhelmingly parental: my father's furniture, his books, his files, his pictures, his whole habit of being. I used to catch myself tidying up, not because I minded the mess our family was making but because he would have. Boots in the hall, old cups of coffee, dog beds, last night's dishes: all of this would have summoned from him that particular, half-audible, rather sibilant under-the-breath whistling, usually a tune from My Fair Lady, which was the signal of contained impatience and anxiety. A shift into "Lili Marlene" was not good: major dissatisfaction. So I tidied up to avoid the whistling. And then, terrifyingly, I found myself whistling too. "Why are you whistling under your breath?" my daughter Rosie asked. "Because I like the tune," I said, exactly what my father would have said, and just as untrue.

On top of that, we had to deal with the National Trust, which at times was like having a third, even more supervisory parent. We were undoubtedly a difficult new presence for them. Instead of a single, self-contained, beneficent, and peace-loving octogenarian, they now had on their doorstep a family consisting of two busy, untidy grown-ups, a Land Rover that leaked oil all over the National Trust cream- and caramel-colored tarmac, two daughters with bikes that were leant against yew hedges, three dogs that needed to do what dogs need to do, two adult rabbits (brother and sister) and their six babies, which were currently smaller than the mesh of the wire we had put up to enclose them. None of this was within the National Trust guidelines. The rabbit run we created looked like something on the back edge of some rundown housing outside Swindon. But what can you do if that is the sort of family you are?

And then in January 2005 the Trust sent me a "Draft Occupancy Agreement," which seemed to confirm the worst. Sarah was to have no rights to live here if I died. All of us needed permission to go into any part of the building except the part we actually ate and slept in. We were to "notify Trust staff if guests of the family will be entering the garden." Our children were not to go anywhere near the greenhouses or nursery. We could have people to lunch only on closed days and only then "with the prior agreement of the Trust." Any photographs we took inside or outside the house were to be Trust copyright. The Trust was to be informed if we were away for more than two days or if anyone came to stay. We were to park our car with the exhaust pointing to the west. The occupation of the house was "at the discretion of the National Trust"—in other words, we could be thrown out at any time it liked. The agreement my father had made with them in 1967 was no more than a list of his wishes. It had no force in law.

I reeled from this document, sunk in gloom. I have talked about it more recently to Sally Bushell, the Trust's property manager, and she has explained it from her point of view. They didn't know us at the time. For them, we were new arrivals. They needed to be careful about security and safety. The yew hedges had to preserved from exhaust fumes. And it wouldn't have been nice for our friends to have been challenged in the garden. At the time, though, I was in no mood for understanding. I wrote an angry letter to the Trust's area manager, who had signed the document. "There is no sense that any of my family belongs to Sissinghurst," I told him,

nor that we grew up here, that we think of it as home, that we know it and have known it more intimately and for longer than anyone else, that it is a place to which we are deeply attached. This draft agreement might well have been proposed to someone who had just strolled in from Arizona or Mars. Many of its clauses treat me and my family as though we were simply unwelcome here, to be contained and enclosed, and not to be trusted.

I would like you to imagine addressing the kind of proposals you have made to my father. Would you have dared do that? I don't think so. I can see my father now, if I showed him what you sent me, holding his head in his hands and saying it was unbelievable. It is an almost complete betrayal of any spirit of cooperation or trust we might have had. And if not to him, why to us?

This was bleak; it felt like the moment of dispossession. "How lovely to be at Sissinghurst," people would say, but it wasn't lovely. Doubly or even triply, it felt like borrowed clothes: first because it was my father's house, then because it was his parents', and thirdly because it was the National Trust's. A three-layered baffle lay between us and any sense that this was home. It made all too obvious the acknowledged fact that the status of "resident donor" is difficult. Even the phrase reveals the difficulty, as if one were living in a body whose heart had been given away. It's your home but someone else's business, a place that is yours emotionally but very far from being yours in terms of who owns it, runs it, pays for it, works at it, and conceives of its future. For my father, who was responsible for the act of giving Sissinghurst to the Trust, this did not arise. He had saved Sissinghurst by giving it away.

If I had been a National Trust employee, working hard all year to keep the place in prime condition, I might not have liked us either. There is something structurally unlikable about a "donor family." They swan about as if they own the place, but they don't own it. They contribute nothing financially. They think they know how things should be but they don't do much to keep them that way. For all the heart-drenching beauty of Sissinghurst, it felt a little cold. At times it felt like living in a theater. One tends, at those times, to see the mechanisms rather than the show.

The Trust reeled in turn from my letter. I saw Sue Saville, the regional director, who did her best to mend the damage that had been done, smiling at me and rather sweetly touching my arm in reassurance. She said that visitors to NT properties liked the idea of a donor family living there. That the NT liked donor families because they often provided an instinctive feeling for a place that an administrator would have to guess at and feel for. That this occupancy agreement had been a mistake, a failure on the Trust's part to imagine themselves into our shoes. Finally, one day that summer, Sir William Proby, the chairman of the Trust, came with Merry, his wife, to talk to me and to apologize. We sat in the garden together, looking at the azaleas, their honey scent blowing over us. The Trust had got it wrong and Sir William was sorry. I know, poor man, that part of Sir William's job is going around the country soothing donor families in these situations, but he did it well. There was no more talk of occupancy agreements.

1930s: *South Cottage from the Tower.*

Nevertheless, it hardly changed the atmosphere on the ground. Through the course of 2005, I gradually worked my way to understanding what needed to happen here. That summer, going for a walk with the dogs, on the path just between the Priest's House and the barn, apropos of nothing, I had an idea. The restaurant at Sissinghurst serves tens of thousands of people a year. Why not grow on the farm the food that the restaurant cooks and sells to the visitors? What does a good lunch need? Some lamb, beef, chicken, eggs, pork, sausages, vegetables, bread, butter, cream, fruit, pastry. If the farm here could supply these things again, as it once had, the place would, almost inadvertently, reacquire the vitality and multiplicity it had lost, not as a smeared-on look, but from its bones. Above all, there would be people working the land here again, people for whom the soil of Sissinghurst was of vital importance, who would get to know it and look after it as carefully as their own children. That stupendous list of tasks performed on the Captain Beale farm would again become at least half necessary. A good lunch would make a good landscape. Grow lunch. That was all it needed.

In the wake of the idea came its drawbacks. This was not a lovely blank canvas. More than two hundred people—employees, residents, volunteers—were directly involved in the working and management of Sissinghurst as it stood. That big and complex business, with its own multiple tensions and high profitability, had to be kept going while this new cluster of ideas—a market garden, an organic farm, a restaurant dependent on very local produce, a labor-intensive use of the land—was pushed into the middle of it, with the same management team having to make the changes. It would not be easy. The new Sissinghurst enterprise would have a ready-made market on its doorstep—the stream of visitors to the garden—but that benefit came at a huge price: the need to convert everyone from the old system to the new. What was good about the idea was also bad.

In October that year, one of the National Trust's committees of the great and good—this was the Gardens Panel, chaired by Anna Pavord, the writer and plant historian—was coming to Sissinghurst anyway, to see how things were going. It was a routine visit, something that happens every two or three years. I decided I should talk to them about my idea. Here was a chance to get change into the bloodstream of the Trust. I rang Anna. She said I could have ten minutes.

I have never written anything more carefully in my life. I knew I had to say it to them with some conviction, but I printed it out as well, so that the committee would have something to take away with them, a physical object that could make the idea stick. The meeting was to be held upstairs in the old granary, whose windows I had shot out with my air rifle one bored ten-year-old morning. It was now part of the varnished pine world of the National Trust restaurant. There were about twenty-five people there, arranged around a giant table, tweed jackets, ties, professional, slightly curious. I distributed my sheets of paper, stapled together, along with copies of the poem called "Sissinghurst" that Vita wrote soon after arriving here. I then stood to address them. This is what I said:

> Sissinghurst is more than a garden. It is a garden in the remains of a ruined house and that house is at the heart of its own piece of Wealden landscape. It is a deeply rooted place and its meaning and beauty depend on its working not only as a garden but as a place that is fed by those wider and deeper connections.

That was code for a major transformation of the place. If connections were what mattered here, then the whole way it worked had to change. Vita's vision of the place had spread far beyond the horticultural. Garden, buildings, farm, woods, history, Kentishness, the land: these were the necessary ingredients. "This husbandry, this castle and this I," she called it in her poem. It was a place, she wrote, where she found "in chain / The castle, and the pasture, and the rose." That chain, that sense of connectedness, was what Sissinghurst needed to embody. It was a garden in a farm and it should seem like that.

I told them about the four different tenants, the lack of anyone working on the farm full-time. No animals attached to Sissinghurst, no farm buildings used as farm buildings, no one farmer who thought of Sissinghurst Castle Farm as his. The result was a certain efficient heartlessness, decisions made about this land not for the place but in the context of the four farm businesses of which it formed a part.

The garden at Sissinghurst is the crowning element of a land-scape which needs to be polycultural. It once had apples and pears, blackberries and strawberries, hops, a herd of Guernsey cattle and another of Dairy Shorthorns, farmers who were attached to it as a place, as well as orchards, cereals, sheep, pigs, chickens, and ducks. That is the landscape described in VSW's poem, and that is the landscape to which we should aspire. I am sure the pursuit of such a rich and various landscape would bring the aesthetic changes to the landscape which the garden needs. Sissinghurst the place would become the poem which Vita envisaged.

How could we do that? By growing the food for the 115,000 people who sat down to eat something in the restaurant and café here each year. Lunch would make its own landscape. And for that we needed a business plan.

The farm would need to employ people. It would strengthen this community and would restore some vital connections to it. I think we have an opportunity here to make something of great rarity and beauty, a poem of connectedness, something of which we would all, in five or ten years' time, be exceptionally proud.

There had been some nodding of heads as I spoke and people clapped when I sat down, but I had to leave the room for the discussion that followed. I wasn't quite sure where the question had ended up. Afterward, I spoke to Jonathan Light, the Trust's area manager. "The one thing I am absolutely determined I am not going to do is string an albatross around Sissinghurst's neck for the next twenty years," he said. "And there's another point. The landscape looks like it does for a reason and that is because economics and the market has driven it to look like that over the last fifty years. If we try to do something different, we will be swimming against the tide." Negative, then? I asked. No, not at all. "If we can demonstrate you can have a beautiful landscape, a mixed farm, and make money, then that really will be something we can show to others."

The next day I had to go to Cheltenham to give a talk. On the way there, in the car, my phone rang. "I have Fiona Reynolds for you," her secretary said. I had met the new director-general of the Trust before, but being called on the mobile in the car was a first. "I hear you've set the cat among the pigeons," she said. Friendly, warm, busy, amused. "I've had some excited phone calls. Do you think you could send me a copy of what you said? I am not saying anything, but it sounds interesting." It was the best of signs. As I drove back home, I couldn't stop smiling. Just think: this thing I had been half remembering and half imagining was still alive.

I walked out across the farm that evening, taking the dogs through the autumn woods, kicking up the leaves in the trenches that the old roads had left in the wood floor. A rising moon hung at the end of the long rides and autumn filled the air like a soup. It seemed possible, then, that there might be no disconnection between the future and the past here, that the passing of time wasn't mere diminution. In the car I'd heard a woman on the radio say that we met the world only once, in childhood, and that everything afterward was only memory. I knew well enough the attractions of that idea, the Wordsworthian regret, the sense of significance being invested only in the past. But here now, maybe, there was something else: the ability to fold the past over into the future, like turning the blankets and sheets over at the top of a bed, or digging over a piece of ground, turning the sods, grass down, and breaking the exposed soil to make a new tilth. Walking through the wood that evening, with the dogs prodding for rabbits among the chestnut stools, and that moon climbing through the branches, I knew I had never felt such buoyancy, such deep and rooted buoyancy, and I wished my father had been there to tell him.

CHAPTER *4*

Origins

I T IS AN ARTICLE OF FAITH with me that a place consists of
everything that has happened there; it is a reservoir of memories,
and understanding those memories is not a trap but a liberation, a
menu of possibilities. The richer the knowledge, the wider the options.
Multiplicity is all. The only enemy is narrow, singular definition. And
Sissinghurst, perhaps like any place that people have loved, is layered
with these multiplicities. Even now, anyone who lives or works here
soon develops an intense relationship to it, none of them quite the same,
none quite distinct, none of them quite secure. Our different histories
are buried and half known but we all think we own the real thing, or at
least want to. It is a place drenched both in belonging and in the longing to belong.

I ALWAYS KNEW THAT ITS FOUNDATIONS were in clay, silt, and
sand—clay at the bottom end of the farm, through which the Hammer
Brook runs, sand on the higher ridges above it, and silt scattered through
all of it. The clay is late land, always lying cold and reluctant, heavy and
wet. It is where the fertility lies and where cereals do have some kind of
a chance, at least with modern equipment. Hops, which are hungry
plants, were always grown down on the heavy land by the Hammer

Brook. In summer the clay is capable of turning to concrete—and then dust—as soon as the sun starts to shine. In winter, it makes for thick and cloggy ground. If you walk across one of the clay fields when it has been plowed, it gathers in lobed elephantiasis clumps around your boots. Teams of six or eight oxen were always needed to pull a plow through these fields. Even in midsummer the roads were "right deep and noyous." If heavy goods had to be brought in—in particular the bells for the churches—or timber taken out, the oxen labored for days. I asked a farmer who had worked all his life on the clay lands to the north of here what his farm was like. "Not boy's land," he said.

Clay, born in the wet, remains a friend to it. Surface water turns into streams. The streams cut away at the clay country, leaving the better-drained sand and silt standing proud as ridges. It is that physical difference that has cut the physiognomy of Sissinghurst. High is open and relatively dry; low is wet, secret, and thick with clay. A hole dug in the clay ground here becomes a pond. No lining is needed. Clay smeared with a digger-bucket seals itself. In the forty thousand acres of pure clay lands to the north and east of Sissinghurst, I have counted on the map very nearly four thousand ponds. They are usually no more than holes where farmers have dug, more often than not for the slightly limy clay called marl, which was used from the Middle Ages onward to sweeten these generally acid soils. The holes have simply filled with water, but each has its character: overhung with ancient oaks, the outer fingers of their lower branches dipping into the dark surface; smartened in the garden of a newly gentrified farm; or eutrophic, clogged in the middle of an arable field with all the green slime that comes from too much fertil-izer draining into it.

The sand is the clay's opposite: thirsty, capable of drying out in anything resembling a summer, without the nutrients on which good crops rely but making for easier and lighter country. Clay and sand are the polarities of the place, although in reality the situation is not so clear. The two principles mix and muddle across the whole of Sissinghurst. The soils roam from silty sands and sandy silty clays to silty clay loams and on to solid clay itself, perfect for the bricks that were made at least since the eighteenth century in the Frittenden brickworks just to the north of Sissinghurst. Patches of lightness appear here and there in the middle of heavy fields, and sudden wet clay sinks can be found in the middle of soils that are otherwise good and workable.

Only here and there do the two extremes appear as themselves. On the hill above Bettenham, there is an old sandpit, perhaps where the sand for the mortar used in building Sissinghurst was dug, and where now you can find little flakes and pebbles of the sandstone pulled out by the rabbits. It also appears in another small pit in the Park, just next to the old road going south, a friable, yellowish stone that crumbles between your thumb and finger. Here and there are thin iron bands within it. But play with a pebble for a moment and all you are left with is smooth, talcum-like dust on your skin. There are small pieces of this stone, included as yellow anomalies, among the bricks next to the entrance arch at Sissinghurst. On the high dry ridge at the western edge of the farm, there is a field still called Horse Race because it is sandy, well drained, and had the best going for the gentry in the seventeenth century and the officers of the eighteenth-century militia who used to race their horses here up until the 1760s. But it is not as building stone that this sand is significant. It is for the lightness it has given some of the soils here, far lighter than many places in the Weald.

At the top of the big wood there is a light, almost purely sandy patch, where a big group of sand-loving beeches grows. These are the most climbable trees at Sissinghurst, and not one of their kind appears down in the damp clay land. A third of a mile away, at the other end of the ridge, a cluster of sand-loving Scots pines was planted here in the 1850s by George Neve, the improving Victorian tenant. It was here that my father, as an anxious young man in the 1940s, proposed to the beautiful and entirely alluring Shirley Morgan, the only girl he ever loved and who would never accept him, despite a campaign lasting years. It was a well-chosen spot: if he had decided to lay her down on the damp, sticky clay soils at the bottom of the farm, he wouldn't have had a chance. At least he got the geology right; but geology wasn't enough. How much easier it must be for men who live on perfectly drained, downland turf, with endless vistas across their spreading acres, to convince the girls they love. My poor father could only point to distant views scarcely visible between the trunks of the surrounding trees. Over there, on a good day, he would have said, you can almost see the tower of Canterbury Cathedral. It wasn't enough; Shirley married a brilliant and handsome marquess whose beautiful house in North Wales has a view across its lawns of mountains and the glittering sea. My father never ceased to love her.

Sissinghurst, in its roots, is a little second-rate. This part of Kent has never been smart England, and its deepest of origins, the sources of its own soil, are decidedly murky. I love it for that. This is ordinariness itself: no volcanoes and no cataclysms, just a slow, deep gathering of what it was. The first moment when Sissinghurst came into being, when the stuff you can now hold there in your hands was there to be held, was about 120 million years ago. Britain was at the latitude of Lagos. Dinosaurs walked its river valleys, and a range of old and stony hills lay across the whole of England to the north. Forests of horsetails and giant ferns shrouded the valley slopes. Two steaming rivers flowed south out of those hills, their tributaries grinding away at the old rocks of which the hills were made. The rivers ran fast and carried with them a load of coarse-grained sand. As they emerged from the hills, just south of London, they flowed into a huge and swampy delta, covering perhaps thirty thousand square miles and stretching to the south of Paris, a dank, tropical place with many soft islands within it. Here the current slowed and dropped the sand in wide banks across the estuary.

As the rivers coming south from the uplands in Hertfordshire and Essex wore away at their hills, they slowed and became sluggish, carrying now only the finest of grains. What had been delta sands turned to thick gray mineral mud. The grains settled closely together in a gluey morass, a brackish and hostile place. It was a fossilized quagmire, impenetrable, a trap for anything that wandered into it, burying entire trees and whole animals, a graveyard of gummy secrets. This was the origin of the Wealden clay.

When I was a boy, I used to play with the clay in the summer. You could dig it out of the side of the lake banks, wet and slithery in your hands, your fingers pushing into the antique ooze. If you held a small ball of it in your fist and wetted it and squeezed it, two slimy snakes of clay, like a patissier's piping, would emerge top and bottom, curling, ribbed, while their miniature cousins came out between the joints of your fingers. It felt like ur-stuff, stuff at its most basic, as good as dough or pastry, squeezable, makeable, lovable. Occasionally, we molded it into pots, one of which I still have sitting on my desk, unglazed and unbaked, a rough lump from the basement of existence. My shorts and shirt after one of these mornings would be unwearably filthy, my hands and legs washable only under a hose.

This was the clay that in the sixteenth century gave modern Sissinghurst one of its essential substances and colors: brick. No record survives of the great brick building programs here, either from the 1530s or the 1560s, but there can be no doubt that the clay for the pink Tudor and Elizabethan palaces at Sissinghurst came from the stream valley just to the south. When Vita and Harold wanted to put up new garden walls in the 1930s, they commissioned bricks from the Frittenden brickworks only a mile away on the other side. But the bricks of those walls never looked right: too brown, without the variable, pink, iron-rich, rosy flush the sixteenth-century builders had found.

If the Sissinghurst process followed the pattern elsewhere in the Weald in the sixteenth century, the clay itself would have been tested and selected by an expert, a traveling brickmaker. In the autumn or early winter, gangs of laborers would then have dug the raw clay out of the valley and spread it out over what are now the Lake Field and Long

Orchard, so that autumn rains could get into the lumps and the frost split them. All winter the clay lay there on the fields, a dirty orange scar, like the embankment for a railway or bypass under construction. In the spring, the clay was rewetted and then, with more gangs of day laborers, trampled underfoot. Raw clay is full of little stony nodules. If they are left in the clay when it is fired, they overheat and split the bricks. For weeks, probably in large wooden troughs, the clay was kneaded and the little stones removed so that the brickmakers were left with a smooth and seamless paste that could be pushed into wooden brick-sized molds, usually here nine inches long, four wide, and two deep, the long, thin, smoked-salmon sliver-shaped bricks of sixteenth-century Sissinghurst. I remember seeing molds of exactly that form in the Frittenden brickworks when I was boy, but they have disappeared now. The clammy raw clay bricks were then turned out of the molds and left to dry in stacks for a month. In Frittenden there were long, open-sided wooden sheds for this, with oak frames and tiled roofs, but the scene in the fields of Elizabethan Sissinghurst would have been more ad hoc than that: bricks drying in what sun there was on offer. The whole process would have relied on a good fine summer.

Only at the end of the drying, when the bricks would already have developed some of the cracks and wrinkles you can still see in Sissinghurst's walls, would they be fired. Specialist brickmakers would arrive again, hired for the purpose, and build temporary "clamps," clay-sealed kilns in which the bricks were baked in a wood fire. It was a local and not entirely consistent process. Those bricks that were at the windward end of the clamp were more thoroughly fired than those downwind. The clay itself had wide variations in iron content. Different clamps, some with drier timber than others, some even using brushwood, burned at different temperatures. And so the flickering pinkness of Sissinghurst's walls emerged from the ground, everything from red to black, the near-white pink of flesh to the pink of camellias, wine red, apricot, even where it is rubbed a kind of orange, but in sum, across a whole wall, always with a rosy freshness, a lightness to the color that denies its origins in damp and fire, and scarcely reflects the whole process, the transmutation of an ancient eroded swamp. Not that the Elizabethans would have liked the variability. They would have admired and required precision and exactness. It was only because there was no stone here with which to build that they turned to the clay. The idea of bringing any quantity of stone from the quarries in the greensand ridge eight miles to the north was unthinkable, in time and expense, on the wet clay roads. Clay ground, thank God, meant a brick house, a subliminal joining of a high-prospect tower to the ground it surveys.

1930s: *Nigel and Ben Nicolson in front of the South Cottage.*

✦ ✦ ✦

EVEN SINCE HUMAN BEINGS FIRST ARRIVED HERE, 750,000 years ago, seven ice ages have come and gone, driving the people, the animals, and the plants far to the south, to their refuges in the warmth of southern Europe, and leaving this place, if not icebound, at least a frozen tundra, bleak and treeless. If I shut my eyes, I like to see it then, just at its moment of emergence, at the end of the last ice age, about twelve thousand years ago. It is a rolling windswept plain, continuous into Europe. Nothing coats the horizon but the grasses and the moss. There is cold to the north. Storms cross it in winter. In summer, as it does the steppe, the sun dries and burnishes it, fashioning a Ukrainian pelt concealing the earth. Ten thousand years ago, the average July temperature in Kent was already in the mid-sixties Fahrenheit. With that warmth, into this huge savanna more developed forms of life came rippling up in the wake of the retreating cold. First, the great herds of grazing animals, what may appear now like a North American scene but was indeed the case in northern Europe as the ice withdrew. Roe deer, red deer, no bison but the huge wild cows called aurochsen (of which the last, a Polish cow, died in 1627, and one of whose horns is still used as a communal drinking cup in a Cambridge college), elk or moose and herds of wild boar: all of these in their hundreds of thousands thrived on the great grassy treeless plains, where the wolves and lynxes pursued them. Bears would have fished for salmon and trout in the Medway and the Beult, the Hammer Brook and its glittering, unshaded tributaries. Foxes, cats, martens, otters, and beavers would all have been making their way up from the south, a spreading tide of appetite and complexity.

The birds came with them and with the birds the trees. In the pollen record, those trees whose seeds are dispersed by birds are the first to appear in the wake of the shrinking ice. Snow buntings, the Lapland bunting, and the shore lark all now spend the summer in the tundra on the edge of the Arctic and the winter farther south. They would have carried the first tree seeds up to subarctic Sissinghurst, perhaps the blackthorn and hawthorn, whose berries they would have eaten in the Dordogne or the Lot and would have dispersed here to make the first shrubby patches in the grasslands. The nutcracker has been found carrying hazelnuts ten or twelve miles from the trees where they picked them up, and perhaps, ahead of the wind, the nutcrackers were responsible for the big hazel woods that were the first to grow on the grasslands here. A thousand miles at ten miles a year takes only a century.

Quite slowly, with the help of the warm south wind, the wood thickened. First, the willows, the pioneers, set up in the damp patches, the fluff of their seeds drifting up in the summers. By 8000 BC the birch had arrived. Five hundred years later, the oaks came, their acorns almost certainly carried north by jays. The elm had also come, growing only on the dry land, not down in the damp of the clay. ("The oak unattended by the elm," J. M. Furley, the great nineteenth-century historian of the Weald, wrote, "betrays a soil not prized by the agriculturalist.") By about 6000 BC alders had colonized the stream margins, where they are still to be found, reliant on the water flowing steadily past their roots. The ash came at the same time. Not until about 5000 BC were there any beeches here, and then only, as now, on the drier hills. The hornbeam came even later and the chestnut not until the Romans brought it.

All of them had come north from their ice age refuges in France, wandering up on the wind into the increasingly friendly environments of Kent. It is like the cast of a play coming onto the stage and finding a seat there. As you walk through the wood and stream margins of Sissinghurst today, it is of course possible to listen to the ensemble, just to drink in the flecking green light of the wood in summer, but you can pick out individual lines of the instruments too and find here now, perfectly articulate if you listen for it, the story of their arrival.

March 2008:
*Hammer Brook
alders in flood.*

The thorns were the early pioneers. In a rough and neglected sliver of Sissinghurst Park Wood, where some giant alder stools have overgrown themselves and crashed down onto the wood floor, leaving a hole in the canopy behind them, blackthorn has invaded to make a thick and bitter, self-protective patch. The long, sharp thorns are poisonous. If one of them pricks you and breaks off in your flesh, the red-flushed wound festers for days. The blackthorn patch is everything the word "thicket" might imply, tangled into a hedgehog of denial and involution, clawing at itself, a crown of thorns thirty feet across. A big hawthorn standing coated in mayflower in a hedgerow is one thing—and well-grown thorns certainly make outstanding firewood—but the essence of a thorn is this thickety resistance to all outsiders, a miniature act of self-containment that the medieval English called a spinney, a spiny place, designed to exclude.

As children, we were always taught that you must try to sympathize with the spiky and the spiny, to understand what it was that did not allow them the open, displaying elegance of the beech or the confidence of the oak. Why are thorns so bitter? What can be the point, in such a calm English wood, of such unfriendliness? You feel like asking them to relax, even if relaxation is not in their nature. But everywhere in the woods at Sissinghurst there is one repeated clue to this foundation-level exercise in tree psychology: at the foot of almost every oak there is at least one holly nestling in the shade. Why? Why is the spiky holly drawn to the roots of the oak? What sort of symbiosis is this? But the question, it turns out, may be the wrong way round.

Why does the oak live with the holly? Because the holly, when they were both young, looked after the oak. Its spiky evergreen leaves protected the young acorn seedling from the browsing lips of the ever-hungry deer. The oak had a holly nurse, and only after a while did the young tree outstrip the protector that now shelters in its shade.

That too was the role played by the early spinney thickets. In an England filled with roaming herds, new trees needed to adopt one of three or four strategies to outstrip the nibbling lips. Either a spiny blanket that would mean they weren't eaten themselves, or sheltering within someone else's spiny blanket, so that by the time they emerged from it they were big enough not to be eaten. Or, like those other pioneers, the willows, growing so fast that at least one or two could outstrip the ubiquitous mouths. Or finally, like the birch, just as much a pioneer of new ground as the willow or the thorns, colonizing new areas in such numbers that at least one or two would escape the enemy. The browsing beasts were at war with the trees and the tree strategies were clear enough: hunker down (the thorns); borrow a friend (oaks, elms, beeches, and ashes); keep running (the willows); or blast them with numbers (the birch).

Every one of these post–ice age theories of defense—spike, cower, rush, or proliferate—is there to be seen in the Sissinghurst woods today. A few years ago, one of the great beeches on the high ridge of the big wood collapsed in a gale. Nothing was more shocking to me than to find it that autumn self-felled and horizontal, its stump a jagged spike ten or twelve feet high, looking more ripped than broken, as if someone had taken a pound of cheese and torn it in half. My father always used to bring us here in springtime when we were small and lie us down on the dry bronze leaves and mast below the tree. The new leaves sprinkled light on our faces. Each leaf was like a spot of greenness, floating, scarcely connected to the huge gray body of the tree. My father always said the same thing: how wonderful it was that this duchess, each year, dressed herself like a debutante for the ball. I cannot now look at a beech tree in spring without that phrase entering my mind.

Later, I climbed this tree often enough, chimneying up between its forking branches, avoiding the horrible squirrel's dray in one of its crooks, finding as you got higher that limbs that had seemed as solid as buildings farther down started to sway and shift under your weight and pressure. Then coming up into the realm of the leaves, as tender as lettuce early in the summer, acquiring a sheen and a brittleness as the months went on, until at last, in the top, like a crow's nest in a square-rigger, where the branches were no thicker than my forearm, I could look out over the roof of the wood, across the small valley, to the Tower, whose parapet half a mile away was level with my eye and where the pink- and blue-shirted visitors to the garden could be seen by me, while I knew that to them I was quite invisible.

Now the whole tree was down. Its splaying limbs had been smashed in the fall and lay along with the trunk like a doll someone had squashed into a box. I could walk, teeteringly, the length of the tree, as if I were a nuthatch whose world had been turned through ninety degrees. Even then, the beech started to rot where it lay. As it did so, something miraculous happened: in the wide circle around the beech's trunk, to which its multilayered coverage of leaves had denied light, nothing in the past had grown. Now, though, the light poured in, and in that circle hundreds and hundreds of birch trees sprang up, a dense little wood of rigid spaghetti trees, a noodle wood, without any great dignity or individual presence but extraordinary for its surge and hunger, opportunists, like pioneers pouring off their ship into a new and hope-filled land.

Within their new wood, the body of the beech lay as a mausoleum of itself, vast and inert, an unburied colossus, yesterday's story, no more than a reservoir of nutrients for the life that was so patently already coming after. The birch surge was, in its way, just as much as the thorn thicket, or the oaks sheltering in the embrace of the holly, or the romping willows on the banks of the lake, a vision of what happened here after the ice age was over, when the cold withdrew and trees reclaimed the country.

As much as the clay, the trees are at the heart of Sissinghurst. To the south and west of here, the woods of the High Weald make up a broken, parceled, varied country, thick with tiny settlements and ancient names, all of them in their own nests of privacy, tucked in among the folds of the wood on the hills. It is still possible, even today, to walk for eighty miles in a line going west from Sissinghurst—if you are careful and pick your path—without leaving woodland for more than quarter of a mile at a time. Not until you reach the Hampshire chalk at Selborne does open country defeat you. Weald means *Wald*, the great wood of England, and although it has been eaten into and nibbled at for at least fifteen centuries, and perhaps for more like fifty, it persists. It is the frame of Sissinghurst, the woods, in Kipling's words, "that know everything and tell nothing."

Wood to Sissinghurst is like sea to an island. Everything in the Weald, in the end, comes back to the wood. Sissinghurst's parish church, at least until the nineteenth century, was at Cranbrook, about two and a half miles away, a short bike ride. It became an intensely puritan place in the sixteenth century, and the feeling in the church still reflects that: big clear windows, a spreading light, the clarity of revelation. But in the church, miraculously preserved, are the remains of an earlier and darker phase. On the inner, east wall of the tower are four "bosses"—large carved wooden knobs, originally made to decorate the intersections of beams in the roof high above the church floor. These are from a late-fourteenth-century chancel roof that was

GREEN MAN 1   GREEN MAN 2

WOOD GOD   WOOD BIRD/DRAGON

April 2008: *Fourteenth-century roof bosses in Cranbrook church.*

replaced in 1868. They are some of Cranbrook's greatest treasures. Each is cut from a single fat dark disc of oak, a yard across and a foot deep, sliced from the body of a timber tree. The carving takes up the full depth of the disc so that there is nothing shallow or decorative about the form.

Each of the four bosses has a different atmosphere, a different reflection of the nature of the wood, and of the human relationship to it.

Green Man 1 shows a conventional, if smiling human face, a young man, wearing a padded hat and a headcloth, surrounded by a mass of curling leaves, a wide border to the face, with no interpenetration between figure and tree. It is, perhaps, an image of reconciliation, of an easiness with the facts of nature, a civilized man (or perhaps a woman?) settled in his bed of vegetation, like half an egg resting on its salad.

The second, Green Man 2, which is aged, bearded, and broken, as if the boss had fallen from the chancel roof onto the stone floor of the church, was clearly similar, a face with leaves, but more troubled, an arch of anxiety across the bearded man's brow, a feeling that in the luxuriance of his beard there is some osmosis across the human-natural barrier. Already here, the civilized man is sinking into (or emerging from?) the vegetation that threatens to smother him.

The other two come from somewhere still deeper, wild and savage things from a world that seems scarcely connected to Christian orthodoxy, let alone to the neatness of modern Cranbrook going about its shopping outside the door. These are the wood spirits that have emerged from the primitive Weald itself:

The third, Cranbrook Wood God, is a huge, near-animal mask, at least twice the size of a human face, with goggle eyes and an open mouth, a face of threat and terror. Between its lips, roughly hewn, uneven peg teeth grip the fat, snaky stems of a plant, which is clearly growing from this creature's gut and from there spewing out into the world. Its chiseled tendrils engulf the head, branching around it, gripping it and almost drowning it, as though the figure were not the source of the wood power but its victim. The whole disc looks like a hellish subversion of a sun god: not a source of emanating life and light but a sink of power, dark and shadowed.

The fourth of the Cranbrook bosses, the Wood Bird/Dragon, is the most intriguing. The same net of leaves, which are perhaps the leaves of a plant that hovers between an acanthus and a hawthorn, crawls all over the surface of the boss, but without regularity, a chaotic and naturalistic maze of leaf and hollow, mimicking the unregulated experience of a wood itself, highlight and shadow, reenacting the obstruction and givingness of trees. Within this vivid maze of life, there is something else, a body, winged apparently, with a giant claw that grasps a stem, and beyond that the full round breast of a bird. There is a head here, perhaps of a dragon, curled round to the top and difficult to make out, a presence, neither slight nor evanescent, both solid and unknowable, the wood bird/dragon, which does not even give as much as the green man, with his terror-explicit face and strangeness-explicit eyes.

These four great Cranbrook bosses were almost certainly paid for by the de Berhams, the family living at Sissinghurst at the end of the fourteenth century, when Cranbrook church was embellished, and whose coat of arms was carved on the west face of the church tower. In their bosses, there is a buried and schematic sermon on our relationship to the natural world. The set of four presents four different visions in a sort of matrix, two human, two natural, two good, and two bad: a sense of ease among the froth of vegetation (human good); anxiety at its power (human bad); the bird/dragon half seen in the obscuring leaves (natural good); and the peg-toothed wood god grinning in the dark (natural bad). Nothing I have ever seen has made the wood speak quite like this.

Of all the trees that this part of the world was in love with, none was more constant than the oak. In the great rebuilding of the fifteenth and sixteenth centuries, oak played a constant part. The hundreds of big Wealden houses on the farms around here are always crammed with as many oak studs in their façades as they could manage.

At what remains of Sissinghurst itself, which is a brick house, consciously set apart from the yeoman timber-framed tradition around it, the timber still shapes the interiors. All my life, lying in bed in the morning or last thing at night, I have stared up at the oak joists and tie beams of its ceilings. In the five hundred years since they were put up there, the oak has lost the orange-brown tang that it has when new and paled to a kind of dun suede, dry and hard, with a sort of suavity to it. There is no way you could bang a nail into this oak now, but it makes no display of its strength. It lies above you as you lie in bed, the grain visible along with an occasional knot, the edges as clean and sharp as

April 2008: *Oak sack hoist, trusses, and rafters of the Elizabethan barn.*

1965: *Elizabethan rafters and braces in the southern end of the front range.*

the day they were cut. I have slept in every bedroom in the house at different times, and each has its different quirks and wrinkles. In some you can see where the sawyers using a doubled-handled saw made their successive cuts. A man stood at each end of the saw, one above, on the timber itself, the other, the underdog, in the pit beneath him. Each downward swoop was followed by an upward cut, and each cut moved the saw a quarter or a third of an inch along the joist. Each of those cuts is visible now in little ridges, not quite aligned, some almost on the ver-tical, some more on the diagonal, where one or another of the sawyers ripped an extra bit of energy into his stroke. The timbers look like a roughened bar code, an account of two men at work one Elizabethan morning.

UNTIL RECENTLY, IT WAS THOUGHT that the original wildwood, the wood of England before man began to change it, was a huge and continuous cover of trees, the crown of each tree meeting those of its neighbors for hundreds of miles so that a squirrel could run from Dover to Ludlow or Penzance to Alnwick without once needing to touch the ground. Universal and mysterious gloom prevailed in this ancient pic-ture. Occasionally a giant tree would crash to the ground, it was thought, and light would come down to the forest floor, but for the most part life was said to crawl about in a romantic vision of everlasting shadow.

All of that, it now seems, may be wrong. In the last few years new thinking, particularly by the brilliant Dutch forest ecologist Frans Vera, has begun to challenge this idea of the ubiquitous, closed forest of the ancient world. According to Vera's ideas, the ancient Weald, the sort of landscape that people would first have found when they came to Sissing-hurst, may not, strangely enough, have looked very different from the Weald as it now is. If I walk out from Sissinghurst, across the Park, into the wood, and out again into the pasture fields beyond it, where the oaks grow spreadingly in the light, I may well be walking through a place whose condition is rather like it was five thousand years ago.

If you take your bike and ride north from Sissinghurst, about seven miles across the clay flatlands of the Low Weald, past a succession of fifteenth- and sixteenth-century oak farmhouses, you come beyond Headcorn to the first rise of the Greensand Hills. Farmhouses, farm walls, barns, and piggeries all start to turn here into the pale gray ragstone of the hills themselves. Just north of Headcorn, where the old road is cut deeply into the slope, you climb to the village of Ulcombe. Here you can look back at Sissinghurst from a place on its own skyline. The Weald lies blue and glossy in front of you. Beyond the ground at your feet, there is nothing but trees. I scanned the whole horizon. In the binoculars—it must have been five miles away—I saw what I hadn't spotted with the naked eye: a kestrel hanging and fluttering in the summer air. Its body was quivering in the eyeglass from the rising heat, a black dot buried in the distance, making its own survey of the land. Beyond the kestrel's body, I could make out the ridges of the Weald, one layer of wood after another, but scarcely a field and no buildings, except, very occasionally, a church tower. There was no hint of modernity, nor from this height even the sound of traffic. Only, far to the southeast and gray with distance, like islands seen from out at sea, the huge blocks of the Dungeness power stations on the Channel coast, and the necklaced pylons strung toward them like toys. Otherwise only the heat, the dot of the kestrel, and the blue of the wood. Even with the binoculars, I couldn't make out the Tower at Sissinghurst, but the avenue of poplars going down from the Herb Garden to the lake, planted by Vita and Harold in November 1932, stood out clearly enough, almost the only verticals in the continuous rounded swells of the oaks.

The view from Ulcombe is a vision of the great wood of England. All the hedgerow oaks in the Low Weald come together to give an impression of uninvaded woodland. It is a view that might have confirmed the old theories of the solid, unbroken canopy of the Weald. Now, though, intriguingly for the later history of Sissinghurst, it seems that this picture of the dark, continuous "closed" forest of folklore may not be the whole story. The critical factor, for Frans Vera and those who follow him, is the large herds of grazing animals. What effect would they have had on the ability of trees to reproduce themselves? Would they not have nibbled the seedlings even as they emerged? Added to that is the strange anomaly of the large amounts of oak and hazel pollen that have been found trapped within ancient muds at the bottom of lakes and ponds. Neither oak nor hazel can reproduce itself in shade. They need plenty of light to establish themselves as trees. If the forest remained dense and dark, with the canopy closed, how come there were so many of these shade-intolerant trees?

Vera's answer combines an understanding of the nibbling mouths with all the defense strategies the trees employ to resist or evade them. The Vera forest is a mosaic of thorny patches in which young saplings are growing; open, parklike savanna in which spreading, many-branched trees stand over well-grazed pastures; fringes of nettle, garlic, sorrel, and goosefoot; and in the center of the spreading woods places where the trees have aged and died and grassland has reestablished itself, with its butterflies and all the birds of the woodland edge. It is not unlike the Park at Sissinghurst now, fringing onto the wet alder and oak wood, with thorny patches here and there (which we call hedges) in which the young oaks spring up, protected by the thorns and looking for the light. If Sissinghurst's well-managed parklands were abandoned, and the grazing mouths withdrawn (by a wolf, say, or lynx), then blackthorn, hawthorn, guilder rose, wild apple, pear, and cherry, together with lots of hazel, would all emerge, to make buttons of young, scrubby wood. The whole place would be in slow and gradual flux under its ancient tension of grazing mouth and germinating tree: not a constant and continuous place, but somewhere in movement, a shifting of high woodland from one place to another, an opening of grassland, a recolonizing of it by scrub.

Seen from a time-lapse camera, suspended over it in a balloon, the country flickers and shifts. The herds come and go, the patches of wood-land emerge as thorny thickets and spinneys, become high, leafy cano-pied oak wood, and collapse in time, the animals moving in again, the grassland emerging, the buttercups flowering in the flush of summer. There were beavers here then, and when beavers build dams in streams and small rivers, the roots of the trees rot and the forest collapses. If the beavers then leave, their dams break and the pools empty. In place of the drained pool, a grassy meadow develops and elk and deer come in to graze it. When Western colonists first went to Ontario they often found beaver meadows up to a hundred acres across and used them to make hay for their own cattle. So perhaps this too was happening down in the valley of the Hammer Brook, beaver dams and beaver meadows, the opening of wonderful damp, grassy glades where the herds of deer would come to graze.

I know that for others, certainly for people who have come to work and make their lives here, Sissinghurst's beauty lies in its fixity, in its resistance apparently to modernity, and as a place that was reassuringly still and even perfect. Why did I not share in that?

Perhaps, I came to realize, because it allowed us a place here too, because a focus on vitality and change, which may look like a rejection of the past, is, if set in this other framework, in fact a continuation of it. It might reestablish at Sissinghurst a sense that this was not a shrine or a mausoleum, but a long-living entity, far older than any one ingredient in it, of which self-renewal was part of its essence.

SISSINGHURST IN ANTIQUITY was not part of the solid, impenetra-ble, and frighteningly dense forest, but threaded with through-paths making their ways between the clearings and thickets, finding them-selves sometimes in savanna-like parkland where the deer grazed and game was to be had, sometimes passing through patches where young oaks were sprouting up between the thorns and the hollies.

The deep past, then, was not, as we are so often encouraged to imagine it, some desperate and dreadful experience colored only by threat and unkindness, but full of possibility, excitement, and beauty in the empty half-open woodlands that were here then. Half close your eyes one evening in Blackberry Lane and those four images from the Cranbrook bosses will come back to you: a relaxed beneficence among the fresh green hawthorns; some anxiety in the shadows; the bird half seen in the obscuring trees; and the big-mouthed grin of the goggle-eyed wood god. It is all here now and it was all here then.

There was one last object that if it had survived might have been the emblem of Sissinghurst two thousand years ago. It represents a little window on the distant past that opened in a Victorian summer and has since closed. George Neve, the distinguished tenant farmer here, a man of parts, contributor to the letter columns of national newspapers, was settled into the large and comfortable brick farmhouse at Sissinghurst that he had built almost twenty years before. The young cedars of Lebanon he had planted on his south lawn were eight years old and doing well. The laurels and rhododendrons in the dell next to his house were beginning to gloom over satisfactorily. It was time to show the county what sort of man he was.

George Neve invited the general meeting of the Kent Archaeological Society to spend part of its day at Sissinghurst. They came on July 24, 1873. Earl Amherst would be attending, as would Viscount Holmesdale, his son. There were about one hundred forty people in all, including a general, an archdeacon, and twenty-five vicars, many with their wives. After a preliminary meeting in the South Eastern Hotel in Staplehurst, they visited Staplehurst and Frittenden churches, and then came on to Sissinghurst in their carriages, where "Mr George Neve, of Sissinghurst Castle, most hospitably invited the whole company to partake of luncheon in a shaded nook upon his lawn, where tables were laid with abundant refreshments."

After lunch, the company reentered their carriages and went on to

Cranbrook church. Before they left, Neve would undoubtedly have shown them his treasure. It had been plowed up five years before, at a depth of about eight inches, from a field near Bettenham, no more specific than that. A few years earlier, in another neighboring field, the men on the farm had plowed up an urn containing some bones. That, unfortunately, had been destroyed, but the treasure found in 1868 Neve had kept, and had even had photographed. An image of it would be reproduced in the volume of *Archaeologia Cantiana* that reported his lunch party. It was a gold ring, made of two gold wires, twisted together. One of the wires was thin and of the same diameter throughout; the other was three times as thick but tapered along its length to a point.

It was a piece of Celtic jewelry, belonging to someone about two thousand years ago who spoke a version of Welsh or Breton, the kind of ring that is found all over Europe, from Bohemia to the Hebrides. Its twistedness is the mark of a culture that liked complexity and the way in which things could turn inward and mix with their opposite. It was a beautiful thing: private not public, suggestive not assertive, symbolic not utilitarian. Perhaps it was a wedding ring, a binding of two lives, in gold because gold is everlasting. At some time in the last one hundred thirty years, this precious object disappeared, but at least we have the image of it and the knowledge of its existence. I see in the Bettenham ring the culmination of this first phase of Sissinghurst's existence. It— and the fact of a burial being made here—confirms a certain view of the ancient Wealden past. This was not, at least by the time of Christ, some godforsaken, Tolkienian forest in which trees loomed and rivers dripped, where people trod rarely and fearfully. Far from it: people knew Bettenham and Sissinghurst as theirs. Stream, meadow, wood, and track, long summer grasses, spring flowers, the spread of archangel, stitchwort, campion, and bluebells on the edge of the wood, the flickering of light down onto the water, the flash of the kingfisher, the pike in the dark pools, the songs of the nightingales and the woodpeckers, the swallows and house martins dipping onto the ponds, the fluster of pigeons, the flicker of kestrel and sparrowhawk: they would have known it all—and more, not in some marginalized way, scraping a desperate, squatter existence from the woods, but with comfort, gold, elegance, and the symbolizing of love and mutuality in a ring. They would have farmed here. Even two thousand years ago, Sissinghurst was home.

CHAPTER *5*

Testing

F ROM OCTOBER 2005 ONWARD, I slowly tried out the ideas
I had for Sissinghurst. Following my nose, asking my friends for
hints and tips, I began to engage with the realities. I have nearly
always worked alone and have loved that, the silence and privacy of it,
the space that solitary work allows for ideas to accumulate and thicken
like crystals dangling in a solution. On your own, understanding comes
not by argument but accretion. It's quick.

I always knew this was going to be different: the meetings, the hierarchies, feeling my way past embedded difficulties, seeing my own
ideas from other people's point of view. All of that was the price of getting something to happen for real, of pushing it beyond the limits of
longing or regret, beyond the written.

I knew from the start that any scheme here had to be commercially
viable. This couldn't be a fantasy park. Any exercise in vanity farming,
in aesthetics or window dressing, would mean nothing and anyway
would smell wrong. In modern terms, it had to survive in the market,
providing something that people were actually prepared to buy. I felt
sure they would. But we needed, first, a feasibility study. It would cost, I
discovered, between £15,000 and £20,000.

Jonathan Light, area manager for the National Trust, Sally Bushell, the property manager at Sissinghurst, Sarah, and I had a meeting in
our kitchen, the first of hundreds: Sally gentle, warm, organizational,
consensus-conscious, increasingly investing in a hope and belief that
this idea might work, always friendly to us; Jonathan a precisionist with
a razored haircut and the straightest of backs, who in an earlier life was
a chartered engineer with the giant British chemical congomerate ICI,
now married to a lawyer, always working out his requirements before-
hand, distinguishing between desires and needs, a careful, note-taking,
systematic man, economical in what he said but with a sharp line in the
sardonic remark, the embodiment of consistency and courtesy, precisely
the calming and sustaining presence Sissinghurst needed; and Sarah
and I both slightly anxious in meetings, not quite having the meeting
language and so tending to look amateur and impetuous, the "flaky cre-
atives," as Sarah called us one day.

That wasn't entirely fair. I had run a small farm in Sussex for ten
years and a small publishing company before that. Sarah had started
and built up her own mail-order business, selling seeds and everything
needed in a garden, combined with a gardening and cookery school.
She had made a name for herself as a gardening and cookery writer,
promoting a direct and bold style that had caught people's imaginations.
Before that she had been a medical doctor, a junior renal specialist. We
weren't exactly innocents, but this particular set of circumstances at
Sissinghurst was different. With the label of "donor family" hanging
over us, it wasn't entirely easy to be our usual businesslike selves.

Nevertheless, we four were calmly getting to know each other, dar-
ing a joke now and then, gathering a trust in each other's capabilities
and good intentions. At the beginning, Jonathan asked whether I could
put together an Outline Proposal for a Draft Project Brief for an Investigation of the Business Case to go out to Tender for a Consultative
Exercise on the Ideas I had? Those were not quite his words, but I said I
could and it took a morning.

The ideal was of a kind of mixed farming that was traditional in the Weald until the 1960s, when the combination of an increasingly globalized market and the arrival of artificial fertilizers made it unviable. That kind of mixed farm was the frame in which the garden at Sissinghurst was originally set. The study needed to examine how far it was possible to reinvigorate the farming methods at Sissinghurst, with a view not to distant markets but to the value that its own restaurant and farm shop could create. The massive retail potential at Sissinghurst made the old landscape possible. The full polycultural variety should be the goal: raspberries and strawberries, blackcurrants, apples and pears, hops, dairy cattle, as well as cereals, beef cattle, pigs, sheep, chickens, pigeons, and ducks.

1950s: *Guernseys on the Plain.*

There were a thousand questions. How would Sissinghurst sell the products of its landscape to its visitors? Could the farm really provide the restaurant with everything it offered its customers? What would the economics be of a farm shop at Sissinghurst? Could the restaurant and shop, at the beginning of the year, "order" their requirements from the farm? Could Sissinghurst make its own ice cream, bread, cakes, scones, and jams from the dairy cows, fruit fields, and wheats and ryes grown in the fields? Could the woods produce pea sticks, hurdles, chestnut fencing, and furniture to be bought by customers? Could people take hop bines away with them in their cars? Was pick-your-own a possibility, perhaps of flowers as well as fruit? Could a chicken run provide the eggs for the omelets the restaurant would make? Was there a place for a bakery with a takeaway counter? Bringing animals back to the farm, the repatriation of farm management to Sissinghurst, the growing of vegetables, and the setting up of a farm shop would all need buildings and equipment. Where should they go? And how would they fit with the tourist business?

Alongside that was the question of a business structure. Were the profit margins to be set in advance? Or could the Trust tolerate a lower level of profit here in return for the landscape benefits? Was it necessary to stick with the idea of farmer as producer and restaurant as client? Or should a single enterprise become the tenant of the farm, the restaurant, and the farm shop? How integrated, in other words, could the retail and production arms at Sissinghurst be? Could a loss on one be set against the profits on the other?

Driving blind—and not knowing the true situation—I guessed that the Trust would have little money to bring all this about. But I also knew that it had raised £360,000 in two years at Sheffield Park in Sussex from visitor contributions—with the same number of visitors per year as Sissinghurst. That money was for repairing some collapsing lakes rather than this more nebulous and commercial scheme, but still it was no more than one pound a visitor. Would the Sissinghurst visitors want to pay for the setup costs of this?

There was also a question of land. The farmed area at Sissinghurst looked as if it might be too small at 259 acres. More land was probably needed, either rented or acquired. I knew, of course, of the neighboring Bettenham and Brissenden farms, which once belonged to my grandmother and now belonged to a ninety-two-year-old law professor, Thomas James, who lived at Benenden. I rang him one evening. "Ah yes," he said, "Nigel's son? You know he sold me those farms?" I did. "A terrible price, terrible, really terrible." For you? I asked. "No, no." He laughed. "For him." My poor father had sold those farms, now worth £3.5 million, for £15,000 in 1964. "To do up his house, wasn't it?" Professor James asked. I didn't go into the details but instead risked my question. "Do you think there is any chance, Professor, that when you die you might consider leaving those farms, or some of them anyway, to the National Trust, to reunite the estate as it was before the 1960s? We have great plans for the farm here." A pause on the other end of the phone. "If there is one organization in England to which I would not leave my property, it is the National Trust." He had been appalled, a few years earlier, when the Trust, which had accepted land on Exmoor on the condition, among others, that stag hunting would continue across it, had agreed under pressure from its own largely urban and antihunting membership to ban the hunt from its land. This was a question of honor, Professor James said, allied to one of uncertainty. How could he be sure that any agreement he made about these farms would be observed after he was dead? I said we would all do our best to see that agreements were honored and how we had nothing but the best interests of the land in mind. "No, no, no," he said, swatting away a puppy. "Anyway, Robert Lewis, who has farmed it for many years for us, he's the man for that land." So Bettenham and Brissenden were severed from Sissinghurst, perhaps forever. We would have to live within our limits.

Sally, Jonathan, Sarah, and I worked our way through the suggestions. I added a need for aesthetics. "Whatever is done must both look and feel right for Sissinghurst, and enhance rather than detract from what is already here. Aesthetics cannot be a last-priority bolt-on." Jonathan added the need for "reversibility." If it went wrong, nothing we had done should be undoable. The scheme "must not land a white elephant on either the NT's or Sissinghurst's back." And any scheme must be "revenue-neutral." Sissinghurst as a whole must earn as much after any changes we made as before.

Having looked at the leases of the four farming tenants, Jonathan also found some good news. There was a break clause in all of them that meant that if we had a coherent plan together by September 2006, the Trust could give them a year's notice to quit, which meant that by September 26, 2007, the land at Sissinghurst could be back in hand and the project could begin to work. The Trust had recently had some disastrous publicity when it had amalgamated two farm tenancies in the Lake District, and so it would have to tread with immense care around this issue. But this gave us a deadline and a timetable.

Fiona Reynolds had asked me to talk to the National Trust Annual General Meeting that November in Brighton. "Don't frighten the horses," Jonathan said, and so I spoke to them after dinner in big generalities. What was the National Trust for? It came down, I told them, to a new understanding of what was meant by the word "place." That word is enshrined in the name of the Trust; it is a National Trust for Places. And what is a place? Not just a location.

> The Trust does not own "sites" in the way Asda or BP does. It doesn't plonk down its identity on a neutral spot. Nor is a place an idea or an image. It is intensely concrete, the opposite of anything virtual, something that is thick with its own reality. And, more than that, a place is somewhere with a quality you might call "inner connectedness." That is a subtle but powerful thing, which is related to a kind of self-sufficiency, a feeling in a place that its life is not borrowed or imposed from elsewhere, but is coming up out of its own soil.

The old debate, I told them, had always set commercialism and enterprise against poetry and conservation. But that was missing the point. People had a growing hunger for authenticity and the enriched place. The enormous proliferation in the modern world of slickly and thinly communicated meanings had generated a demand for the opposite, for the sense when you arrived somewhere that not only did it look wonderful but was wonderful, that it wasn't just a skin. Gertrude Stein had famously said of Oakland, California, "There is no *there* there." For the Trust, and for all of us, *thereness* and turnover could be the same thing. All the NT had to do was make sure it was constantly cultivating and rejuvenating the thereness of the places it owned and its customers would flock in.

I did not feel in private quite as sanguine. I had underestimated the way in which these ideas would ruffle feathers at Sissinghurst. Anxiety was already raising its head. What people loved here was its "tranquillity." And people were worried that my ideas would disturb it. Trucks, intensification, multiple demands: none of those felt very Sissinghursty. Nobody much liked the idea of chickens or pigs because of the smell. Already, just creaking open like a board splitting in the sunlight, the cracks were appearing between those who had the easy ideas and those who were expected to make them work.

In December, one freezing foggy Sunday, Sarah and I went to see Jacob Rothschild. The Rothschild house at Waddesdon belongs to the National Trust, but the Rothschilds, because they are able to subsidize it to the tune of £1 million a year from a family trust, are able to decide pretty well everything that happens there. The garden writer and designer Mary Keen, who is a friend of the Rothschilds, had asked him to ask us to lunch. I wore a suit, which was a mistake as everyone else was in shirts and jerseys. A butler told us to park our dirty Land Rover next to a Swiss-number-plated Range Rover. Lady Rothschild gave us champagne. "Or would you prefer something else?" A classical pavilion of a house. Guardis on the wall. Lunch in a French rococo room. I felt like a suited prune amid such riches, but Lady Rothschild was warmth itself. "Barbara Amiel said that Jacob marrying me was about as likely as the emperor of Japan marrying a Hottentot," she whispered at lunch.

Rothschild was regal, huge in his red jersey, loping, looking at the world from a great height but full of grace. Just audible beneath the surface a great deal of idling, ticking-over horsepower in reserve, but generous in his eyes, exuding interest. Sarah grows a bulb called *Gloriosa superba Rothschildiana*. I couldn't get the phrase out of my head. After lunch we talked about the Sissinghurst scheme. He thought the Sissinghurst Trust idea bad because it set up two power bases and an inbuilt tension. "Why not take the whole thing over, including the garden?"

Impossible, I said.

"Why?"

For a million and one reasons. The great difference was that the Rothschilds had their huge fund hosing money into Waddesdon, and the National Trust was happy to accept anything they were prepared to pour down its throat. We were not in that position. But he was also discouraging about the prospect of raising any money. "It is much, much more difficult than you imagine." There was a kind of shy directness to him, and he was funny. "I couldn't sack a daylily," he said.

At home at Sissinghurst a couple of days later we gave a drinks party for everyone living and working there. Sofas pushed back, hot mulled wine, a big fire. Sometime into the party, a woman, flushed with the warmth, came up to me. "You really think you're the lord of the manor now, don't you? Well, Adam, I can tell you something: you are not." So here it was: the sunny visions of perfection exposed to a cold and withering wind. There were people at Sissinghurst who considered it theirs, who had devoted their lives to it, who loved it quite as much as I did, and who felt that Sarah and I were more interested in our own welfare than in Sissinghurst's. "Are we helping you do what you want," someone asked me, "or are you helping us do what we want?" I thought even then that perhaps we should simply leave them to it and they could make it in their own image.

We had a final meeting just before Christmas with Sue Saville and Jonathan Light. Sue said the Trust was happy to put some money into a feasibility study. A feasibility study! Have three words ever sounded quite so sweet? And how will it be paid for? I asked. "Sissinghurst will pay for it," Jonathan said. How, though? "The clause your father inserted in the 1967 agreement has meant that Sissinghurst is what we call a Special Trust in Credit. It has a large reserve accumulated against a rainy day." The disciplines exercised over the last fifteen years or so have meant that the size of the Sissinghurst financial cushion is astonishing. While the world has been borrowing, Sissinghurst has been saving, and the accumulated reserve now allows substantial annual expenditure with no diminution of the invested capital. People rarely applaud the National Trust for its financial management, but this policy has been exemplary. Not a single aspect of the scheme this book describes would have been possible without it. As Jonathan said that afternoon, the farm project could not be allowed to lose money on its current account in the long term, but, within reason, it was not going to be constrained by shortage of capital.

Together, Jonathan, Sally, Sarah, and I worked our way through the early part of the year. I made a list of target qualities for any scheme:

Authenticity
Richness
Rootedness
Connectedness
Vitality
Delight

Jonathan and Sally drew up a huge and careful tender document. Consultants came and made their bids for the work. We walked them around the place in the late winter, some in the rain, some on wonderful mornings when there was a frost on the moat, just a skin, not enough for a moorhen to walk on. The first spikes of the narcissi were up in the orchard and the aconites were out under the hedge between Delos and the White Garden, casually there like beautiful weeds. Against the light blue of the March mornings the consultants had ideas and questions. The old dairy and the barn next to it might be the farm shop and café. The Horse Race hedges would have to grow up if the fruit trees were to go back. Could the farm be enlarged? Could the restaurant expand into the barn? Did it have to be organic? There was a sense above all of potential in the air. Some of the reports were a bit highfalutin. "I don't see why, when we know we've got our feet in the treacle," Jonathan said after reading one report, "we need to have our heads in it too." Helen Browning from the Soil Association took a bit of the soil away in a napkin I gave her. It felt like a kind of spring, tentative, only half there but, still, half there.

I went for walks in the early woods. The colors were changing, the purple of the alder catkins now mixed with the hazel and then the goat willows coming on like lights, the "palm trees," as my nanny Shirley Punnett always used to call them. The geese were clanging away across the farm, their voices a long, deep echoing you could hear a mile downwind. Sissinghurst was full of one of the miracles of spring: the light suddenly penetrating to the floor of the wood, for the first time since the previous year, reaching into its depths as if into an aquarium or an unfinished house.

It was a heady time for me. I felt excited at the prospect of my idea becoming a reality. This was different from how it had been for a long time. I had become used to the idea that changes would happen at Sissinghurst without my knowing about them in advance. My father as he got older had increasingly accepted the decisions being made around him. I remember finding him once almost in tears, sitting at the kitchen table, having come back from a walk down by the lake. He had found that the wood he had loved all his life, fringing the lake and the stream that runs beside it, had been cut down. No one had told him. He did not like an argument and had said nothing. That silent acceptance of unannounced change had seemed like the prevailing reality. Now I felt the

National Trust responding to my ideas. Under Jonathan's hands they were taking on substance, and the experience was vertigo-inducing. I realized I had never wielded influence here before.

To my relief, the Soil Association, the champion of the organic idea, was awarded the contract, and their glamorous team turned up: Helen Browning, powerful, strong-minded, clear-voiced, a big farmer in Wiltshire, chair of a government committee on animal welfare, a partner in her own organic food business; alongside her, Katrin Hochberg, a cool, taut, courteous German in her twenties, with high cheekbones and eyes the color of the North Sea in February. Both of them glowed with the kind of health that was a billboard for the organic idea. And Phil Stocker, a Bristol man, once a big-time chemical farmer who went to work for the Royal Society for the Protection of Birds, saw the organic light, and now devotes every hour of his life to persuading the farmers of England to go the way he has gone. Every sentence he speaks delivers straight, persuasive idealism. When these three arrived, I felt as if I had bought a new car. With them we could go anywhere. No weariness and no viscosity, nor any sense that they were in service to some antiquated or inherited idea. They looked like ushers to the future.

We walked around the farm on a sunny day in April. Spring was coming on and the blackthorn was out in the hedges. An occasional wild cherry was a white flash in the wood. The higher trees had not yet leafed up but in the garden the magnolia petals were lying browned and scattered among the lungwort at their feet like the scales of a fish. There was color in the world. The pigeons were sitting in the trees like fattened Christmas decorations. From out in the arable fields, where the soil was still as bare and brown as it had been at the end of August, the daffodils, the forsythia, and the cherry blossoms in the orchard blazed away. You could smell the soil drying in the sun as if it were some kind of vegetable mass.

With Helen and then again with Phil I walked across the empty arable fields. Nothing was growing in them. Nothing had been planted and the weeds had been sprayed off. Everywhere around us, the celandines were emerging in the hedge banks and the garlic along the stream, the anemones and the first of the bluebells were out in the wood. The cuckoo was cuckooing, there were yellowhammers and blackcaps, and some larks were singing high above us, embroidering their song on the glowing air, but the earth beneath our feet was lifeless, a dusty and degraded place. Phil had a spade with him, and in one arable field after another he dug into the surface. Everywhere, in Frogmead and in Lodge and Large, even in Banky on the far side of the Hammer Brook, the spade went in an inch or two and stopped. That top couple of inches was loose and friable, but below it the earth had compacted into solid and impenetrable clay. There were some wormcasts here and there on the surface, but when Phil dug deeper and revealed a section in the side of small square hole, he showed me how nothing living was penetrating deeper than the surface inches. Here were the results of decade after decade of extractive agriculture. Some farmyard manure was still spread on these fields, and they were occasionally broken up with a subsoiling plow, but in essence they had been squeezed and compacted to within an inch or two of their lives. The Soil Association is called that for a reason: the basis of organic farming is attending to the well-being of the soil. It is the matrix in which life— bacterial, vegetable, and animal—has its beginnings. Here the matrix was little better than a polystyrene block, the sterilized background into which artificial fertilizers could be injected and high-intensity grains grown. That pale, lifeless soil was a picture of everything that had gone wrong. You only had to look at it to see that an organic system here, one that rested the land from time to time in fertility-building leys, that restored organic matter to these lifeless soils, was the only way this scheme could go. Organic was the obvious and default option.

Only in one place did Phil's face light up. Just outside the restaurant, in the Cow Field, where the dairy herd had always been turned out after milking, I dug Phil's spade in. If you had been watching it in slow motion, you would have seen, with my first plunge, its worn and shiny leading edge slicing down into the green of the spring grass, slowly bury-ing the full body of the blade in the earth and traveling on beyond it so that the spade came to rest with the ground level an inch up the shaft. Nothing wrong with that. I sliced out a square of turf and lifted it over. A delicious tweedy-brown crumbling soil appeared, a Bolognese sauce of a soil, rich and deep, smelling of life. Inside the small square trench, juicy beefsteak worms writhed in the sunlight. Here was James Stearns's "best bit of dirt on the farm," the stuff in which he had said we could grow anything we liked. "It's got to be the veg patch, hasn't it?" Phil said. Smiles all over his face. Peter Dear, the NT warden, came with his dog, and the three of us lay down on the grass there, looking across the Low Weald to the northeast, chatting about the birds, and how they loved the game crop in Lower Tassells. There were two larks making and remaking their song high over Large Field below us. How could we ensure the new farm was as friendly to birds as that? It was a moment when I felt I could see something of the future, that slow, exploratory, otter-like feeling, which you recognize only as it rises to the surface in-side you, that an idea might be one worth having.

It was clear from the beginning that the consultants' task was more than to provide a set of plans and figures. Anything new had to fit with the old. Helen said to me almost as soon as she arrived that none of it would work unless both Sissinghurst and the Trust subscribed to it. So we were to have meetings, partly to hear what Sissinghurst thought of the ideas and partly to tell Sissinghurst what the ideas were.

Late in April 2006, we all gathered in the lower part of the restau-rant, the whole Sissinghurst community, which almost never gathered in one place. The anxiety was palpable in the room. I was nervous and I knew both Jonathan Light and Helen Browning were too. Helen had brought with her some facilitators, two glowingly beautiful, clear-eyed young women in plum and lime-green cardigans from the Soil Association. I told Helen afterward how marvelous they were. "I've got shedloads of those," she said.

We split into groups and discussed what meant most to us about Sissinghurst. Jo Jones, one of the gardeners, summed up the best of Sissinghurst as "established slowly over time; vulnerability; fragility; tenderness." Claire Abery, another gardener, liked the feeling of a whole estate but said she would be glad if the visitors never turned up. People loved the sense that the place was full of its stories, that Sissinghurst somehow had an emotional existence beyond its bricks and lawns.

Then we came up with some ideas for the future. Several people said, "Do nothing," and "Make no change." The anxiety had its origins, I think, in a fear that any changes could only be for the bad. For many years the gardeners had defended Sissinghurst against what they had seen as excessive commercialization from NT Enterprises, the Trust's business arm, and thought of themselves as the guardians of Sissinghurst's soul. On top of that, the years of reduced spending had meant that the gardeners' eating and washing facilities had not been updated since the 1960s and were frankly disgraceful. The restaurant building had not been improved since the early 1990s. The offices and workshops were far below the standards expected in everyday commercial life. Many people working at Sissinghurst had been clamoring for these improvements for years and nothing had been done. Now here, apparently, as soon as Adam turns up, there was money a-go-go for consultants, plans, changes. Why was that? And was it fair?

Many months later, the head gardener, Alexis Datta, apologized to me for the "negativity" she had shown to these ideas over the months. The roots of the hostility between us were in some ways very simple. We both thought we knew what the essential Sissinghurst was, and both felt proprietorial about it, but the two visions didn't match up. What I was suggesting had its roots deep in the historical soil of Sissinghurst, but no one here had ever seen any of it. They did not know what was missing. What I thought of as old and better they saw as new and suspect. Nor did they see any lack in the farm. "What could be better than that?" Alexis asked me one day when pointing across the grass of the

Cow Field and the big arable fields beyond it. "I want it to be kept like that," she said. Her friend the gardener Jacqui Ruthven told Alexis that Sarah and I coming to live at Sissinghurst was "like having white trash move in." It is not particularly easy to be told that, but I recognized well enough that we represented disruption, unneatness, a departure from the way it had been for the last ten or fifteen years.

I had not understood one crucial point. Everything I was suggesting drew its inspiration from what I had known and seen forty or forty-five years ago. My plans seemed to me like a regrounding of Sissinghurst, a return to the condition—or a version of it—in which it had existed for centuries. To almost everyone else, though—if not my sisters and not the Beales, Stearnses, or Cliffords—it felt like a major disruption of something that, in their experience, up to seventeen years in one case, had "always" been as it now was. My return to source was for them a destruction of perfection.

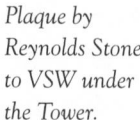

Plaque by Reynolds Stone to VSW under the Tower.

There was some recent history to this. Under my father's stimulus, and an unrelenting publicity campaign, publishing volume after volume about his parents' intriguing lives, visitor numbers had peaked at 197,000 in 1991. The whole place and everyone working in it were stretched beyond any sense of ease or comfort. It was felt that the "spirit of the place" was being damaged by its tourist business, and a new strategy was set up: stop all publicity, reduce visitor numbers, introduce timed tickets to the garden, and cut expenditure so that Sissinghurst could begin to accumulate a financial reserve. The income from that reserve would mean in future that Sissinghurst no longer needed to rely on a huge visitor flow. By 1992 visitor numbers had dropped to 151,000, and went down to 135,000 in 2001. Meanwhile, the strategic reserve was steadily growing. The threat of crass commercialization had been averted and the ideal of stillness and quiet, a steady state, had come to replace it.

What I was saying seemed to be overturning that, and it would continue to be difficult for months. At times it became personal. When I sat down opposite one of the gardeners at one meeting, she said, "Oh God, do we really have to have you here?" In May we had two gardeners come for the day to do the flower beds in our part of the garden, which we had left untidy. "Thank God someone is doing something about this garden at last," Alexis said to them. "But don't do it too nicely, will you? Why don't you go to the farm they used to live on and make that garden a little bit nicer and with any luck they'll leave us and go back and live there."

My head told me that it was a question of washing away the fears. And that there was also a perfectly hard set of constraints: Sissinghurst did not need any more visitors, nor too much of a drain on its running costs. Any plans had to be careful about not damaging what was already here. But in the face of all this it was difficult to maintain buoyancy and conviction. People higher up the Trust were prepared to countenance our plans; at Sissinghurst I felt increasingly besieged. I cherished tiny breakthroughs. Early one morning, Claire Abery told me that she had been given Sarah's book about growing vegetables, she was loving it, and was planting up raised beds in her garden. "Most of the time people don't join up the aesthetics with growing the veg, but Sarah has done it," she said. I said Sarah was keen to help in growing the vegetables here. "Do you think I could do it with her?" Claire said. I could have kissed her.

At the end of April 2006, I asked Simon Fraser, a good and wise friend of mine, what we should do. He was sanity itself. I should put my ideas and energy into setting things up now in the way I thought they ought to be. Be patient. It takes time for ideas to become clear. Make sure the farm was combined with the farm shop and restaurant so that they were mutually supportive, not in some kind of market competition with each other. Don't get financially, managerially, or practically in-volved, as that would end in grief and upset. Sarah and I should remain as members of the Sissinghurst Farm Board, to trim the direction it would take in the future. Eliminate risk, have no areas of conflict, give Sissinghurst what you can, and then leave the National Trust to it. That was all we could do. It belonged to them and they would have to man-age it. We shouldn't ever put ourselves in a position where we were claiming more than they could possibly give. Gauge that gap. Go where there is a door to be opened. Don't think of demolishing walls.

I realized, as Simon spoke, that this was an exercise in adulthood, in understanding the nature of organizations, and perhaps of places. It was unlike writing, where all you had to do was get the sentences and paragraphs in a clarifying and pleasing order. This was about having an idea, getting it in order, and only then creating a culture—in the sense of a laboratory culture, a growing environment—in which the ideas could take root and flourish. It was going to be slow and would never follow a straight line. And it needed the other side to speak. Nothing would happen unless everyone involved in the life of Sissinghurst made their claims on these ideas. It wasn't a question of recovering Sissing-hurst but the opposite: allowing it a life, giving it what we could, gradually easing the concerns of people who worked here, understanding that we had to adapt our ideas to the sense of tranquillity that they cherished. The coexistence of vitality and tranquillity: that was the ideal, a kind of balanced health. And then confessing to ourselves that Sissinghurst had a life that stretched far beyond us.

I could feel myself being educated by this process. My previous experience of organizations had been either at the top or at the bottom. As a journalist, I merely did my best to provide what the paper wanted. A reporter is only a tool in the proprietor's hands; he certainly does not run the machine. And when I had run the small publishing company with my cousin Robert Sackville-West or helped Sarah run her Garden and Cookery School, we had made the simple decisions ourselves, with small staffs and clear, single purposes to fulfill. Sissinghurst could not have been more different: viscous, anxious, convoluted, not entirely articulate about its needs, slow to respond, occasionally crabby, yet at other times warm, friendly, receptive, nurturing, and generous. It was, in other words, rather old in the way it did things, and that oldness and embeddedness, its maturity, had to be understood. New oldness: that was the goal.

CHAPTER 6

Occupation

FROM OUT IN THE CLAY VALE, a mile or two away, Sissinghurst appears as a low, wooded ridge on the southern horizon. It
looks, perhaps, like anywhere in the distance or on a map, full of
promise and intrigue, a place, if you were given the chance, you might
like to occupy.

There are places in the Sissinghurst woods that looked like that
when I was a boy: huge oaks collapsed into dark, anoxic bogs where the
streams had leaked outside their banks; if you walked into the wet, the
mud would suck itself up over the top of your boots and fill the air with
rot; streamers of green-leaved honeysuckle were the only sign of life in
the decaying, mineralizing wood; what had been living and vegetable
was now falling apart, biology going back to its chemical constituents.
The blackened and slimed timbers, whose fibers you could pull apart
with your fingers, lay in the strangest and most exotic of pools, red,
metal-stained, where groundwater seeping out through the nodules in
the clay had taken on a rich, tomato-soup brilliance from the buried
iron, but clearly poisonous, with swirls on the surface, slicked up and
bleared, as if diesel had been dropped in the water.

That is how I think of the world of this ridge fifteen hundred years
ago: damp, dark, and disintegrating. It was called *Cadaca hrygc* then, the

second element of that name meaning back, spine, or ridge; the first, in which every "a" is pronounced long and thick—*Kardarker*—meaning "of the jackdaws." There may be something in the name itself that hints at marginality. The Anglo-Saxon word *cadac* or *cadaw* and its equivalents throughout Europe were always used as a metaphor for a pilferer or petty thief. Jackdaws are little avian foxes. Like their cousins the magpies, they steal any bright, glittery thing. So perhaps this was the meaning of Kardarker Ridge. At the place where the crumbling Roman road began its climb into the wooded folds of the Weald—I pass it every day taking my daughters to the station on the way to school—there, among the trees, in the fifth century, a band of outlaw, jackdaw pickpockets preyed on anyone who dared to come this way. Perhaps that was Sissinghurst then, named like a place in a western: Thief Ridge?

Maybe. It would fit with the early days of the post-Roman Weald, when the officials and functionaries of the Roman fleet had withdrawn and the authority of any early English overlord in the north of the county scarcely stretched this far into the forest. But if it was a moment of disintegration and lawlessness, it was also the start of the great medieval movement that would transform the Weald.

The end of Roman authority allowed a new, expansive, and even entrepreneurial culture to flourish in Kent. Like other heavily wooded parts of England, an independent culture grew up here of men and women reliant on themselves, on their axes and plows, owing few duties to any feudal superior, able to own property and sell it, capable of leaving it to whomever they liked in their wills, and looking for their well-being not to some lord but to their own struggles with the soils around them, a struggle that over many generations they succeeded in winning. It was a way of life treasured by Kentish people and here it was called "the custom of Kent."

Beginning probably in the fifth century, the first of the English were coming to settle this part of the Weald. They walked or rode in from the northeast, down the sinuous droves, across the chalk, and then over the Chart Hills, the routes that people and animals had already been using for thousands of years: down Sand Lane and Blackberry Lane, or along the track past Three Chimneys, which is still in part hedged well back from the road, wide enough to accommodate a driven herd or flock.

How did they arrive? Who were they? How did they establish themselves? How were these places made? In some ways the history of that settlement is particularly opaque. It seems that each drove led people from different parts of the periphery into the ancient forest. Around each drove, large, separate commons developed, a slice of Wealden lands, each common arranged to converge like the segments of a tangerine and each pushing in toward the center of the Weald from a great manor on its northern boundary. To the north of Sissinghurst one large common led in from the manor of Hollingbourne through Sutton Valence and on to Staplehurst. To the east, another came in from the manor of Wye through Smarden and Biddenden. Converging on Sissinghurst itself from the northeast were two commons based on the manors of Faversham, coming down through Headcorn and Frittenden, and Sturry, following the line of the Hammer Brook from the direction of the Chart Hills, whose level brow is the horizon seen from Sissinghurst to the northeast.

That is the administrative picture—and it remains full of queries. How was it decided who should go where? Were people told to go? Or invited? On all of that there is nothing to say. But there is another level at which these questions can be asked, and the place-names are the key to it.

There are a million acres in Kent. Scattered across them are more than eight thousand names marking places that have been occupied for more than a thousand years. No other part of England has anything equivalent to this density of ancient nomenclature, and that is because a thousand years ago and more, this was the landscape of individualism: no clustering; no early villages; little sense of community; a very early fragmentation into separate places, families spreading into all corners of the Weald. It is the landscape of private ownership.

This detailed gazetteer of anonymous lives is distributed across Kent at a density of one to every 125 acres, in effect a name per farm. It makes for a country of private and secluded places, as if each place has a taproot diving into the past. The big villages are no older than the hamlets, the hamlets no older than the farms, the farms no older than the name of a wood or a stream. It is country alive with detailed memory. Each tiny place is more significant to itself than to the parish or village of which it is a part. From the sandy hill between Sissinghurst and Bettenham, I can look across the neighboring farms: Bettenham itself, Brissenden, Whitsunden, and the manor farm at Frittenden. Just beyond the woods, obscured only by the trees, are Copden, Branden, a farm called High Tilt, others called Comenden and Camden, perhaps originally part of one place. The far side of Hocker Edge, Hawkridge, and Hartridge (three thirds of one holding?) are Tolehurst, Lovehurst, and Snoad, Friezley, Buckhurst, Wilsley, and Angley, Flishinghurst and Glassenbury.

These small places are the foundation of the Weald: I love them for the rounded angularity of their names, as Wealden as the timber-framed buildings still to be found on them, and as pure a litany of Wealden Kentishness as could ever be written. None is famous beyond itself. All have conducted their private lives across the centuries, wringing a living from difficult soils, all of them an interfolded mixture of wood and coppice, meadow and stream, all of them bedded into the sands and clays that underlie them.

This is the world in which Sissinghurst and its name also have their origin. Like all those other places, Sissinghurst is the landscape of its own privacy, continuous with its past. It is a place, like everywhere else around it, that is worn and used, as Edward Thomas once described

The old Rosa gallica "Sissinghurst Castle," discovered by Vita Sackville-West in 1930 growing among the weeds and rubbish of the ruined site. It had probably been planted here in the 1560s.

The Hammer Brook where it runs through the Sissinghurst farmland: like a vein under the skin, a place of privacy and escape.

The Sissinghurst woods in May: bluebells under the chestnut coppice,
oak standards above them.

Blackberry Lane, the oldest thing at Sissinghurst, in use for perhaps
the last three thousand years.

OPPOSITE: Sissinghurst's greatest tree, an oak pollard that was young
when Queen Elizabeth I came to stay in the 1570s.

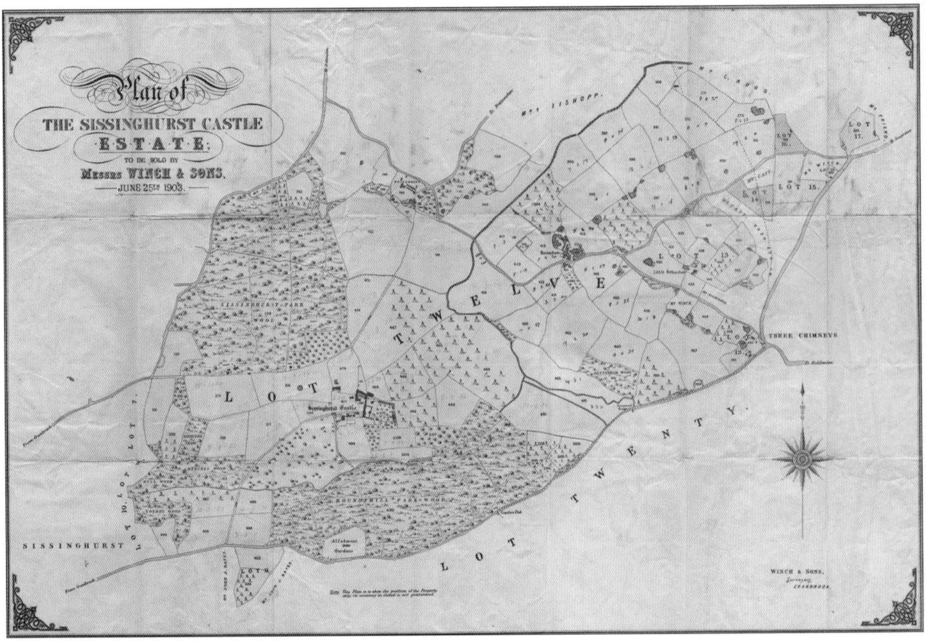

The Sissinghurst estate in 1903, the product of high Victorian farming and woodsmanship.

Sissinghurst in its environment: farm, parkland, and the distant hills of North Kent.

The view from the Tower over the purple border, the oast houses and cattle sheds, the fields and woods beyond them: a garden in a ruin in a farm.

Vita Sackville-West's workroom in the Tower: the gravitational center of Sissinghurst, its presiding secrecy.

An early summer morning, mist in the stream valley and in the edges of the wood,
Vita's luxurious planting, Harold's strict design.

"Iceberg" roses and the wild Chinese rambler Rosa mulliganii over the
central crossing in the White Garden.

Summer 2008:
the first lettuces for the restaurant in the new vegetable garden overlooking the arable fields of the northern part of the farm.

Summer 2009: *Sarah Raven with lettuces, squash, and parsnips for the restaurant and Amy Covey, the National Trust's vegetable gardener, behind her.*

July 2008: "*I find in chain / The castle, and the pasture, and the rose. / Beauty, and use, and beauty once again / Link up my scattered heart.*" V. Sackville-West, "Sissinghurst," 1932.

a stretch of country he knew and loved, "like a schoolboy's desk that has blunted a hundred ingenious knives."

Beyond that general understanding, though, and using the research done before the last war by J. K. Wallenberg, a Swedish etymologist from the University of Uppsala, one can start to read in these farm names the contours of a lived past. They record the phase after the bleakness of Cadaca Ridge, and represent a moment when once again the landscape became humanized and settled.

The twenty-five square miles around Sissinghurst cross the boundary between the clays to the north and east and the higher, sandier ridges of the High Weald to the west and south. Within this little local province, five miles square, with nowhere more than three miles from Sissinghurst, there are, remarkably, seventy-four places that acquired their names at least a thousand years ago. What is here now, for all the roundabouts and golf clubs, the prison and crayfish lagoons, the private schools and the carpeted pubs, is in essence a depiction of what was here in the millennium before last.

The names of more than a third of Sissinghurst's neighbors (twenty-six of them in the twenty-five square miles) end in the suffix -den. Dens surround Sissinghurst on all sides. The name means "a pasture for pigs," and so this, deep down, is swine country, which is one of the reasons I am so keen to have some pigs back at Sissinghurst. That does not mean that it was exclusively woodland. Pigs were and are the key ingredient of peasant farming throughout northern Europe. They breed quickly, they are omnivorous, and, although certainly hungry for acorns and beechmast, cannot live on them alone. Pigs fed only with that kind of tree nut sicken and die. They need the worms and beetles and greenery they get from rooting around in a multiple and diverse environment if they are to thrive. They like the waste from kitchens. They are rather good to be with. Their meat can be preserved by smoking and salting (there were giant salt works on the north Kent marshes throughout the Middle Ages). They are the great generalists, relishing the acorns they would have got from the Wealden oaks but needing a mixed landscape. Of all farm animals, they are the natural companions for anyone deciding to make their way into new country.

1950s: *Pigs at Bettenham.*

Alongside the swine pastures are sixteen -*hursts*—from *hyrst*, meaning a wood, probably on a hill, perhaps enclosed. The hurst is the natural companion of the den, the surviving fragment of woodland, perhaps coppiced for firewood, alongside the open, treed pastures in which the pigs (cattle, horses, oxen, chickens, goats, and sheep) are grazing. The existence of a place known as a wood can only mean that much of the landscape was not wooded around it. Most of the hursts are to the north and east of Sissinghurst, away from the great blocks of forest to the south, standing out in the largely cleared land of the Low Weald.

The third element, of which there are nine examples here, most of them concentrated to the southwest of Sissinghurst, on the high, light soils going toward Cranbrook, are places ending in -ley, a rubbed-down version of the Old English word leah. Its etymology is connected to "light," a clearing, and the name is a sign of country made up of "woodland with glades," perhaps the fragmentary edges of the forest, where corridors of pasture led into the thicker woods to the south.

Even at this most generalized level, it is an intriguing picture from the Dark Ages. These place-names describe almost exactly what you would expect from the descendants of Frans Vera's open, browsed woodland: some pasture, perhaps cleared; knots of slightly denser wood; and passages of country, particularly on the lighter land to the southwest, that mark the transition between the two, the Kentish parklike savanna.

These names are the hyphen between now and then. Hurst, den, and ley make for a human landscape, one in which the atmosphere of Kardarker Ridge has been left far behind. A subtle, interfolded life was being lived here. Undoubtedly, the Germanic English coming into the Weald were expert carpenters. In the absence of many arable crops for thatching straw, they would have made oak shingles for the roofs of their large, rectangular timber houses, in which smoke rose from a central hearth to the height of an open hall. They could turn cups from blocks of applewood and field maple. Archaeologists have found Dark Age flutes made of hawthorn. The first Wealdsmen had hammers, adzes, drill bits, gouges, planes, draw knives, saws, and wedges with which to transform timber into their houses and furniture—all of these have been found. But this was also the world of *Beowulf*, and in both landscape and poem it was the axe that was the instrument of destiny, for felling trees, lopping and topping the trunks, and perhaps occasionally for imposing violence and asserting will. The axe was followed by the heavy plow, the team of oxen and the dogged plowman behind it, described in one Old English poem as *"harholtes feond"*—the gray enemy of the wood. Here, on a kind of internal frontier, the expansive and acquisitive culture of the early Middle Ages was taking in the forest.

They would have hunted too, especially perhaps in the ley lands, the glades leading into the heart of the forest, some of which, around Angley near Cranbrook, were later in the Middle Ages to be converted by the archbishop into a park reserved for his hunting. In Saxon hunts, hounds were used to drive the wild boar onto the points of spears and javelins held by men standing in its path. Both roe and red deer were hunted through the English woods and wolves pursued, often into specially dug pits, where they could be killed and skinned, for the most glamorous coats known to Anglo-Saxon England.

The place-names are a guide to this landscape, and one can chase them down to another level of detail. There is variation, flickerings of happiness and failure, of individual enterprise and fiercely staked identity, the cast of an ancient epic still distributed across the fields and woods. At their simplest, the names do no more than describe the places as the new arrivals found them. There is a Hartley the other side of Cranbrook, which means "the glade of the deer." Two Buckhursts, one on either side of Sissinghurst, look as though they might also be deer woods, but they are in fact a corruption of *Boc-hyrst*, meaning beech-wood. The modern owners of one of the Buckhursts have planted a beech avenue as an act of vegetable memory. There's a Maplehurst—a beautiful wood on a little hill that still does have maples in it—an Exhurst (ash—no wood at all there now), a Hazelden, an Iden (yew), and an Ibornden, which is a swine pasture by a stream with a yew. Others are simpler still. Hareplain near Bettenham is what it says it is. Rogley, on the edge of Hemsted Forest to the south, is a rough *leah*. Wadd, now a large and beautifully timbered fifteenth-century house on the way to Staplehurst, is the same word as Weald, meaning something like wood or perhaps wood-pasture, and it does indeed have a large hornbeam coppice next to it. Two Chittendens, one toward Benenden, the other near

Staplehurst, were pastures where growth sprang up, the same word we now use for chitting potatoes, and The Freight, a luxurious house outside Cranbrook, where lawns spread and roses tumble between the yew hedges, comes from an Old English word that means the furzy growth on what had been cleared land.

This is the natural landscape, variegated and full of life in the margins of wood and pasture. The gaps between the old droveways were starting to fill, as if color were flooding into the outlines of a drawing. Sewn into this natural world is a layer of places named after what people had done to them. These names, of great simplicity, are thought to be early, part of the first colonization of the wood and its margins. So there is a place south of Sissinghurst that is simply called Hemsted, meaning homestead, the first place there that anyone had made their home. What is now called Sissinghurst village was until the nineteenth century known as Milkhouse or Milkhouse Street, a name older than it sounds, meaning a dairy settled around the old straight Roman road than ran through it. The farm called High Tilt, on the next ridge south from Sissinghurst, all tennis courts and gravel drives today, was originally called Tilgeseltha, which meant something like a collection of shacks by the tilled ground. (Tilt is the same as tilth.) And around High Tilt the soils are still good enough today for arable crops to be grown between the blocks of wood.

Then the individuals come up out of the ground: places named simply after the people that settled there. Bubhurst—now a beautiful house near Frittenden just off the old drove to Headcorn—is the wood of a man called Bubba. Frittenden itself and Friezley near Cranbrook were both settled by someone called Frithi. Branden, next to Copden, was originally called Berryingden, meaning the pasture of Berry's people. And at Bettenham there was a Betta or even a Betti, perhaps the first woman to own property here. The -ham element of the name—still pronounced as "ham," not "em"—comes not from -ham, a farm, but from the Old Frisian for a flat meadow by a river, *hamme*. That is exactly where Bettenham is, on what are now arable fields but were until the nineteenth century a long string of lovely damp meadows by the Hammer Brook. The name of the stream itself may also be a memory, not of the much later ironworking hammers in Hammer Mill but of ancient meadows, the Hamme Brook, the name preserving almost uniquely the voiced second syllable of the Germanic *hamme*. So Bettenham was Betty's Meadow on the Meadow Brook: could anything be more alluring than that?

A recognizable world seems to balloon up out of the names, as if a constancy and normality had survived the massive transformation of the intervening centuries. Already, in the very beginning, the generations were passing. Lovehurst down in the clay lands toward Staplehurst means "the hurst that was left to someone in a will": Legacy Wood. Its near neighbor, Tolehurst, originally called Tunlafahirst, means something like Heir's Farm Wood. Inheritance and all the implications it carried of legality and order were already fully at work in what had become the highly legalized world of the Anglo-Saxons.

There is a final, surprising layer in this joint land-biography of a forgotten age: the place-names around Sissinghurst are full of jokes and taunts, nicknames and insults thrown across the woods and fields by one set of neighbors at another. It is an element that brings the spark of life to this wood-margin-farming world. Out in the wet of the vale, where even now on a winter's day the water lies dead in the ditches, there are two neighboring places called Sinkhurst and Hungerden. They are low in the damp ground, never where you would have gone if you had the choice, and their names clearly reflect what everyone else must originally have thought of them. (Hungerden did well in the hop boom of the nineteenth century and its ancient Wealden house was replaced then with a fine Victorian farmhouse. Sinkhurst still has nothing much to show for itself beyond a few cottages.) Both look like places in which it would be easy enough to sink into hunger and despair. Just as damp and not far away, until the nineteenth century, was a farm called Noah's

Ark. By comparison, their near neighbors on slightly higher rising ground, Buckhurst and Maplehurst, glow with health and well-being.

And Sissinghurst's own place in this dense social network? Its name is among the most intriguing. It is a hurst, a wooded hill as seen from the open meadows along the Hammer Brook. Its second syllable *-ing* means "the people of" or "followers of." And the first syllable, which had become "Siss" by the late sixteenth century, had begun life in the Anglo-Saxon centuries as *Seax*, which can mean any of three related things: a short sword, the *seaxa*, for which in Anglo-Saxon culture there was a reverence and cult, swords being handed down through the generations of a family; a man's nickname, *Seaxa*, his strength, flexibility, and beauty reminding people of a sword; or the people themselves, the Saxons, who were named collectively after the battle weapon they had originally borrowed from the Franks. So what was Sissinghurst? The wood of the men of the knife? The place belonging to a bladelike hero and his followers? Or the Saxon place? You can't tell.

There is one hint in another place-name, just to the west of here on the edge of the forest. It is possible that Angley near Cranbrook was the glade of the Angles. And so in the early English wood, it may be that two ethnically distinct settlements named themselves after the homelands they had left behind across the North Sea. This too is the world of *Beowulf*, an English poem, written and declaimed in England, to English men and women in English halls, but telling nostalgic stories, across the sea in the countries from which they all knew they had come. Perhaps Sissinghurst begins like that, as a colony, a planted place, whose inhabitants brought other memories and habits with them.

The name for me has always embraced the Dark Age world. It is not difficult, in the cold of an early winter evening, when the soil is cloddy and damp and the Hammer Brook is running thick and clotted with brown floodwater from rain on the hills to the south, to feel the presence of these people here: their timber hall, with the dark outside, a fire in the central hearth, the animals housed in the steading, shuffling in their straw or bracken beds, and in the light a tale being told, perhaps one of the great tales of Anglo-Saxon England, of our presence on earth being like the flight of a swallow through a winter hall, coming in from the night through one high window, spending a few airborne moments in the warmth and brilliance of the lit world, before flying out through the other end, back into the endless dark; or like the stories in *Beowulf*, of past heroes and blood, sea journeys and the monsters that stalk the night, in Seamus Heaney's time-shrinking phrase, "as a kind of dog-breath in the dark." That is what to imagine here: the Seaxingas drawn around their fires, alert to horror, held by stories that were intended to make their fears explicit, and to make more real their membership of the blood-band gathered beside them.

It would have been a good place. Seaxinghyrst was no Hungerden. It had some lightish, sandy-silty soils, which could be cultivated without too much labor. In the Park and in the Well Fields to the south of it, you can still see, in a low evening light, the shallow swellings and hollows of medieval strip cultivation on the light soils that modern agriculture no longer considers worth plowing but that in the Dark Ages and the centuries that followed would have been invaluable. Even in what is now the wood, in the winter when the place is bare, you can see the rise and fall of what were clearly the boundaries of medieval fields. Sissinghurst was workable from the start, and it may be that these light soils were open and treeless then. But Sissinghurst also had its woods, for heating and buildings. It had streams of sweet fresh water coming down through those woods and many springs emerging in the hillside to the south. Even in the 1920s, the gentlemen farmers who then owned Sissinghurst, the Cheesemans, used to bottle up the water and take it to families living out in the clay vale, where the people would fall on it as something more drinkable than the murky water from their own wells. And Sissinghurst had, above all, the meadows by the Hammer Brook, well-watered land that would grow grass early in the year, might even produce two hay crops in one summer, and that, until the coming of modern agriculture, was the most valuable land you could have.

✦ ✦ ✦

BY THE TIME THERE ARE ANY DOCUMENTS describing this place, that first folk-settlement phase was over and parts of this wood-pasture world were being explicitly granted to the manors on the good land lying beyond it. That is the moment at which this chapter began. In 843 the king of Kent gave this whole stretch of country to his "faithful minister" as an autumn pasture for his pigs. The king ordained that every year, for ever, Æthelmod's pigs were to be driven up here from Little Chart (along the drove coming southwest to Sissinghurst) to fatten on the acorns from the Wealden oaks. Anyone who interfered with the pigs, the charter makes clear, would suffer "everlasting damnation." The pigs were to stay for seven delicious and terminal weeks, from the equinox on September 21, when by tradition the acorns begin to fall, until Martinmas on November 11, the feast of Saint Martin, the patron saint of butchers, when they would be driven back to Æthelmod's manor in Little Chart to be slaughtered and salted for the winter. Sissinghurst had become a Saxon grandee's pig-fattening ground.

2006: *Chestnut coppice, oaks, and young beeches in Birches Wood.*

Nobody quite knows how all this worked. Pigs don't like being driven and tend to wander off at will. Would they really have been driven the fourteen miles from Little Chart and back again? Surely the journey to Sissinghurst and back was likely to slim them down quite as much as they would have fattened up on the fruits of Sissinghurst's forest? Nor is the situation on the ground at all clear. By the ninth century, the large early pieces of common, such as the original *Cadaca hrygc*, were being divided up into much smaller dens, each of them allocated to different manors. The ownership map of Sissinghurst and its neighboring lands, along with almost everywhere else in the Weald, soon became intensely complicated and has yet to be unraveled. Sissinghurst became a mosaic of wood, field, pasture, and meadow, but of many different landlords' holdings.

Kent was an increasingly busy place in the centuries before the Black Death in the mid-fourteenth century. The skeletal structure of the late Dark Age Weald was filling up. Many of the farms and hamlets surrounding Sissinghurst were occupied by incomers from the north of the county, squatting in the wastelands belonging to the great manors north of the Weald, or encouraged by the lords of those manors to bring the Weald into cultivation. The whole of the Weald had already been shared out, about five hundred dens belonging to one hundred thirty manors, with few fragments of common lying between them. Now, though, from the twelfth century onward, slowly and piecemeal, the third phase began: the emergence of separate manors within the Weald itself, not dependent on lordships in north Kent, but acting as the center of their own worlds. It is the point at which a visible identity for Sissinghurst begins at last to surface.

The name of the place, which until the nineteenth century was always part of the parish of Cranbrook, first appears attached to a man, Stephen. He is called "Stephen de Saxingherste." Fifty years later, his relation John de Saxenhurst is taxed for some lands in the parish of Cranbrook. These lands must have been the manor at Sissinghurst itself, and this John built himself a chapel here, dedicated to John the Baptist. A few years later, in 1242, a man who was perhaps John's son, Galfridus de Saxinherst, appears in a document named as the friend of the head of a priory at Combewell, a few miles away near Goudhurst.

It isn't much to go on, but it is possible—just—to construct a world from these fragments: a manor, pious, refined, just starting to material-ize out of the blurred background of wood and stream. Sissinghurst has come onstage occupied by its own family: the de Saxinghersts. If there had ever been a scattered hamlet of Seaxinga descendants, that mo-ment was now over. This one family owned and dominated the place. It was a manor with its own "rents, services, escheats and heriots"—in other words, a place where these lords could charge others to live and farm, demand work from them, reclaim property if a tenant misbehaved or died without heirs, and charge death duties on the death of any ten-ant. The hierarchies and expectations of feudal Europe had arrived. The de Saxinghersts sat at the top of their own small pyramid, friends of the higher clergy, with their own chapel and lands elsewhere in the county.

The family held an estate that had a central core at Sissinghurst itself, Copton, now called Copden, just over the ridge to the south, and a place called Stone, which has disappeared, but may be remembered either in Milestone Wood, which is just to the south of Copden, or may be the place near Cranbrook Common, recorded in the early eighteenth century when Sissinghurst still owned somewhere called "Milestone Fields in the manor of Stone." Beyond that central clump, the de Sax-inghersts also had some properties in "Melkhous"—the old name for Sissinghurst village—and were the tenants in 1283 of two of the arch-bishop's dens, Haselden just to the north of Milkhouse and Bletchenden in Headcorn, which their ancestor may have owned a hundred years before. "The heirs of Sissinghurst" were also in possession of a place called Holred. They paid five shillings a year for the "game they take there," easily the most rent paid to the archbishop by anyone in the

Weald. Among the archbishop's papers there are records of Kentish partridges caught by hawks, only a few pheasants, and some rabbits, as well as geese and swans, with woodcock in the winter woods, where they still come today, lurking in the thorns of the hedges, seen in the headlights when you come back late.

So the picture thickens: a small but high-quality estate distributed along the old grain of the country, the ancient droveways into the Weald from the northeast, with some good hunting attached, in what might perhaps have been a park near the house. Today, if I walk out the door at Sissinghurst, the possible site of Holred (a wood) is seven minutes away by foot; it takes me about a quarter of an hour to get to Copden (a house in a wood to the south); the same to the village; ten minutes beyond that to the site of Stone (many modern houses on small plots), which is next to Haselden (a medieval house). Bletchenden (now a wonderful half-moated medieval house and barns) is an hour and a half's walk in the other direction, up the old drove toward Canterbury, past Brissenden and Bubhurst, on a track that for part of the way is now no more than sheep-mown grass between ancient hedges.

It is one coherent world, a country of lands and manors cut out of the Weald. But what was it like? That is the repeated question. What did it feel like then? In return for protection and as a means of dominance, the de Saxinghersts would have imposed duties on the peasants who worked the land for them. It was a life of unremitting labor for the poor. They had to thresh the corn and cart the manure to the fields; maintain the lord's buildings; collect the straw; deliver wood; provide men for the bakehouse, the kitchens, and the brewhouse; make hazel hurdles for the sheepfold and then supervise the sheep when in it; fence off the young coppice woods from any marauding animals; mow, spread, and lift the hay in the lord's meadows; carry his letters; drive animals to other manors if required; drive pigs to the autumn pannage; collect the hens due from tenants; collect and carry the eggs; put their sheep into the lord's fold by which the sheep manured the arable ground in the lord's demesne, from which of course the lord would derive the benefit in the years to come.

The woods had shifted in purpose. In an increasingly populated world, the acorns and beechmast for pigs had become less valuable than timber and wood for people. The long story of coppice-with-standards, which came to dominate the Weald and the Sissinghurst woods, was in operation by the fourteenth century. The long-growing standard oaks provided the structural timber for buildings; the coppiced underwood the heating and fencing, faggots and tool handles, reinforcements for river banks, and even beds for the poor. Woodland was worth about the same per acre as good arable ground, not as much as meadow, and over a coppice cycle the value was not in the standard trees but in the repeated cropping of the underwood. It was a wood world: wooden shoes, wooden tools and instruments, wooden wheels and cogs for mills, wooden vehicles, wooden furniture, wooden houses, wooden heat, wooden shutters, wooden fencing, wooden hurdles. As late as the 1950s, the families who came from London to pick the Sissinghurst hops were given beds in their huts made of straw palliasses placed on an underlayer of hazel faggots from the wood. Mary Stearns has a wonderful photograph of her son James driving a trailer-load of them up the lane.

James Stearns transporting faggots, 1950s.

The great trees, which had originally been the source of the acorns and were often pollarded when young to produce a big head of acorn-bearing boughs, continued to belong to the landlords as a source of timber, even when the ground below the trees had been let to the tenants. The archbishop's bailiffs were fiercely defensive of the trees their master owned, prosecuting the tenants of Bettenham and seven other dens in the early fourteenth century for cutting down an extraordinary six hundred oaks and beeches, forty of them at Bettenham. This was one of the longest-lasting customs of the Weald. Even in the leases drawn up for my grandmother in the twentieth century, that ancient practice continued. When the farm was let to Captain Beale in 1936, he agreed to "keep all hedges properly slashed laid and trimmed in a workmanlike manner according to the best practice known in the district and to use no wire or dead thorns for repairing any quick hedges." All "timber and timberlike trees sellers and saplings" were to remain Vita's property and Captain Beale was to pay her five pounds for every tree or sapling he cut down.

In case this was still unclear, he agreed to "preserve all timber and other trees pollards and saplings underwood and live fences from injury and not to lop top or crop any of the timber timberlike trees or saplings likely to become timber." Unknown to either of them, it was a form of agreement that was at least seven hundred years old when they made it.

Among the woods, in the fields, or at least on the drier ground at the top of the farm, the Kentish men and women living here, speaking in their strange half-Dutch, would have striven for survival. Medieval England had no root crops. It was a world without potatoes, turnips, or parsnips. Instead, on the light land, they might have grown barley for brewing and as the staple for bread. On the best demesne lands wheat was grown for sale in markets (Cranbrook had one from 1289), but it is unlikely they would have grown it here. Instead, on the damp and heavy land they could have grown rye, which is drought-resistant and survives in dry years, and oats for animal fodder, which can tolerate wet and heavy soils. By the mid-thirteenth century, even here, legumes were be-ing introduced: peas, beans, and vetches to renew and refresh the soil, fixing nitrogen from the atmosphere as we now know, but then thought at least to be an improved version of a fallow, with the added benefit that stock could be turned into the pea or bean fields when they were ready. The yields were pitiful: for wheat you might harvest three grains for every one sown, spring barley two and a half to one, oats maybe three and a half to one. These figures meant that hunger stalked them. As the population grew and the poor soils were driven harder, they sank ever deeper into a fertility trap: not enough goodness going back into the soil, too much land going into feeding the draft animals on whose muscle power they depended, declining yields, more people, fewer nutri-ents per person. By the early fourteenth century, famine and chronic malnutrition prevailed across the whole of Europe. The Black Death arrived in the 1340s at a landscape and a population that were ready to welcome it.

In this system, nothing would have been more important than the draft animals. On the archbishop's manor at Bexley in north Kent, there were 312 farmed acres, a little bigger than Sissinghurst, and on better land, but broadly comparable. There were two hundred ewes, all-purpose animals, from which milk, lambs, wool, and skins for parch-ment could all be had. The sheep was the mainstay of mixed farming. Bexley also had twelve cows and a bull, but what is most surprising is the number of working animals, the tractors of the medieval enterprise: twenty plow animals, both oxen and horses, driven in teams of eight, often mixed, with one or two horses leading the ranks of oxen behind them, and sixteen draft oxen on top of that. They needed feeding, and of Bexley's farmed area, very nearly a third, ninety-six acres, was de-voted to meadow, to the grass on which these animals could survive.

Oxen were valuable: in 1264 four were sold at Bethersden for 7s 6d (seven shillings and sixpence) each. But meadows were more valuable still. They were richly treasured by the archbishop's estate managers, and it seems as if archiepiscopal farms were focused entirely on the availability of meadowland. On the archbishop's riverside estates at Westgate itself, outside Canterbury, at Otford, Maidstone, and Charing, and even at the outlying den of Bettenham, which was still attached to Westgate, meadow looms large in the accounts. Rent for a well-watered meadow per acre was double the rent on arable land and perhaps three or four times as much as on ordinary pasture. Meadows meant riches: more hay, which allowed you to keep more stock, including more oxen, and so more animal power to plow and harrow the land, more manure with which to enrich it, more cereal crops, more grains, and more food. The meadow was the route to well-being.

The meadows at Sissinghurst had gone by the late nineteenth century, but they continue to have a flickering ghost existence nearby. The neighboring meadows upstream have belonged to the Halls at Hammer Mill since the early twentieth century, but they certainly belonged to Sissinghurst in the Middle Ages and right up until 1903, or at least to its subsidiary manor of Copden in the wood beside them. They are there as a kind of reproach, still grassy, damp, alluring on a morning heavy with summer wetness, or in the dank and dusk of a winter evening when the mist drifts up out of them and the smell of the windblown apples in Mrs. Hall's orchard comes into your nostrils, musty and sweet. I have often been for late walks there, secretly, while the owls hoot in Floodgate Wood, beyond the banked channel that fringes the grass, and the lights in Hammer Mill Farm glow as yellow as apricots. If you can feel a lust for a kind of land, I feel it for those meadows, wanting more than anything else to return the Sissinghurst margins of the Hammer Brook to that condition. Instead, where our meadows once were, we have, at the moment, a dead and dreary arable field, which has suffered one cereal crop after another without break for years, where the soil itself is heavily compacted, and where in the winter the rain doesn't soak into a delicious, light, open soil structure but lies on its surface in sad-eyed pools. Only the name of the field recalls what it once was: Frogmead, a damp

and froggy place, along the banks of the meadow brook, a name redo-
lent of everything a Wealden John Clare would have loved here, a kind
of thick-pelted richness, with secrets buried inside it.

Frogmead is something of a test of Sissinghurst's condition. It was
once a marshland, a wet willow and alder wood. There are some heavy
willow pollards and giant alder stools here by the stream, eight or nine
feet across. The alders must be centuries old. Every year, they throw out
vigorous, purple-budded seedlings into the edges of the arable crops,
which survive until the summer when the combine shears them off an
inch or two above the soil and the power harrow mashes their roots.
Without that annual destruction, this would be a wet wood within a
decade. The first settlers would have loved the prospect of lush meadowland and would have cleared the alder wood for the grass as soon as they
arrived. Alder scarcely burns (I have tried: even after a year in the shed
it molders and hisses in the fireplace, giving out more damp smoke than
any heat), but it looks good as furniture, and they could have turned
cups and plates from it. Frogmead would then have remained an endlessly self-renewing meadow for centuries, perhaps even for thousands of
years. It may have gone back to wet woodland at the end of the Roman
period, but the early English would have cleared it again, and hay crops
would have been taken here throughout the Middle Ages and on until
the nineteenth century. The hay for the great brick barns built at
Sissinghurst in the sixteenth century would have come from these
meadows, but in the 1860s the feeder channels bringing water into the
meadowland were bridged over and filled in and a hop garden planted
here. When the hops were abandoned in 1968, Frogmead became an
arable field, which it has remained ever since. No hay comes off it anymore and the barns remain empty from one year to the next. Frogmead's
story is Sissinghurst's biography in miniature: after the ice age about
eighty centuries of wild marsh, twenty of meadow to sustain this place,
one of hops for the London thirst, and approaching half a century of
subsidized cereals for a global market. Only in the wettest depths of the

winter, when the Hammer Brook floods and brown rivers of clay-thick water leak out over the fields, do you see again the old multiple beds of the meadow watercourses very lightly creased into the land, invisible when dry, but made apparent when the Hammer Brook once again reclaims its own. Knowing this and seeing this, on the maps and in the floods, I determined to persuade the Trust to restore the meadows that had been here for so long.

At the center of the interlocked medieval world was the manor house and the high-gentry family to whom it all belonged. Judging by others that have survived, it would have been a timber-framed building, with a hall and a chapel, a private wing for the family, and a cluster of service buildings around it. At some time toward the end of the thirteenth century, the line of the de Saxinghersts failed and they disappear from history. Their place was taken by the de Berhams, a family with other holdings in Kent, perhaps related to the de Saxinghersts by marriage, and of great distinction. With them Sissinghurst achieved its late medieval flowering. They made this their principal seat and through them something of the quality of late medieval life can be felt here. It was still as remote a place as England knew. In 1260, Cranbrook church was described as being "in a wooded and desert part of the diocese through which the Archbishop has to pass and where no lodging can be found during a long day's journey." Even in midsummer, the roads were not clear. When the great warrior king Edward I came through the Weald in June 1299 (as he had two years before and would again almost at the end of his life in 1305), the royal exchequer issued "money paid by order of the King to seventeen guides leading the King when going on his journey." It was a busy royal cavalcade, distributing four shillings a day in alms to the poor, accompanied by messengers sent off each evening on royal business. Edward had his cook and sauce-maker with him, as well as William de Rude, the king's foxhunter, and two helpers, all dressed in English russet, along with John de Bikenorre, keeper of the king's hawks. Greyhounds, deerhounds, harriers, and beagles accompanied the horsemen. In the middle of June, this impressive party came down the old drove road from Charing, through Little Chart, past Smarden, and on the evening of June 19, 1299, arrived to spend the night at Sissinghurst.

Can one say what the king and his companions found there? Certainly a pious family of high status. One of the de Berhams was a major official of the archbishop's office in Canterbury. Another was knighted. A third, Richard, became sheriff of Kent, the county's chief law enforcement officer, married a Cranbrook girl, Constance Gibbon, and was one of the knights charged with command of the local militia. As well as Sissinghurst, he gathered estates on the Chart Hills, up the droveways in Charing and Pluckley, and was worth forty pounds a year.

A higher, finer version of the medieval world begins to emerge among the woods and fields. Among the de Berhams' neighbors are people called Nicolas and Petronilla, Bertram and Benedicta. From the tiny Trinitarian friary at Mottenden near Headcorn (now a farm called Moatenden) they had two friars to celebrate mass in the Sissinghurst chapel, an arrangement made decades earlier by the de Saxinghersts. One or two manuscript books survive in the Bodleian in Oxford from the Mottenden Priory library—works on medieval logic and grammar—and it is not unreasonable to imagine that the visiting friars may have brought them here too. The friars assisted the chaplain, an employee of the family.

There is one document above all that for the first time brings to Sissinghurst a sense of the interiors and even of interior life. It is a will made by Elisia de Berham in April 1381, now in the National Archives. She was the mother of Richard, who was to become sheriff of Kent, and was clearly a cultivated woman of fine sensibilities and deep piety. She asked to be buried in Cranbrook church and left money for prayers to be said for her soul. The vicars of other churches on the edges of Romney Marsh received legacies from her, as did her chaplain at Sissinghurst, Robert Couert, the friars in Canterbury, and the Carmelite friars at a small friary at Lossenham near Newenden, which is now a farm. The friars and master at Mottenden, who would have known her well, all received money.

Once she had catered for her soul, Elisia de Berham attended to those near her, perhaps those who had looked after her. For the first time, ordinary people living at Sissinghurst acquire their names. Robert Goldyng, Simon Addcock, Thomas Herth, Alice Addcok: small legacies of 6s 8d (six shillings and eightpence) to each of them. Then the precious objects in her life:

> To Johan Herst my daughter 10 marcs one of the best towels and a napkin. To Alice Creyse a blue bed and a saddle. To the wife of Thomas Hardregh a towel with napkin. To Elisia Addcok 10 marcs and a bed in which I lye with one "curtyn" and over-cover and a casket with little garments (*parvis velaminibus*) within.

This is not a world of high luxury but one in which the lady of the house gives something she cherishes to the women with whom she has lived. Finally, and poignantly, to her son:

> To Richard my son 10 marcs and a white bed complete and my Matins book and six silver spoons and one broken piece of silver, a good towel and napkin.

Here, then, is medieval Sissinghurst, a place not of riches but of great dignity, with precious beds in various rooms, some silver objects, but not so many that a broken piece is not valued. This is a place both deeply engaged with the sanctified life of pre-Reformation England and somewhere that exudes its own kind of gracefulness and clarity.

The de Berhams certainly contributed to the beautification of Cranbrook church. Their arms, along with those of the archbishop and the de Bettenhams, are on the west face of the church tower. What this means, intriguingly, is that the wonderful distilled lucidity and simplicity of Elisia de Berham's will, its delicacy and distance, are almost exactly contemporary with the wild-green-men bosses in that church, which the de Berhams almost certainly helped pay for.

Nothing much survived from that moment. The two friaries were dissolved, Mottenden in 1536 and Lossenham in 1538. Their vestments, a chalice or two, the bells, the kitchen equipment, and some of the friars' hay was sold off and the land leased out. At Sissinghurst itself, the de Berhams lasted probably until the 1530s, when they sold up, no one knows why. It has often been written that they sold Sissinghurst in the 1490s, but I can find no evidence of that. Only in 1533 did a newly rich family, the Bakers of Cranbrook, buy from them the manor of Sissinghurst and its lands, and with the Bakers Sissinghurst entered a new and dramatically different phase of it existence.

Almost nothing remains from those years. The moat, which now defines two sides of the orchard, is likely to be medieval in origin, even if adapted later. On an autumn day, its "black mirror of quiet water," as Vita described it, is another of the places into which the acorns steadily fall. There is nothing to be seen aboveground of the medieval house. The stone lip of drain possibly connected to the well in the court of that house can still be found in the wall of the Moat Walk. That well, just outside the South Cottage, was excavated by George Neve, the farmer and amateur antiquarian, to a depth of thirty-five feet in the nineteenth century, when human remains were found in it. It has now disappeared, but instead Peter Rumley, a Kent archaeologist and building historian, has made a new suggestion: the timbered buildings visible in a drawing made by one of the officers guarding French prisoners here in the 1760s might in fact be the de Berhams' medieval house, or at least an Elizabethan adaptation of it.

Big brick Elizabethan chimneys have been added to the timber frame, but the fretted bargeboards on the gables, the jettied-out upper stories, and the sense of accretion, of parts being added and adapted, as well as the close-studded oak timbers in the façades, all hint at this being a medieval building. In the washy pen and ink of a certain Captain Francis Grose, with the sentry boxes of the Hampshire militia in the foreground, this is probably as near as we can ever get to Sissinghurst before the Renaissance and its money changed it. (See page 166.)

1950s: *Oaks overhanging Sissinghurst moat.*

CHAPTER 7

Rejection

E ACH SPRING, SISSINGHURST CLICKS BACK into its public life. Before it opens to the public in March, there is a flurry of preparation. The garden beds are forked over, the lawns are given their first mow of the year. Paths are swept, the sign asking people not to tread on the flowers is wiped down and put out under the arch. The shop is restocked, the new restaurant staff are trained up in the arcane and complex systems of the kitchen and self-service counter, the warden has ensured that no tree is about to fall on any visitor, the stewards are asked to learn or relearn about the contents of the rooms where they stand guard, and the volunteers in the car park are trained in asking for the £2 parking fee. There is a sort of pre-party buzz, a place reawakening from its winter ease and privacy. It is a highly evolved and interlocking system, with more than two hundred people working here as permanent staff, seasonal staff, or volunteers. You only have to walk around this preoccupied, busy place to see that changing it was never going to be a question of simply having an idea.

Throughout the spring of 2006, the meetings on the farm project rolled on as before. Meetings! I have never sat around so many tables in my life. Jonathan said he had never taken part in anything that had involved so much consultation since closing down a factory with a workforce of four hundred. From time to time, someone would voice the idealism of it all. Caroline Thackray, the Trust's regional archaeologist, said, "The garden is there because the landscape is there. The setting is what lit up Vita's mind." Sarah Roots, the Trust's head of marketing in the southeast, told us all one day that "people should be walking through cowpats to get to the garden. They need to smell the farm as they go into the garden." Katrin Hochberg from the Soil Association said we should be "steered by a sense of community," and Sally Bushell that we should try to feel we had "the freedom to experiment."

The anxiety about change was never far away. I often felt I was trying to push a fat clay-mucky lump of otherness into the neat and productive workings of a clock. Ginny Coombes, the restaurant manager, was at full stretch, with 115,000 people coming through the restaurant over six months, a third of them in the six weeks between the Chelsea Flower Show and mid-July. The head gardener, Alexis Datta, didn't like the idea of vegetable-growing. "Horticulture is not as pretty as what we've got now," she said at one meeting. "I would prefer grass. Horticulture won't enhance the farm. I don't like the idea of polytunnels. But I don't want it looking deliberately old-fashioned either. I don't want to attract more people." She had big worries over visitor numbers, housing the people who were coming to work here, buildings, where they were going to be built, water supply, car parking, the capacity of the lane, what it was all going to look like, the effect on the surroundings. "I feel we are rushing into it," she said. "I don't want to sound negative. I don't really mind veg but I do mind the view from the top of the tower." Later she told me she was worried that some of the smaller fields I was advocating were going to look like "one of those privately owned stately homes where the owner is trying to get the punters in by having a few rare breeds in a little paddock."

Difficulties clustered around the business questions. Under the NT system, Sissinghurst retains all its own profits to invest in the future of the property. To maintain the flow of funds, the NT likes to see a

40 percent return on its restaurant turnover. Anything like that was looking very difficult under the new scheme. Could Sissinghurst be allowed, within the National Trust system, a special derogation so that it did not, at least for a year or two, have to generate quite such a high percentage of profit? That might be difficult, it was said, because other properties would complain.

Phil Stocker of the Soil Association produced some figures that laid out precisely what sort of farm resource the restaurant would need. The surprising fact to emerge was just how productive the land, even when managed on a low-intensity, organic basis, could actually be. The restaurant, with 115,000 customers a year, could be supplied from:

86 chickens laying eggs
2 dairy cows in milk at any one time
25 beef cattle
3 sows
a tenth of an acre of lettuce
half an acre of potatoes
a fifth of an acre of carrots
3 acres of wheat

The problem was not that Sissinghurst was too small; it was too big. But the economies of scale meant that a farm working with the quantities needed by a single restaurant would never be viable. A single sausage would cost ten pounds. The farm had to sell more elsewhere in order to reduce the cost of the produce sold to the restaurant to a reasonable price. To make the farm viable, it would also need to sell 48,000 eggs, 3,400 kilograms of beef, and 170 tons of grain. We all thought that much of this could go through a farm shop. But a farm shop with nothing but eggs, beef, and flour would be a sorry thing. So most of the farm shop would have to be stocked from elsewhere, which would mean that the village shop in Sissinghurst would have a competitor on its doorstep, tails would be wagging dogs, and a local crisis would erupt. I may have thought that what was needed at Sissinghurst was a little more connectedness. What each of these exercises revealed was the intricately knotted and knitted condition of life as it was.

We were confronting head-on precisely the problems that had produced the sort of landscape from which small farms, and even mixed farms of any size, had largely disappeared. These intractable difficulties were what lay behind the erosion of the world I had known as a boy. On top of all this, there were deep suspicions from some parts of the Trust about the viability of an organic system. Some people thought organic farming was worse for the environment. The commercial arm said their customers were not interested in organic produce. In 2005 the Trust had sold a million pots of local jams and honey, and it was clear from market research that most people thought the Trust was organic anyway. Wasn't going organic in danger of putting the whole Sissinghurst scheme at risk?

Clearly my ideas would be no good if they did not fit real-world conditions. It was all very well recovering the atmosphere of medieval Sissinghurst, but what good was that if the modern world could not accommodate those ideals? These were real objections, not mere anxieties or neuroses. The Trust understood the virtues of what I was suggesting, but they didn't want to end up looking stupid.

EARLY IN JUNE I WENT to a meeting held in London by the National Trust for all its donor families. It was a beautiful early summer morning when the sunlight stuck out from the side streets in diagonal mote-filled slabs. We were to meet in Spencer House, the great eighteenth-century private palace in St. James's, restored by Jacob Rothschild. I walked there from the station through the richest streets in Europe. Swallows cruised the length of the tarmac and early white roses were in flower on the edge of the park.

Spencer House is in the part of London where in the eighteenth
and nineteenth centuries every great family used to live, in a narrow
street but with a façade looking over Green Park. It is like a palace in
eighteenth-century Rome. A stone hallway. Upper-class men in soft,
well-cut suits, their skin as pampered as the wool. Ties that start out at
the horizontal buckle beyond the knot and dive for gold pins. Cufflinked
cuffs, tugged and adjusted. Burnished, pointy black lace-ups. The deepest level of the English establishment that, for all the changes of the last
century, seems to be as established as it ever was. Some women also in
wool, sub-Chanel. Giant diamonds. A gathering of the most ancient of
England. I talked to an old friend of my father's, the woman with the
most wonderful name in England: Mrs. Horneyold-Strickland. She had
been having trouble with the Trust over the flag at Sizergh Castle in
Cumbria. On a table were badges for everyone, a catalog of the peerage
and its wives, ranks of earls and viscounts, with their properties named
beneath them, or to be exact, their ex-properties, their ancestral places,
which now belonged to the Trust. I had never seen so many titles gathered together. It looked like the Congress of Vienna or Agincourt. I
pinned my badge on: "Adam Nicolson—Sissinghurst."

The NT high-ups were there: Fiona Reynolds, the director-general;
Sir William Proby, the chairman; Simon Murray, the director of opera-
tions; Sue Saville, our regional director. "I always introduce people at
this thing," Sue said to me, "but they always know each other already.
Freddy? He's my mother's second cousin. None of them have the faintest
idea who we are." So, indeed, I met my first cousin once removed, John
St. Levan, who lives on St. Michael's Mount, a National Trust house in
Cornwall. And my second cousin once removed, Robert Sackville-West,
my oldest friend, who lives at Knole, Vita's beloved childhood home and
now a National Trust house in Kent. A colonel of the Grenadiers asked
me, "How long have you put up with the Trust?" A couple of years, I
said. "You wait," he said. "It won't be long before you're not quite as

cheery." Coffee came round. Jacob Rothschild saw me. "How's the scheme?" Fine, I said. Paintings from the Italian Renaissance on the walls, a perfect private palace, like a hotel that wasn't scuffed in the way of hotels. We sat on rows of little chairs in the great dining room. Robert and I were together in the front row, a wonderful team feeling to have him there. Simon Murray said the Trust wanted to delegate, to push decision-making down to the regions. Then the grumbling began.

The only reason these people were there is that they had been taxed into these chairs. The NT mechanism had provided them, or their fathers, with a way of continuing to stay in their houses, to pretend that the world remained as it was before 1911, before modern tax laws began to redistribute the extraordinary wealth this room had once represented. Now these dinosaur donors had the illusion of significance but not the substance or the power. The low whine of impotence came from the ranks behind me. The NT staff were hopeless because they were poorly paid. The NT was taking a purely commercial attitude with its estates and should understand something about communal coexistence. One famously cantankerous lady could barely contain her rage, about what was not clear. Someone asked how the Trust could think of buying new properties such as Tyntesfield, the huge Victorian country house near Bristol, when they couldn't pay their property managers enough. Murray explained the difference between grant-funded capital expenditure and daily running costs.

It was a pitiable scene. What was intended, I suppose, as an airing of views, even a gesture by the Trust to show that the dinosaurs mattered, felt in the event like a demonstration of their irrelevance. The very meeting in this glamorous London palace set up the Trust as a large, powerful, centralized body, and the lords and ladies assembled in the room as an old, nostalgic, and emasculated audience, saturated in self-pity. I thought, first, as I sat there, how much I would prefer to be at the National Trust table looking at us than in one of our little chairs looking up at them. But then I remembered that every occupant of every chair in that room had their own Sissinghurst, their own book like this one bundled up inside them, written or unwritten, thought or unthought, and that these thin, wheedling complaints were only the voices of attachment and the love of place somehow translated into the wrong tone and the wrong language. I wondered then whether the Trust's relationship to its donors was correctly framed. There was so much buried passion in this room, but apparently so little engagement. It was framed as an opposition, but could it not be framed as a partnership? Perhaps these crusty men and women could become in effect "inheritance consultants," the experts in buried meaning, in the folding of the past into the management of the future? If the Trust didn't do that, the result was this: complaint, a jangled joylessness, the old, long-repeated idea that things weren't what they used to be.

At lunch, on one side I was next to a well-primped lady with angry opinions and antediluvian views, loathing the Trust on class grounds, making no pretense that she didn't, as she ate their lunch and describing at length the "agonies" of building an extension to her house. On the other side was Sarah Staniforth, the Trust's historic properties director, wife of the leading environmentalist Jonathon Porritt. She talked about how houses had to be slept in if they were to be known. I talked to her about Gaston Bachelard and his idea that the purpose of a house was that it allowed one to dream in peace. If you got that right, everything else would be right. Maybe the tenancy of the Priest's House at Sissinghurst, I said, might become the prize for an arts competition? A year's tenancy with a poem or a painting as the rent? She wasn't completely averse.

After lunch I talked to the Cornish colonel again. He and his brother had twinned estates. They were too rich to feel comfortable in the position they were in but not rich enough to do anything about it. It was clearly best to be either a Rothschild—with enough money to call the shots—or a Nicolson, with no money and happy in the end to receive whatever might be on offer.

✦ ✦ ✦

LATER THAT WEEK, SARAH AND I had what Claire Abery, the gardener, called our "famous day." We invited a cluster of people to come to Sissinghurst to discuss the ideas we had been chewing over: garden designers, chefs, experts in retailing and restaurants, journalists interested in the new food culture, organic growers, people with a passion for the meaning of the landscape. It was in effect a company strategy day, an attempt to enthuse Sissinghurst and the people who work there with the sort of thinking that all these outsiders were dedicated to, and who in their different ways represented new attitudes to land, food, people, and the connections between them. Was it naïve to think that Sissinghurst might take to their suggestions with alacrity? In retrospect, I think it might have been. People really don't want to be told to do things differently, whoever is doing the telling.

The Rose Garden at Sissinghurst, Tower in background.

The outsiders all gathered at Sissinghurst on a beautiful evening early in June to spend the night here and talk the following day. It was a strange summer. The irises and the roses were out at the same time, which was rare, playing havoc with the color system in the garden. But the southern end of the White Garden was in full fiesta, the lovely white Sibirica irises, the white poppies, the little white roses like something from a Persian miniature all covered in bees. The orchard was thick with sorrel and buttercup-sprinkled grass.

Sarah had filled the house with flowers from the garden at our farm twelve miles away in Sussex: sweet-smelling stocks, the firework alliums called *Schubertii*, creamy speckled foxgloves, some crinkled Iceland poppies, and dark purple columbines. The doors of the house were all open and the light came flooding into spaces that all winter and spring had been dark. Just to look at it filled my balloon of optimism. Surely, here, from this, people could find their way to a better future.

But Sissinghurst seems inseparable from anxiety. We had first the worries over the seating plan at dinner. The scheme was to surround each of the people who work here with the people who had come from outside, hopefully with inspiring ideas. Katrin Hochberg from the Soil Association was convinced that this was going to backfire. The people who work at Sissinghurst, she told me over the phone, were going to think, "What the hell is going on? Who are these people swinging in here telling us what to do?" There was the danger that after so much careful buildup and so much consultation the thing would explode in acrimony and resentment.

There were drinks under and on top of the Tower. Kent was looking as beautiful as the day my father had showed it all to the secretary of the National Trust forty years before. The Italian chef Antonio Carluccio and his wife, Priscilla Conran, were warmth and encouragement. Jo Fairley, who invented Green & Black's organic chocolate, said I should have courage. I said I was overbrimming with it. Guy Watson, who grows organic vegetables on a large scale at Riverford in Dorset, and Will Kendall, who made a national success of the Covent Garden Soup Company, both said, "It's just so obvious. None of us can work out why we are even here. Why don't they just do it?" I told my old university friend, the writer and gardener Montagu Don, what they had said. He said everybody thought the same. Here was one of the central aspects of this story. An individual entrepreneur would feel in his bones that he should just do it. But somehow institutions can't behave like that. They have to commission studies, articulate the opportunities and risks, weigh the strengths of an idea against its weaknesses, and bring every aspect of a scheme into fully examined light. That, to me and these friends of mine, looked very like sclerosis, a furred and clogged decision-making system, when what was needed was simple, quick decisiveness. But I couldn't avoid a disturbing thought: institutions may be unable to just do it, but institutions, mysteriously, are what do it more than anything else *in the end*. None of these famous media and business entrepreneurs had three and a half million members behind them, but the National Trust did. What was the relationship between these things? Was the Trust slow to decide because it was big and old? Or was it big because it was slow? Had it lasted because it was slow and careful? Was there a relationship between the viscosity of institutions and the power they wield? And was this lack of spontaneity the reason they survived? Or was it just big-organization conservatism: we've always done it like this, so there is no reason to change?

I sat next to Fiona Reynolds and for the first time had a talk with her about the deeper motivation for these ideas. She told me how when she was at Cambridge she had been entranced by *The Making of the English Landscape*, the book by W. G. Hoskins that had invented the idea of landscape history. It was a book I had fallen in love with at exactly the same time. And then I talked to her about Sissinghurst, what we were trying to do. It was a chance to encourage people into a new way of seeing things, I said. She undoubtedly saw the Trust as an organization for leading people a bit further, for providing the enrichment that comes from beautiful places. She had spent four years sort-ing out the Trust's finances and governance. Now, maybe, I said, was the point when something else could come to the front, when the Trust could be renewed as something that reconnected itself to other, newer, older, more inspiring ideas, where it wasn't just a middle-class comfort zone. Meaning? she asked. Would she consider, for example, experimenting with Sissinghurst as a place in which financial targets set from elsewhere in the Trust might be suspended? Where we could look to set up a garden/farm/shop/restaurant system that focused more on the place's own well-being than on the straightforward bottom line? Where a glowing ideal of a landscape and a life wasn't hung up on gross profit margins? Her reaction to that was an "Mmm," but with a rising inflection . . .

We had our long, enjoyable, and sometimes slightly angry meetings in the sunshine the next day. Everyone agreed that there should be no hint of the farm being a demonstration farm, with signboards or the rest of it. It should simply function and be, remaining subsidiary to the gar-den. Its new fields and buildings should understand the historic form here but not be a slavish copy of them. It needed to work. Tom Oliver of the Campaign to Protect Rural England argued for the landscape as a place of life and mobility, nothing should be tarted up, and the land-scape designer Kim Wilkie said that "the aesthetic framework should be poetry, not painting—not just a seen picture but a whole-body, all-senses experience." Decisions about Sissinghurst should be made at Sissing-hurst; the landscape identity would then emerge from the place itself. The farm should be brought in "peninsulas"—Kim's word—close up to the garden boundaries. The connection should be visceral and felt. The garden should never be brought into the farm. The farm should always be its own self-motivated place.

That was the easiest of the groups. Others, talking about the res-taurant, found it more difficult to reach common ground. The real-food champion Hugh Fearnley-Whittingstall made an impassioned speech on behalf of authenticity and freshness. How do you really bring the landscape into the restaurant? How can you make it feel as if the food comes from here? But the task was to accommodate 115,000 visitors a year inside that real-food ideal. It could never be an upscale, London-chic, River Café–style experience. You couldn't have waitress service with such numbers. Food had to be collected from a counter and food sitting on a counter had to be different from food served on a plate. But lots could be done about the ambience. Herbs could be grown in pots outside the door. The veg garden should be beautiful and visitable. There could be outside seating in the summer. In winter there could be special game evenings. The chefs could be trained up to relish this river of produce streaming in from outside. Ginny Coombes said the excite-ment in the team outweighed the anxiety. "But *please* let's have some support." Stuart Richards, the big wheel in National Trust Enterprises, confirmed that Sissinghurst no longer needed to turn in a 40 percent net margin as profit. Fiona Reynolds had told him that. The Trust had decided, in other words, that the landscape benefits of the idea were worth buying.

The Soil Association now had to pull together a model for the farm/restaurant/shop. They were working to some exceptionally tough NT ceilings. No increase in revenue was to be allowed from an increase in the number of people who might want to visit this new farm. And because of the demands imposed by a National Trust environment—beautiful materials, elaborate approvals, sensitive surroundings—a cow shed that might have cost £100,000 on an ordinary farm would cost £200,000 here. As a result, the numbers just weren't adding up. Overall, the total investment, if you included the use of working capital, came to £1.2 million. I couldn't quite tell if we were in cloud cuckoo land.

I went for magical walks that summer with the National Trust war-den, Peter Dear, a man still in his thirties, with whom I felt the closest possible identity of purpose and mind, and who knew more about the wildlife of Sissinghurst than anyone else alive. He had made new ponds

February 2006: *Sarah Raven, Molly Nicolson, and Rosie Nicolson in Upper Moat planting the oak circle in memory of Nigel Nicolson.*

in which beetles and bugs proliferated. We scooped them out with nets. He guided me to a knowledge of the damselflies and dragonflies on a level I had never guessed at before: the Cinnabar moths and the four-spotted chaser, the black-tailed skimmer and the Beautiful Demoiselle, whose dazzling body Peter called "emerald blue." He found a White Admiral on the marsh thistles whose underwing was a rare and delicious creamy orange. He knew there were Purple Emperors in the wood, but they lived in the upper canopy of the oaks and so we never saw one. But he showed me where the trout were still hanging in sunlit pools in the Hammer Brook. He planned out, and would later plant, stake, and fence with my whole family, a ring of twelve oaks in the field across the moat, as a memorial to my father. He wrangled with me as we walked through the shadowy thickness of the summer wood over the benefits and drawbacks of organic farming. He rigged up for me one evening a net of ropes—he climbs rocks in his spare time—in the oldest tree at Sissinghurst, a four-hundred-year-old oak pollard buried in the chestnut coppice, and I spent a day in that tree from dawn onward, clipped to Peter's webbing slings, enveloped first in the barrage of summer song, then drifting in the midge- and spider-thick world of a great silent tree, its skin of leaves a globe above me, while the pigeons walked about like beadles on the wood floor and treecreepers ran up the trunks, corkscrewing their way along one beetle-rich line after another. Black-and-white woodpeckers hammered crazily into the dry dead branches, unable to settle or decide. Squirrels skittered past without the first idea I was there, but still taut, quivering, looking over their shoulders. Rabbits played anxiously in the grassy open rides below: a second or two in one spot, a skip to the next. There was no ease in the wood. All life here flickered and jumped. I lay stretched out on the sloping branches of the oak in a world that knew nothing but tension. The great patience of the tree stood there in silence, an ideal nothing else could seem to manage.

I thought about what we had done in all our year of meetings and I knew that our solutions and suggestions only restated the problem: the beautiful idea looked as if it was too expensive. The application of real costings meant the world of Sissinghurst would remain diminished. The circle wasn't square, and my instinct that we could do something new and good here was looking like an empty hope.

I was in Scotland when the answer came. It was toward the end of July. My mobile rang. Jonathan Light: "I just wanted to tell you the out-come of the Regional Planning Group's meeting," he said.

Yes, I said.

"The top and the bottom of it is that the Group are not going to recommend either of the schemes to the Regional Committee on the third of August." Sinking. "Yes," I said to him. "I thought that might be the direction you'd take. When I saw the £1.2 million low point." "Of course," he said, "we might be able to salvage something—an orchard, some sheep and some new hedges, maybe some veg and chickens, and that would push Sissinghurst in the right direction, wouldn't it?"

I put the phone down, devastated by the point we had reached. Intuitively, viscerally, my idea felt right. It attended to the appetite for local food and real food, for a sense of authenticity in the landscape and the feeling that the best places are deeply fueled by their own agendas, that they are richly themselves. The idea in its development had generated a great deal of tension but also some excitement and enthusiasm at Sissinghurst. It had become, to an extent, a shared view of how the future there might look. There was a luster to it.

Now, at the end of all this, we had arrived at a rejection. Risk was the problem. The questions asked had defined the answers. It was as if the pilot of a plane, anxious about arriving at his destination, had loaded up with so much spare fuel that the plane had become too heavy to take off.

What it meant, though, was that the heart of the idea had been stripped out. Maybe there still would be some apple trees grown and chickens raised at Sissinghurst. But it felt as if a mediocrity filter had been applied. That it would be safer to supply food in vans from elsewhere. That the visitors could continue to be patronized, and that other unvisited farms could continue to provide the revenue on which the place relied. It was a victory of safety over imagination. That is why it was disappointing, because it set a frame of ordinariness for Sissinghurst. It didn't feel like a missed opportunity; more like an opportunity carefully presented and willfully denied.

In August 2006 the whole project looked like it was lying dead on the floor.

CHAPTER 8

Glory

I PLUNGED BACK INTO SISSINGHURST'S PAST, to look for
the aspects of Sissinghurst that stretched beyond modern tensions
and difficulties. I hoped to find Sissinghurst in its glory, in the
sixteenth century, when it leaped up out of its rooted and Kentish
condition and became for a moment a place of power and glamour. Intriguingly, it turned out that Sissinghurst was never a more troubled
place than then.

IN THE DECADES BEFORE 1500, the Wealden villages around Sissinghurst boomed. Money surged into them. The Weald was not part of the
strictly regulated, seigneurial world of the good lands in the north of
the county, and so the people here had long nurtured their liberties.
The ability to rent and buy land; small dues owed to distant overlords; a
habit of dividing property between all children; a poverty in the soils
that created the need for a mixed system of farming: all of this made for
a radical independence of spirit and a competitive, entrepreneurial
world. There was a long history here of rebellion and resistance to authority, stretching back to the Peasants' Revolt in 1381. Nowhere else in
England did the new Protestant ideas take such quick and vivid root.

A modern land market was fully operating by the fifteenth century.

Estate agents, auctions, dodgy dealing, short-term rentals, buying to let, speculation, and mortgages were all at work in the Kent Weald, embedded in a rapidly modernizing and commercializing world. Business and farming were deeply intertwined here. Cranbrook was the largest town in Kent (with over two thousand inhabitants) and the parishes around it were one of the busiest parts of England. Most of it was occupied by a free peasantry, who farmed holdings made up of small fields or closes, almost never in single blocks but scattered across parishes and between them. It was cattle country, with few sheep and only a little arable land. Wheat and oats were grown but no barley and no hops. Beef cattle were the source of cash. A trade was maintained with north Kent, along the old droveways, by which beef walked north and barley came south.

No records survive for the farm at sixteenth-century Sissinghurst, but they do for another gentry estate belonging to the Culpepers at Bedgbury in the neighboring parish of Goudhurst. There in 1542 they planted fourteen acres of wheat and thirty-four acres of oats, about twenty acres lay fallow, and there were about one hundred and sixty acres of grassland—some pasture for grazing, some meadow from which hay was taken—on which about thirty breeding cows and their followers and forty ewes and their lambs were raised. Gradually I came to realize that if we were ever to introduce a system to Sissinghurst that would work, it would be not unlike this. The land itself would dictate our use of it.

In the early sixteenth century, the parishes around Sissinghurst were doing exceptionally well, the population rising decade after decade. By the 1550s, this was the most densely occupied part of Kent, with the families and immigrants afloat on an extraordinary industry: the manufacture of about twelve thousand luxury woolen broadcloths each year. The wool did not come from here and the cloths were not sold here. A group of large, protocapitalist clothiers bought the wool (usually in London markets), had it shipped down the Thames and then up the Medway to Maidstone, and from there carted it south on the old Roman road. Unlikely as it might sound, this amphibious route remained the recommended way to come to Sissinghurst from London, particularly for goods, at least until the end of the seventeenth century. Shiploads of wool, 30,000 pounds at a time, 450 tons of wool a year, were brought down to these parishes and converted into cloth, which was shipped back out to London, Antwerp, and the markets in France, Spain, and the Mediterranean. Dyes came from Brazil and Africa (indigo and co-chineal) wood from France, Seville oil from Spain, much of it shipped in via Rye.

A fuzzy boundary existed between smallholder, laborer, and artisan. There were dozens of holdings no bigger than seven acres. Little orchards were planted next to modest one-up, one-down houses. Chickens and pigs were everywhere. There were yeoman farms of some thirty acres—not many and rarely in a single block—and only one or two per parish that were bigger than that. Almost everyone who worked on the land also had a trade. This landscape was almost suburban in character, the cloth business sewn into every corner of the country. Nor was it a place of great rootedness. Although most people living here came from Kent, most of them, according to their wills, did not die in the village where they had been born. It was, in other words, a surprisingly modern world. Elizabethan Cranbrook had shoemakers, carpenters, tailors, glovers, masons, butchers, truggers, eight shopkeepers, a barrel-maker and smith, three barber-surgeons, a haberdasher, and a milliner.

The town and the surrounding villages were animated with the trades associated with clothmaking. At least thirty or forty people were involved in the making of each cloth: carding, dyeing, and spinning the wool, weaving the cloths, fulling them, raising the nap, shearing them. A finished cloth, twenty-eight yards long, weighing ninety pounds, was worth as much as fifteen deer. "Clothing in the Wylde of Kent," according to one petition from the clothiers to the queen, "is the nurse of the people."

A tenth of all English cloth manufacture came from six parishes around Sissinghurst. These Wealden cloths were famous for their colors:

scarlet, russet, damson, ginger, blue medley, gray, orange tawney and "rattescolour," pheasant, pepper, and mallard. The boys at Eton were dressed in "sad Kent" from Cranbrook, and there were undoubtedly quantities of money around. No one should imagine it as a world of delight. It was rough, raw, and exploitative. The large clothiers' houses had apprentices sleeping in the attics at night, working by day in the filthy, hot, wet dye houses at the back. In outhouses and those attics, vast piles of wool, wood, and finished cloth were stored. One person in five was a spinner, at the poverty pay of twopence or threepence a day, often paid many months late. Whenever clothiers died, they owed money to the spinsters, the poorest of the poor who had nowhere else to turn for work or sustenance in an overpopulated country. The soils were not good enough and most of the people were dependent on the clothiers, who acted as bankers, entrepreneurs, employers, controllers, landlords, and magistrates. Life expectancy was still low; most deaths still occurred in the "hungry gap" of March and April. Across the sixteenth century as a whole in the parish of Cranbrook, for every eighty people who died in August, one hundred and thirty died in April, twice the modern seasonal difference. People in the sixteenth century were still as vulnerable to the turning of the year as a population of weasels or rabbits.

This hard-driven, commercializing world is the one from which Renaissance Sissinghurst, in the hands of the next Sissinghurst family, now emerges. The Bakers, like their fellow townsmen, were men on the make. One of their ancestors, a Thomas Baker, had been taken to court in 1371 for illegally cutting down the archbishop's trees. A hundred years later, it had become a pious and well-established family. In the late fifteenth century, another Thomas Baker owned lands in several parishes running south into Sussex, and when he died left money for masses to be said and the churches to be repaired in all of them. The little friaries at Mottenden and Lossenham had legacies and his daughters had some silver, feather beds, and cushions. He left his best cow to his wife and to all his sons small pieces of land. Although Edward Hasted, the great eighteenth-century historian of Kent, wrote, and it has often been repeated, that this Thomas Baker first acquired at least part of Sissinghurst, there is no evidence that either he or his son Richard did so, and Sissinghurst appears in neither of their detailed wills.

The surge begins with Thomas's grandson, John Baker, Richard's son, born in about 1488. When he was about fifteen, he was sent to London with ten pounds a year to keep him at Lincoln's Inn, where he was trained as a lawyer. It was the moment when the Bakers began to lift away from the Wealden entrepreneurial society and enter the boom conditions of Tudor London. John Baker thrived, becoming a leading barrister, an undersheriff, recorder, and member of Parliament for London. It was a familiar track for a clever and ambitious man, and everything that is now at Sissinghurst, all the grandeur and riches that were once here, even if now worn and crumbled, had their origins in this man's enterprise.

Sir John Baker (c. 1488–1558). A print of a painting that has now disappeared, last heard of in Norwich in 1820.

In the early 1520s he married Catherine Sackville, the daughter of a Sussex knight. One of her brothers, Thomas, was married to Anne Boleyn's aunt. It was the kind of invaluable connection that pushed John Baker into the mainstream of the English court and Reformation. That four-hundred-year-old Sackville relationship to Sissinghurst was one of the factors playing in Vita's mind when she decided to come here in 1930. At Anne Boleyn's coronation in 1533, Baker made a speech to the young queen on behalf of the merchants and financiers of the City of London, where he was still the recorder. Within a couple of years he had begun to make his way into the coils of government and power. In 1535 he had become an attorney in the pay of the Crown. A year later he was attorney general, pursuing papists on behalf of the reforming king, executing instructions prepared by Thomas Cromwell, the king's first minister, who was in full, self-enriching career. When Cromwell fell in 1540, finally destroyed by the enmity and jealousy of those around him, Baker was there to benefit. He became chancellor of the Exchequer, was appointed to the Privy Council, knighted, and, most important of all, became chancellor of the Court of First Fruits and Tenths, the court through which taxes that had previously gone to the pope now came to the Crown. Baker stood at the sluice gate through which the new money-river flowed into the royal Exchequer, a flow into which Baker could dip his cup whenever he liked. He became speaker of the House of Commons, a royal appointment. The electors of Kent refused to have him for one election in the 1540s, but the royal officials found him another seat. He slid on in these jobs through the reigns of Edward VI and his sister Mary, and at every turn the lands and riches on which Sissinghurst would come to float steadily accrued around him.

He already had his grandfather's lands in Sussex and Kent. His first acquisition, bought from the de Berhams in 1533, was Sissinghurst itself, with its subsidiary manors of Copton and Stone. Five years later, when the Priory of Hastings was dissolved, the king gave his loyal attorney slabs of Sussex "to have to him and his heirs for ever." Two years later, when Cromwell was dismissed and bloodily executed, Baker gratefully received lands all over the Kent and Sussex Weald that had previously belonged to his chief. On through the 1540s, scarcely a year passed without Sir John acquiring another manor or two. When Catholic rebels against Edward VI were condemned to death, Baker had some of their lands; and when Protestant rebels against Queen Mary fell and were executed, he had some of their lands too. Many places he bought with the money that came his way from his chancellorship of the Court of First Fruits.

The result was that by the 1550s the Baker estate was one of the largest in Kent and Sussex, its archipelago of lands and manors stretching from beyond Eastbourne up to Maidstone and from Winchelsea to Pluckley. There were other manors in Hampshire, Oxfordshire, Gloucestershire, and Essex, houses in Southwark and in the City of London, but the core was in the central Wealden parishes around Sissinghurst. It may, in all, have stretched to something approaching fifteen thousand acres, a spread of land that would be worth £75 million today.

Those are the economic and political facts of his life, but there are further elements that add depth and color to Baker's story. The first is what he did at Sissinghurst after he had bought it from the de Berhams in 1533. In the 1930s my grandmother thought that Sir John had built himself an enormous brick house here, with an entrance range, a tower, and a large courtyard beyond it. It seemed to make sense that the acquirer of the lands had created the monument at its heart. But in the 1960s my father looked into it more carefully and it became clear, first of all, that Sissinghurst was not all of one phase. He consulted various architectural luminaries, including Sir Nikolaus Pevsner, Jim Lees-Milne, and Sir John Summerson, and came up with a building history that has been the orthodoxy ever since. According to my father, in the late fifteenth century the de Berhams abandoned a stone medieval house by the moat (said to have resembled Ightham Mote, a romantic building near Sevenoaks) and built themselves a brick house to the west of it, around a courtyard, and resembling instead Compton Wynyates, the great medieval brick house in Warwickshire. When John Baker bought this house in 1533, he is said to have inserted a modern Tudor gateway into the late-fifteenth-century entrance range. And when John Baker's son Richard inherited the house in 1558, he was said to have knocked down all except that earlier entrance range and built a huge Renaissance palace in the place of the demolished Compton Wynyates, with a tower in its center and its further reaches stretching out into the orchard.

I, in my turn, with help from architectural historians and archaeologists, have now had another look at this story. There seems to be, first, no evidence of any Ightham Mote–like house. The medieval house almost certainly occupied only the southwest corner of the orchard, not the whole of it, and was almost certainly timber-framed, perhaps with some stone footings. Its tall bargeboarded gables are probably shown in the drawing of the back of the house made by Francis Grose in 1760. Nor is there any evidence of a house resembling Compton Wynyates built to replace it. These were the two great early English houses my father was most in love with, and he seems simply to have imported them into Sissinghurst because he liked the idea.

The entrance gateway, from the style of its chimneys and their playing with geometrical forms, can be firmly dated to the 1530s. Inconveniently, though, the long wings of the front range on either side of it were not built then. Dendrochronology commissioned in the 1980s put the beams in the late sixteenth and in one case the eighteenth century (probably a repair), findings my father refused, with some passion, to accept. He liked to be able to tell Americans who came to stay that the bedroom they were sleeping in had been built in 1492.

So what did happen? The simplest suggestion is that when in 1533 John Baker bought the de Berhams' house on the site of the present orchard, he kept it. It was an important manor house, with a history of distinguished occupants and its own chapel. It had a moated garden beside it. What he undoubtedly added was a small, dignified, and wingless modern gatehouse, decorated with its fashionable chimneys. The gateway would have led into a large walled "base court," at the far end of which, a good three hundred feet away, stood the medieval house. Such a huge empty courtyard may seem odd to us, and certainly would not fit with later, Italian-derived ideas of proportionality of space, but could be found in many Tudor houses.

This simple picture fits both the man and the moment. It is essentially conservative. In John Baker's will, he asked his executors that his "funeralls be done and made in honest maner with out pompe or pryde according nevertheless as vnto my deggree apperteyneth." That was the style of his house too: dignified but not extravagant. The timbers used inside his gatehouse are not, intriguingly, of the best. Many were reclaimed from other places, with slots and peg holes marking their earlier use, and with nothing like the consistently high quality of oak that can be found in other, later parts of the building. The house he had bought was saturated in real, medieval, inherited status and was good enough to entertain both the French ambassador and, on one occasion, Queen Mary. John Baker was not a man to blow everything he had so carefully accumulated on a grand and a pretentious gesture; far too careful for that.

John Baker's enormous will, proved at Canterbury and preserved in the National Archives, is a measure of his methods and his ideals. It is, in fact, a picture of the Sissinghurst through which he moved, one that, not by chance, looks like a depiction of a great medieval household. "I John Bakere of Cessyngherst in Kent Knyght one of the Kinge and Quenes Majestyes previe Counsell" presided over an entire community at Sissinghurst. It is the statement of a great territorial patriarch and magnate. Alms were to be given to the poor, masses and dirges sung for his soul in sixteen churches across his estate, and the old Roman road from Sissinghurst to Staplehurst was to be mended.

There was no question here of dividing the great inheritance into equal parts, as the custom of Kent had been. Baker had "disgavelled" his lands so that the bulk of the estate could remain whole and in the hands of a single heir. To his second son, John, Sir John gave "Goddes blessinge and myne and £200 and such stuff I have in the Citie of London," and "to you my doughters Marye, Cecyle and Elizabeth I gyve Goddes blessyng and myne requyringe you aboue all things to serve God and to be faithfull, assured, true, humble, lovinge and obedyent wifes vnto yor husbands." They were off his hands. To his eldest son, Richard, who was in his late twenties when this will was drawn up, he left the great prize that he had spent a life accumulating: the vast estate and Sissinghurst at its core.

Sir John's will is a paternalist vision, perhaps an old man's sentimentality, of what his world should be, with Sissinghurst as a place where many would be employed and his own relations looked after, a family widely connected with the higher gentry and with an ideal of stability and completeness standing outside the turmoil of Reformation England. Almost nobody knows of this paternalist Sir John Baker because his name will be forever bloodied by one of the great triumphs of Elizabethan Protestant propaganda, John Foxe's *Acts and Monuments*, usually known as *Foxe's Book of Martyrs*. This twenty-three-hundred-page compendium of crimes committed against the Protestant martyrs of the English Reformation, particularly in the reign of Mary, was more widely read than any book except the Bible. In Elizabeth's reign it stood by order of the archbishop in every cathedral in England as the companion to the translated scriptures. Cranbrook had opted hard and early for a fairly strict form of Protestantism, and it is certain that in the independent-minded, entrepreneurial culture of the farmer-clothiers, there would have been many copies of Foxe's book, at least in the richer houses scattered through the surrounding parishes. And Foxe, in one incident after another, drawing on personal testimony and eyewitness reports, damns this great man as a cruel and intemperate persecutor of Protestants. It is the dark side of his desire for the order and consolations of the old world.

1760s: *Francis Grose, the back of medieval Sissinghurst.*

The story that comes closest to home, dramatizing the condition of Sissinghurst in the middle years of the sixteenth century, and its separation from the surrounding country, concerns Edmund Allin, a miller, who lived at the beautiful Maplehurst Mill in Frittenden, a mile or two north of here. He was a man full of concern for his poor neighbors and "in a deare yere, when as many poore people were like to starue, he fed them, and solde his corne better cheape by halfe then others did: and did not that only, but also fedde them with the foode of life, reading to them the scriptures, and interpreting them." The radicalism of the Reformation, its distrust and loathing of instituted authority, came in Allin's hands sifting into these fields and lanes.

Allin and his wife were reported to the priests, arrested, and brought to Baker at Sissinghurst, where he kept them prisoner in his "house the one from the other." Where was that? Almost certainly in some back rooms of the de Berhams' building in the orchard, now disappeared. Baker then began to play with his prisoner and "entreated the sayd Edmund Allin to come to Masse in his Chappell the next day." This must have been the chapel that had been there since the four-

teenth century. After much persuasion, Allin agreed to go to chapel
with Baker the next day, who then allowed him to

> goe lye with his wife that night, and desired him to perswade her
> to come also, and he would deliuer them both out of prison.
> When [Allin] was come to his wife, he told her what he had
> promised, and she with teares sayd, hee shoulde go alone for her.
> Then he likewise lamentyng the same, sayd, he would go with
> her to death.

I feel a kind of vicarious shame at this story, at this suffering imposed on young Kentish idealists, here in this house five hundred years
ago. The next day, Baker came to Allin, asking him to keep his promise and come to chapel with him. Allin said, "I will not: do what you
will with me." Then Sir John called out Allin's wife, Katherine, and
berated her:

> "Thou old whore, thy husband would be a Christian but for
> thee." Then he beate her very sore with his staffe in his hand,
> and sent them both to prison the next day, sending with them a
> cruell letter that they shoulde be burned out of hand.

The manuscript notes from which Foxe wrote up this story (given
to him by the vicar of Cranbrook) have survived, and it is clear that
Foxe did not alter the evidence he had received.

Allin and his wife escaped to Calais, but there his conscience troubled him and he returned to Frittenden to continue his secret ministry.
He and his wife were arrested again, his house was ransacked by Baker's
men, and in June 1557 Baker was given another chance to "taunt and
revile him, without all mercy and pity," as Foxe says, at a hearing in
Cranbrook, at the George Inn. "We are al kings to rule our affections,"
Allin told Baker. One day, walking in Frittenden churchyard, the miller

had realized he could never believe that a communion wafer was any-thing but a symbol. "He considered in the Churchyard with him selfe, that such a little cake betwene the Priestes fingers could not be Christ, nor a materiall body, neither to haue soule, life, sinnewes, bones, flesh, legges, head, armes, nor brest." Baker could have no truck with this. "Away with him," he said. On June 18, 1557, Allin, his wife, and five others, all tied to a single stake, were burned on King's Meadow in Maidstone, one of them a blind girl called Elizabeth and another "a vertuous maiden cauled Jone Bradbrege." As the wood was being laid around them, Joan

> turning to the people sayed, "What is it a clocke?" They sayed, "Ten." Then she sayed, "Thanks be to God! Bye xi we shalbe with our God." And then, turning to the blinde mayde, sayd, "Now sister Besse, be of good cher. Thou dyd never see, but soone yow shalt see Lord Jesus Cryst." To whom she answred, "I trust so."

Is it any surprise that these stories sank deep into the psyche of the Protestant people of the Weald? Or that this exercise of orthodox power and the suppression of liberties should give rise to terrible, half-mythical tales, still current in Sissinghurst and Cranbrook, of John Baker as Bloody Baker and Butcher Baker, a Bluebeard murderer, rapist, and oppressor? I remember my father telling me one as a boy, taking me to the place, in the old brewhouse, just on the other side of the arch from our kitchen. There is an early-sixteenth-century staircase there, with a rubbed and worn newel post at its foot. At the top, shadowed and spooky when I was young, a big door gave onto a room that had been my father's bedroom when he was a boy. This, he told me, had been Bloody Baker's own room, and it was on this staircase that the most terrible crime in his long and terrible life had been committed. He was in the habit, my father said, of ravishing young virgins from the village. "Do you know what *ravishing* means, Adam?" I did. And *virgin?* I did. Bloody Baker would summon them, they would come to the foot of the stairs, and he would take them up to that room and in there *do his worst* with them. "Do you understand *do his worst*, Adam?" I did.

One day a young woman arrived early. She was approaching the stairs when she heard someone coming down them and hid in the cupboard beneath. *This one here.* It was Bloody Baker carrying the body of his latest victim. As he reached the foot of the stairs a ring on her hand caught the newel post and in a rage of frustration Baker drew his sword and sliced the hand from the wrist. *Look, Adam, here, where the sword cut into the wood.* I saw how the newel post had been slashed and hacked as if with a hatchet into a worn and eroded stump.

June 1962: *The stairs, broken newel post, and cupboard all said to have played their part in Bloody Baker's mutilation of girls. VSW's boots are on the chair.*

Although this story and the many like it are all untrue, nothing I had heard had ever seemed more real. It is the kind of story told by the powerless about the powerful. It relies on the strangeness and distance of authority and the way in which power can suddenly land, terrify, and destroy its victims out of a clear blue sky. It is a measure of the distance between Tudor Sissinghurst and the world around it.

IN 1558, THE OLD MAN died. In his will, he addressed his son directly from beyond the grave:

> To myne oldest sonne Richard Bakere goddes blessinge and myne and all suche my plate of siluer and gilt &e. and all other stuffe and utensiles of houshold in my manor mesuage and house of Cessyngherst. And I charge the[e] my sonne Richarde that above all things thowe serve God and thy soueraigne lorde and ladye the Kinge and quene, applye thy lernynge, be curtesse and gentill to euery bodie, be aydinge and lovinge to thy naturall Brother John Bakere and to thy susters Mary Cecile and Elizabeth, love well they neighbours, counsell, cherishe and help theym in theire necessities as righte and good conscience will requyre, avoyde Brybery, extortion, corruption and dissimulacon, eschewe Idlenes, applie the[e] to vertuose exercise, be faythfull and true in worde and deede and holly putt thy truste in Almightie God with humble callinge to hym for grace with laudes and thanks for all thy benefits and he wilbe thy keper and defender from all daunger, perill and evill.

The implication is clear: the aging father, replete with his vision of strict social wholeness, distrusted his son. He was right to do so. In the most spectacular of Sissinghurst's generation shifts, Richard Baker, still in his thirties, with a huge income from the inherited estate of at least £650 a year, took Sissinghurst in hand and drove it in a new direction:

not ancient propriety but aestheticized glamour, not conformist strictness but Elizabethan romanticism, not rooted Kentishness but highly cultured, Italianate arcadianism, with a sophisticated interaction of building and landscape, large, grand, and expensive, far beyond anything anyone had ever done here. Between 1558 and 1573, Richard Baker made of Sissinghurst an Elizabethan palace at the center of its own dream world. It was the flickering ghost of that place, with all its ancient Sackville connections, that drew Vita here, to make a garden among the ruins.

There are many forms of evidence for what Richard Baker did: the remains of the buildings themselves—the Tower, the South Cottage, the Priest's House, the barns, the long front range; plans of other contemporary buildings that bear strong resemblances to Sissinghurst; drawings made of it in the eighteenth century that show the great Elizabethan palace from various points of view; accounts of one or two eighteenth-century visitors; the verbatim record of a monthlong investigation made in 1761 into crimes that had been committed here, whose pages inadvertently describe the Elizabethan house's geography; the claims made by the owners against the government for damage done by prisoners held here; the marks left on the surrounding landscape by Richard Baker's great and encompassing scheme for the whole place; accounts of court cases held at the end of the century, which describe the relationship of Sissinghurst to the surrounding population; a very early, 1610 census of people living in Cranbrook and the surrounding parishes, house by house, which takes in Sissinghurst; and finally the accounts of Queen Elizabeth's visit here for three days in August 1573.

Although it is a fragmentary archive scattered across the country, in Cranbrook, Maidstone, Lincoln's Inn, Kew, Staffordshire, and Sissinghurst, and although there are no contemporary maps, drawings, or letters, there is richness and suggestion here, which, taken together with other Elizabethan theories of what the beautiful place should be, can be assembled into a coherent picture of what Richard Baker made. He overlaid the medieval inheritance with a mixture of classical detail and ·

a simple version of an Elizabethan fantasy palace. By the time he died, everything was here: a great, many-courtyarded house; a garden beside it; outlying banqueting houses overlooking the park; a prospect tower from which the park could be viewed in its full extent; new barns in which the hay was kept for the park deer; a bank and pale surrounding that park; woods; open grasslands called "launds" (from the French *lande*, a word that evolved into "lawn"); a park-keeper's lodge; and necklaces of ponds dammed along the stream within the park. Evidence for every one of these things remains at Sissinghurst today.

It was all made in the service of a deep and extraordinarily expensive form of play. House, landscape, woods, and meadows were reshaped as theater. Each of the elements was carefully integrated with the others, all contributing to an atmosphere in which the demands of getting and spending did not for a while have to be observed. The parishes beyond the park gates may have been deeply embroiled in the accumulation of capital. Within it, those priorities were suspended. Central to this transformation is the fact that the Bakers were often not at Sissinghurst but at their London houses, either in Southwark or in Lime Street in the City. When a crisis with the local populace erupted in the 1590s, the whole Baker family was in London, and when a survey of communicants in Cranbrook parish was repeatedly made in the first decade of the seventeenth century, the Bakers were only rarely here to be counted. Sissinghurst was their dream place. It became a kind of toy.

Like the other gentry of Elizabethan England, Baker was not indifferent to enterprise or industry, and along with this theatrical construct of the new Sissinghurst was something else: a working and earning landscape. The woods grew coppice wood and standard timber; a large dam was built across the Hammer Brook and a fifty-acre pond made upstream of that dam, its head of energy powering the hammers and bellows of an ironworks; there were other mills, other ponds and sluices that provided extra head for the grain mills farther downstream.

What can be said about the world of this glamour-and-delight palace that Richard, the Elizabethan Baker, inserted into his father's adapted medieval-Tudor manor house? To begin at the center: still standing in the orchard was the de Berhams' close-timbered manor house. Beside it on the eastern side was a large fish pond. Three hundred feet to the west was John Baker's twenty-year-old gatehouse with its out-of-date twisted chimneys. Between the two stretched a large open court. It was a bitty inheritance that needed ordering, regularizing, and aestheticizing.

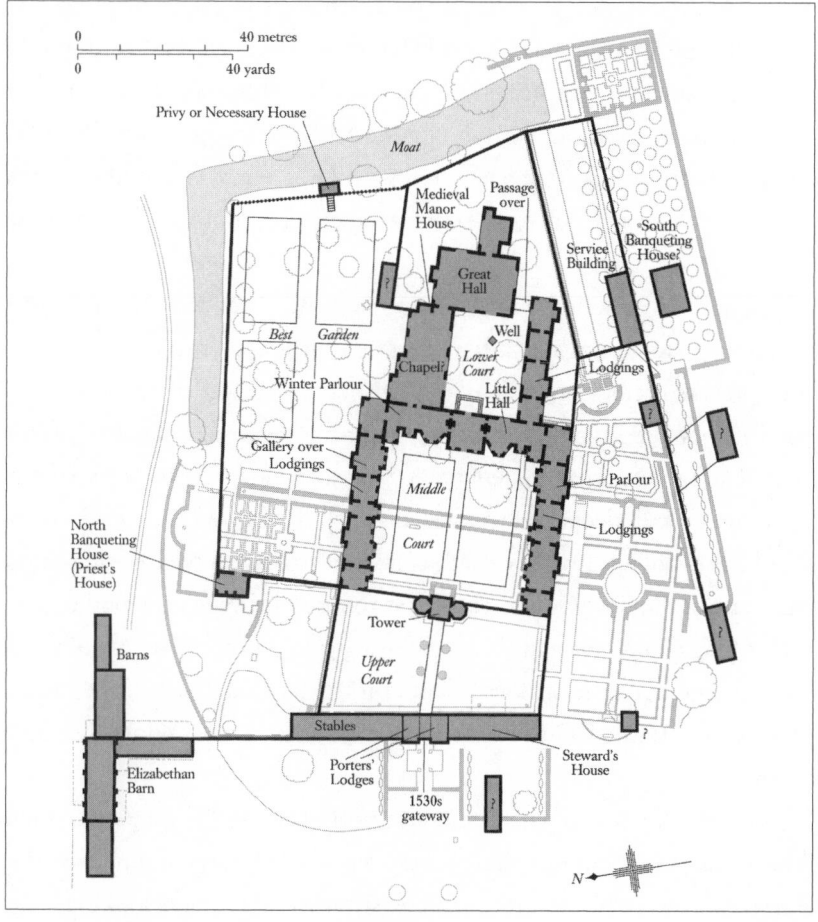

Guess-plan of Elizabethan Sissinghurst by Peter Wilkinson on the basis of a drawing by Peter Rumley, laid over a plan of the twentieth-century garden.

Using an architect whose name has not survived, but whose plans as seen in eighteenth-century drawings bear a strong resemblance to the drawings collected by John Thorpe and now in the Soane Museum in London, Baker inserted between the medieval house and the 1530s gateway a large Renaissance core to Sissinghurst. It consisted essentially of a prospect-tower-cum-inner-gateway with a *cour d'honneur* beyond it. The result was a three-courtyard house: the first a reduced base-court, paved throughout, into which horsemen could enter through the earlier arch. Dendrochronological dating of the timbers in the front range has shown that Richard Baker probably lengthened the wings on either side of the entrance arch at the same time, with stabling to the north and simple accommodation, perhaps for the steward, to the south. Both façades of both ranges were decorated with large black diamond patterns in the brick, visible in early-twentieth-century photographs but now faded.

These lengthened wings exaggerated an effect that has troubled rationalists (including my father and grandfather) ever since: the axis of the gateway is not perpendicular to either the Tower or the court beyond it, nor presumably to the medieval house, which has now disappeared. The unfortunate effect is that the upper courtyard is not rectangular but deeper at its northern than its southern end. Why should this have been? No one has ever been sure: a possible reason is that part of medieval and early Tudor theory of the healthy building— Tudor feng shui—insisted that a gateway should not be directly aligned with the entrance to a house. Doors into the house should be either offset or misaligned so that a noxious wind could not find its way into the rooms.

At the far side of the first court stood the new Tower, still called "the Great Gate" in the eighteenth century. Its form dramatizes the story of its own insertion into a preexisting plan. The side looking back to Baker's father's gateway is pierced with a flattened Tudor arch. But the other arch on the other side of the Tower and the entire façade looking into the great court are strictly detailed in the correct grammar of a Tuscan order, with pilasters, entablatures, elegantly molded cornices, and the perfect semicircle of a Roman arch. As you passed under the Tower, you moved from medieval to Renaissance Sissinghurst. Steps led down then as now into the court. Horse and carriage had been left behind on the other side. You were entering a piazza in which the gentry strolled. There was no muck, noise, or dung. It was the scene for a Kentish *passeggiata*. On either side, large mullioned and transomed windows gave onto apartments reached from separate stairs, much like an Oxford or Cambridge college. A paved path led across the court between lawns. Stone balls marked the breaks in the cornices. Those that had survived until the 1930s Harold put up on the garden walls. Over each doorway, small pediments held the Baker arms flanked by their surrounding dolphins. A fragment of one of those pediments still sits, unregarded, in the arch under the Tower. Another was taken by a visiting Baker descendant to Cranbrook church in the 1830s, where it was accidentally put up in the east wall of the nave, by the chancel opening, thought to be part of old Sir John Baker's tomb.

At the far end of the courtyard was an elaborated columned and entablatured doorway, like the frontispiece for an Elizabethan book. Harold and Vita used the shafts of its fluted and channeled columns, which they found lying in the ruins, to make a pergola called the Erechtheum outside their dining room on the edge of the White Garden, where a white wisteria grows over the frame and a rose spirals up one of the shafts. Part of the cornice is now used as a doorstop at the foot of the stairs up the Tower. Originally, the doorway had led into the screens passage between the hall and the buttery and on out into the third, medieval courtyard, with an Elizabethan range across its western side, and with a well in its center.

Other satellite buildings clustered around these three central courtyards. Two large-windowed, pretty banqueting houses, one to the north (now called the Priest's House), one to the south (on the site of

Circa 1787: *An engraving by Richard Godfrey of the great courtyard at Sissinghurst, published in Edward Hasted's* History of Kent 1788–89.

the Nuttery, still there in 1760 but now disappeared), gazed out over the parkland. Outside the entrance, Richard Baker also built a pair of beautiful brick barns to the northwest of the main cluster. One is still there but the other was demolished in about 1800. Unlike the precision classicism of the Tower and its great courtyard, the barns were built with big strong Gothic archways, medieval buttresses, and air slits through which the hay could breathe. It is a manner and vocabulary that, for a 1560s building, may have been consciously nostalgic, a suggestion in the pointed arches that the barns had been here since time immemorial.

Slowly the ensemble of Elizabethan Sissinghurst begins to gather. Turn off the "Pavement of the Middle Court of the mansion house," as it was called, step inside one of the doorways, and you would find a staircase rising before you. On either side were doors giving into guest lodgings, or those for Baker's relatives. The stairs rising in front of you turned on a half-landing at the back of the range and climbed to the landing overlooking the court. Here on the north side was a long gallery, seventeen feet wide and one hundred and twenty feet long, wainscoted throughout, with a rich entablature and carved marble fireplaces. "The ceiling," according to Horace Walpole, who saw it in 1752, was "vaulted, and painted in a light genteel grotesque." Above it, in the attic, may have been the bowling alley referred to in the 1760s. Other rooms upstairs in these ranges were also paneled, probably with oak, probably with some classical allusion in the ornament. Alongside half an oyster shell, a small piece of classically molded cornice, made of plaster, was found in a drain in the orchard in 2006, nothing very elaborate but cleanly and precisely done.

At the far end of the Middle Court the hall would have filled the right-hand part of the range and the butler's pantry and buttery the other half, across the screens passage. There was probably a smaller and cozier winter parlor upstairs here too. As the account of the prisoners' damage refers to the "great and little halls"—both paneled—it may be that the great hall of the medieval house survived in the medieval court beyond it, and that a small, modern Renaissance hall was installed here in the Elizabethan range. There was nothing low-status about that third court. Here the household continued to use the well. Beyond the medieval court, which still contained the chapel, stretched the garden, running up to the old fish pond as its eastern boundary. It may be that Richard Baker added two new arms, turning the old pond into what looked like an ancient moat.

This Elizabethan garden filled what is now the White Garden and those parts of the modern orchard not taken up by the great house itself. It was walled to above head height and fruit trees were trained against the walls. What this means, intriguingly, is that when Vita came to a bedraggled and broken place in 1930, and found, miraculously, an unknown *Rosa gallica* growing here on the edge of the ramshackle orchard, among the weeds and brambles, it was in exactly the place it would have been planted in the Elizabethan garden. The rose is particularly persistent. Vita claimed she could never eradicate it from wherever it wanted to grow, and it is not absurd to suggest that successive plants of that tough and hardy rose, which Vita named "Sissinghurst Castle," had been growing there for 450 years.

Inside the Tower, Richard Baker had one of the rooms decorated with a set of carved heads of Tudor monarchs. They were still there in the 1870s and shown to visitors, but tantalizingly they had disappeared by 1930. Above them, though, was the real showpiece of the place, then as it is today: the prospect from above. Until the early nineteenth century, each of the two turrets was a room higher than it is now and in each face of those octagonal rooms a window gave the viewers collected there—no more than four or five for comfort—a panoramic view of the lands of which this tower was the node and hub.

1950s: *Sir John Baker's 1530s gateway seen from the Tower showing the misalignment between the two.*

This view from above was a central part of the Elizabethan experience. Big rooftop prospects, rooftop walks, rooftop pavilions, parties on
rooftops, even romantic assignations on rooftops: all this was part of a
sudden new sixteenth-century relationship to a place, not only dominating it from above but, by standing above it, seeing it for what it was
and for what your place within it might be. The sixteenth century in
England was the moment when people first began to draw and buy aerial
views, when the first models of buildings were made by architects for
their clients. And the view from the top of the Tower at the end of the
building campaign of the 1560s would have been full of a very particular
aesthetic pleasure, the experience, it seems to me, around which the
whole ensemble was framed.

At your feet was the intricately made thing, many interlocking
courts, with passageways and doors between them, a house not only as a
machine for living in—there were thirty-eight hearths paying tax here—
but as a kind of enlarged jewel, a device, a cleverly made object. It was
placed in the middle of a landscape from which all apparent human influence had been removed. Beyond the perfect court at your feet; beyond
the stable court to the west and the medieval court to the east; and beyond the little banqueting pavilions to north and south—lower cousins
of this great prospect tower—came the free-flowing lands of the park
through which the hunt could pass. The farm on which the inhabitants
of Sissinghurst had relied for so long, which they had worked and cultivated for perhaps a thousand years, was no longer needed. The fifteen
thousand acres of the Baker estate provided enough money. So while the
new house at Sissinghurst was made particularly refined, the land at
Sissinghurst could be thrown back to an artificial naturalness, which was
both self-consciously relaxed and self-consciously luxurious, a holiday
zone for the well-born, from which the poor and the industrious were
explicitly and often officiously excluded. Intuitively or not, when Vita
and Harold came here in the 1930s, they were responding to a place
that had once been shaped into a model of Elizabethan arcadianism.

The field pattern of modern Sissinghurst is not medieval, but a mixture of late eighteenth century and Victorian. The medieval fields had, in other words, been removed and replaced within the park pale by a relaxed openness, a pretense at nature. It was a set of relations that embodied constraint and ease, order and freedom, the cultivated and wild. Stand on top of the Tower at Sissinghurst in 1570 and you could feel almost literally on top of the world. It may have given the pleasure that nineteenth- and twentieth-century Englishmen got from standing on top of mountains: the perfection of dominance.

An enormously expensive fence and bank—an oak pale—seven miles long had been built around the whole seven hundred acres. The park was stocked with deer and, in a small part, just beyond the site of the Victorian farmhouse, with exceptionally valuable and highly prized rabbits. There were gates into the park where the old roads entered it and stiles here and there over which a man could climb but a deer could not jump. On the northern edge, where the drove road from Charing to Cranbrook crossed the park, an oak-framed park-keeper's lodge was built. It is still there: a one-up, one-down cottage now subdivided and buried under later extensions, but with the field next to it still called Lodge Field.

From the Tower, and to a lesser extent from the two little banqueting houses, Baker, his family, friends, and guests could survey their world, one that, in the heavily commercialized and semi-industrialized surroundings of the Cranbrook cloth business, had been cut out of the new normality and in its adopted and theatrical simplicity made to seem precious beyond price. This is a very early holiday house, or at least a beauty house, a place in which life could be seen and enjoyed like a ballet.

The landscape historian Nicola Bannister, in a survey for the National Trust, has made a richly interesting discovery about the relationship of house and park. She took me with her one day that winter to show me what she had found. For about two-thirds of its length, Nicola had rediscovered the bank on which Richard Baker's park pale had been built. Sometimes it snaked its way through modern woodland. Sometimes it was as much as five or six feet tall, sometimes no more than a ripple in the leaf litter. For much of its length the old drove from Three Chimneys to Cranbrook (now the busy A282) ran alongside it, and for another part the old lane from Frittenden to Cranbrook Common. But the intriguing point was this: for all the length that it survives (about 70 percent of the complete circuit), it is laid along the skyline as seen from the top of the Tower. Both the pale and the tower-top rooms are about 230 feet above sea level. It is unlikely that this a coincidence. It seems as if the height of the Tower was calculated to make the house-and-park effect work most precisely. The deer in the park were to be hunted. The height of the Tower guarantees that from its prospect rooms you would never lose sight of the park. The vision of the Sissinghurst park is precisely like one of the sixteenth-century tapestries Vita brought with her from Knole and that still hang in the corridors of Sissinghurst: open grounds, shady bowers, exquisite pavilions among the trees, and the hunt of the swine or the deer, at which the men with their javelins stand firm, while the horn is blown and all is happily and easily laid out to view.

September 2007:
*Remains of
the bank that once
carried Sissinghurst's
park pale along the
Biddenden Road.*

The park was important to the Bakers. In Richard Baker's 1594 will, his executors were empowered to have any of his woods and underwoods felled to pay off his debts, "except only the okes and Beeches growing within my sayd parke of Sissinghurst." Some things were worth more than money, and the family maintained the park and had the pale repaired and renewed up until the end of the seventeenth century. Only then did it fall into decay. When Horace Walpole came here in 1741, he described "a park in ruins and a house in ten times greater ruins." In the late eighteenth century it was reclaimed for farmland and wood. Only here and there, magically, does a great tree survive. The huge four-hundred-year-old pollard oak in which I spent a day in the early summer of 2006 is a relict from that park. There is another down by the Hammer Brook, almost equally old and more venerable, its giant bole not to be hugged even by four people. The big beech pollards up on the crest, although much younger, probably germinating even as Walpole was looking at them, are from the last days of the park, as are many of the younger oaks in the wood. They are now surrounded by dense chestnut coppice planted in the nineteenth century. Many lower branches of these oaks, which must once have grown out in the open air of a park, have withered and died where the chestnuts have shaded them out so that only the crown and the central trunk of the tree remain green and juicy. These lower oaky limbs hang out barkless and sapless, sticking out from their trees like narwhal tusks, the memory of an Elizabethan dream long since gone.

All this is to take the great house, with its precisionist workings and its surrounding spread of exquisite nature—so unlike the tightly knitted closes of the Wealden landscape—at its own valuation. It didn't look quite the same from beyond the park pale. The court records at the end of Elizabeth's reign are full of trouble between the Bakers, their precious park, their ironworks at Hammer Mill, and the people of Cranbrook.

One young Cranbrook man after another raided the park for its

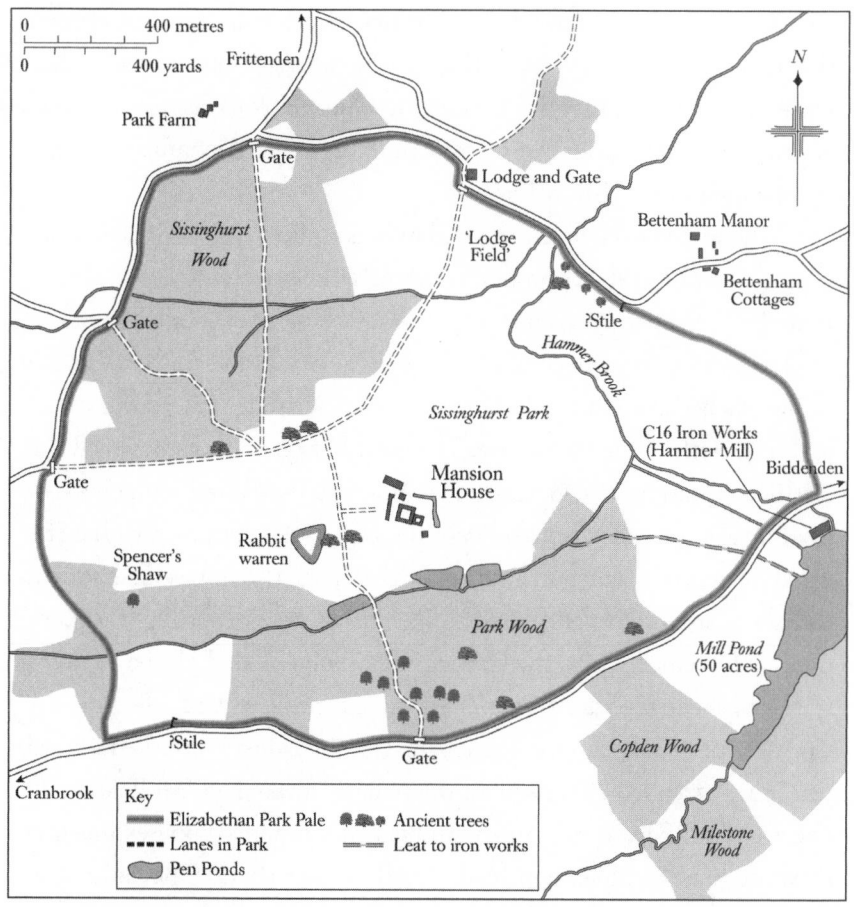

Sissinghurst in the 1570s, on the basis of investigations and a plan by Nicola Bannister.

deer. Jasper Glover, the Bakers' keeper, pursued them to their houses in Cranbrook, waking them in the middle of the night, hauling them before the magistrates, with their mud-covered stockings as evidence of what they had been up to. Others broke into the park with their greyhounds. There were armed scuffles between the Bakers' men and the Cranbrook thieves.

Court cases dragged on for years, the focus of a deeper conflict between the Bakers and the deeply puritan people of the surrounding country. There may have been a sense of religious divide between them—there is some evidence that the Bakers remained secret Catholics—and in 1594 a plot was hatched in Cranbrook to destroy the Bakers' most valuable asset: the furnace and forge that Richard Baker had set up at Hammer Mill in 1569.

The ironworks needed stupendous amounts of charcoal made from coppice wood, largely oak and hornbeam, in the surrounding woodlands. It has been estimated that about four thousand acres of coppice would be required to fuel a furnace and a forge. The woods had to be near the ironworks because charcoal, if carted too far, shattered into dust.

But cloth needed wood too. The great hot boiling vats in which the clothiers in the six parishes around Cranbrook dyed a million pounds of wool a year consumed untold quantities of it. The problem was that the wood belonged, in large measure, to the Bakers, the ironworks had first call on it, and on top of that wood merchants were exporting it to London. By December 1594, the clothiers of Cranbrook and all the weavers, spinners, shearmen, teasel men, carters, and mercers who relied on the cloth business had put up with enough. They had already attacked a wood dealer in Biddenden. A conspiracy was hatched focused on "Mr Bakers mill and woodes." Secret meetings were held in Cranbrook houses urgently debating how "to break upp Mr Bakers Hammer Pond." The authorities began to hear whispers of the plot. Some poor Cranbrook weavers, egged on by the richer clothiers, remaining hidden in the background, were planning "to put up the bank of the ponde." Cranbrook had no wood to burn and so "There is a rumor that they will put down the furnace."

John Baker, Richard's son, was the owner of Sissinghurst when this crisis hit. Hearing of "certaine mutinus speeches tendeinge at the least to greate disorder ensuinge," he hurried down to Sissinghurst from his house in Southwark. Many of the conspirators were arrested, while others were known to have fled.

By mid-January 1595, the crisis seems to have ebbed; it is difficult to say why, but it is clear that Elizabethan Sissinghurst, which perhaps to Vita looked like the moment of perfection, turns out to have been a time of polarized identities: a fierce distinction between inside the great house and outside it; a pretense at ease and refinement within the enclosure; a hard-pressure world of unregulated business beyond it. The whole of the Weald, in the middle of which the parkland and jewel-like house sat, was a negotiated and contested space, full, not slack, taut and tightly patrolled.

There is no portrait of Richard Baker and nothing written by him. We know only that he was a man of wealth and sophistication. He left to Mary, his Roman Catholic wife, "such apparrell as she hath" in his will, "And my better coatch with the horses and furniture thereto belonging." He had a daughter, Chrysogna, whose portrait as a girl survives at the Vyne in Hampshire, a minature person in ruff and gilt lace, with a coral and pearl necklace and a red gallica rose in her hand, not unlike but not very like the *Rosa gallica* "Sissinghurst Castle" discovered here by Vita. Richard Baker had his own silk clothes that he left to his eldest son, John. Richard had been trained up by his father for a political career, but abandoned it as soon as his father died. Instead, he devoted himself to creating a vision of a perfect Sissinghurst. He loved Sissinghurst.

1579: *The six-year-old Chrysogna Baker, daughter of Sir Richard Baker, with a rose in hand, perhaps implying her father was already looking for a betrothal.*

He had taken his inheritance and profoundly reshaped it. Sissinghurst became his self-portrait. What he made of it was a denial of his terrifying, moralist father, a substitution of delight and playfulness for authority and violence. He had retreated from brutal Tudor politics into the play politics of Renaissance aestheticism, a quasi-medieval, quasi-classical world of a pure pink fantasy castle surrounded by its lawns and woods and prancing deer.

This is the place to which, amid an orgasm of anxiety and preparation, the queen and her court came in August 1573. By then the house was surely complete: the rents gathered, the coping stones on, the paving laid, the moat extended and filled, the garden manured and planted, the roses trained, the banqueting houses embellished, the glass polished, the paneling up, the light grotesque devised and painted, the tapestries hung, the chimneypieces installed, the fires lit, the park laid out, the pale erected, the deer stocked, the meadows fenced, the woods coppiced, the entranceways smoothed, the pond-bay dug, the river dammed, the charcoal made, the furnace lit, and the ironworks begun.

In August 1573, the queen had been on progress in Kent for a week or two. She had already stayed with the Culpepers at Bedgbury and knighted Sir Alexander. She stayed with the Guilfords at Hemsted, and knighted Sir Thomas. Finally, on August 14, she and her court arrived at Sissinghurst, coming up from Rye through the atrocious clay-stodged roads. The courtiers were not in the best of moods. Lord Burleigh had written three days before to the earl of Shrewsbury in Derbyshire, saying he had much rather have been with him at Chatsworth than down here in the slums of the Weald.

It was the most dazzling sight ever seen at Sissinghurst. When the court went on progress, its baggage filled between three and five hundred carts. You have to imagine them coming through the heavy gate in the park pale, lurching down the deeply entrenched road through the wood, pulling on to the level ground in front of the gatehouse, streaming in through that gate into the upper courtyard and there debouching their riches.

There is no record of who was with the queen that year, but by chance an account has survived from the following summer of the rooms given to the court when it arrived at the archbishop's palace at Croydon. They had also been there in 1573. Most of the courtiers, as the document records, were given the chambers they had occupied the year before. Where the courtiers on progress differed, a note was made of who substituted for whom. The 1574 Croydon list, in other words, can be used to identify the people who came to stay at Sissinghurst in August 1573.

That summer day the whole cavalcade of Elizabethan courtliness arrived. There was the lord chamberlain, Thomas Radclyffe, earl of Sussex, a seasoned soldier in Ireland and the north, aged forty-eight, now in charge of the Household; the lord treasurer, Lord Burghley, the architect of Elizabethan security, now aged fifty-three, who as a young man must have known Sir John Baker well; and the lord admiral, Edward Clinton, earl of Lincoln. A generation down, and the glamour star of the whole performance, Robert Dudley, recently created earl of Leicester, was here. The youngest of the courtiers here was the brilliant young poet, the earl of Oxford, Burghley's son-in-law, recently married, rich, of ancient lineage, the world at his feet.

The new Sissinghurst would have been built with this moment in mind. Baker would have had tens of rooms to play with: in the great new court, in the Tower, and in the old medieval house. It was not unheard of for the hosts of the court on progress to farm out a few unimportant courtiers to neighboring houses. The key concern, which the earl of Sussex would have overseen, was a set of rooms for the queen in which she could perform her political and public roles; and away from that, on the upper floor, more withdrawn rooms in which she could be cocooned in some privacy. If Sissinghurst followed the pattern in other houses, the court would have used the hall as the Great Chamber to which all had access; the parlor as the Presence Chamber, to which many of the higher courtiers had access; and maybe a winter parlor as the Privy Chamber, to which access was strictly controlled.

On the floor above, probably overlooking both the garden by the moat and the great court on the other side, the queen's rooms would have been surrounded by her core household: Sussex within calling distance, Lady Carew and other gentlewomen of the bedchamber and Lady Strafforde next door, "the lady Marquess" of Northampton nearby. The male counselors would have been accommodated on the far side of the court in the opposite range: with Burghley, Leicester, Oxford, and others over there in tense proximity.

From the first ceremonial greeting at the threshold, surely under the Tower arch, they would have moved on into the great courtyard. Each member of the court would have been shown his or her apartments. Hall, parlor, garden, the room in the Tower decorated with busts of the queen's father, mother, sister, brother, and herself, the rooftop views and those from the flanking banqueting houses, the park with its deer-hunting and rabbit-catching: all this feels like an amalgam of party architecture and landscape design, a complete universe in which life itself was a theater of delight.

Was that the tone here? Or had Richard Baker, like Sir Francis Carew at Bedington in Surrey in August 1599, dressed his cherry trees in canvas tents delaying their season, so that the fruit would be at perfect ripeness on the day the queen came? Or did he drive his park deer into a small paddock so that the queen might shoot one or two without much effort, as happened at Cowdray? Or did he make green houses in the park, the walls of hazels cut and stuck in the ground, roofed in ivy, the interior hung with tapestries and the floor thick with strewing herbs and parsley, as the earls of Pembroke did in Clarendon Park near Salisbury? Did he have a young man serenading the queen under her window as soon as she awoke? Or did the Faery Queen with her accompanying maidens come dancing across the garden toward her, singing a song of flowery delight? Did the queen herself dance, in the high-stepping style for which this smallpox-scarred, wig-wearing forty-year-old was known across Europe? Or did she play the virginals in her own chamber, as she often did "when she was solitary, to shun melancholy"?

All of this happened elsewhere on her progresses. Sadly, none of it is recorded for Sissinghurst. All we know for sure is that Richard Baker gave her

> One standynge cup, the bodie chaste [?] and cover partli christall, garnished with silver and guilt; in the top of the cover is a lion holding the Queen's armes cxvii oz

A rich cup weighing 117 ounces far outdid the offering made by the Culpepers (46 ounces), the townsmen of Cranbrook (47 ounces), and even the Guilfords (55 ounces). After three days, queen and courtiers left, perhaps with trumpets and drums in the court, and three days later, when they had traveled on to Dover, Baker followed them and was duly knighted, the reward that sealed his vastly expensive, entirely Elizabethan, and father-denying efforts to make Sissinghurst a Renaissance palace in an invented park.

CHAPTER 9

Disintegration

MY IDEAS FOR THE FARM had collapsed in the summer of 2006. I wasn't going to let them go, but this was clearly the moment for a pause. One or two moves were made: the prospect of a Sissinghurst dairy herd disappeared, as a hop garden had earlier. Both were unaffordable. The Trust started negotiations to buy a small and slightly run-down neighboring holding called Whitegate Farm. Its buildings would be useful if the larger scheme ever took off. And the break-clauses in the four old tenancies on the farm were invoked. If we missed this window, there would be no chance of changing the farm system here for another five years. But things were scarcely going ahead at full speed.

I WENT BACK AGAIN TO the longer story of Sissinghurst, to what I had always thought of as the long slide of a decline between the days of Elizabethan glory and the moment my grandparents arrived in 1930. Sissinghurst was not Knole. It had fallen from its great height, and that decline and collapse were the part of the story I now turned to. Again I found a surprise: as the great house had imploded, the land around it had thrived.

First, from about 1600 to the 1640s, Sissinghurst had continued as the Bakers' grand and occasionally visited hunting lodge, an increasingly out-of-date palace in a park. It was a period of profound inactivity. The Bakers were based largely at their house in Lime Street in the City of London and from the late 1630s onward in a new, expensively rented and richly furnished house in Henrietta Street, Covent Garden. Generation by generation, the Bakers trained as lawyers in the Middle Temple and Gray's Inn and hung around the edges of the Stuart court—while Sissinghurst remained occupied largely by their servants and filled with their possessions.

There is a hint that the Bakers may have continued as secret Catholics, drawing on the inheritance of the great Sir John, or at least as high Anglicans. In 1639, the chapel at Sissinghurst was, according to Thomas Philipott, the seventeenth-century historian, "re-edified." Sissinghurst was "in the wilds of Kent," and "by reason of deep and fowle ways (especially in winter)" the latest Sir John Baker and his family were "not able without much trouble and danger duly to frequent the church" in Cranbrook. Hence they needed their chapel here. The archbishop's license describes it as "newly built and decently embellished, apart from the ordinary part of the house," and so one can't say whether this seventeenth-century chapel was a refurbished version of the medieval chapel or an entirely new building. The license says it was "below" (infra) the mansion at Sissinghurst, which suggests it might have been in the orchard below the medieval house. One eighteenth-century drawing does indeed show a semidetached building there, with a door giving onto the Elizabethan garden.

A further hint comes in the sermon that was preached by Robert Abbott, the vicar of Cranbrook, at the dedication ceremony in September 1639. The chapel was, Abbott said,

> built and furnished with cost: profit therefore is engaged to give way to the devout worship of God heere. It is built by a garden of pleasure, a parlour of plenty: pleasure therefore is engaged to give way to the devout worship of God. *Iosephs tombe* was in a garden,

to put thoughts of mortality into his delights, and this chappell is in a garden, to be a monitor (in the midst of refreshments) to the way of immortalitie.

Between garden and parlor, a "chapel in a garden": this was the Sissinghurst version of worshipping God in the beauty of holiness.

Abbott addressed "a large crowd," with some markedly Catholic names (Campion, Mounckton, Henley, Darrell) among them. And the chapel was furnished in a far from puritan style. It had a communion table, pulpit, reading desks, and thirteen pews "all of wainscot," candlesticks and a branched candelabra, a "fayre silver bason, a silver pott for wine and a silver chalice with a cover for the communion and a silver plate with a bason for the font, all double guilt." In 1639, this was the highest of church Laudianism, and you can be sure the whole of puritan Cranbrook would have been scandalized. It was probably at this stage that the little Elizabethan banqueting house at the northern edge of the garden was extended so that the chaplain could be housed in it, and renamed perhaps by the locals the Priest's House, a term that in Protestant Cranbrook would have been dripping in contempt.

It was inevitable that this High Church, possibly crypto-Catholic family would side with the king against Parliament in the Civil War. Sir John was already off with the king's army in 1642, and in August that year his lands, worth £2,000 a year, and his "rich furniture in Covent garden" were seized by the parliamentary committees raising money for the war.

I have been unable to find the inventory made sometime in the summer of 1644, when Sissinghurst was raided for everything of value. But there are lists for neighboring gentry houses whose goods fell under the hammer that summer, often sold to the local poor. At the Wottons' house in Boughton Malherbe, rugs for two shillings, "a little round table," a coverlet, a chair, "old pieces of stayres and lumber," "the fruit of the Long Walk and the Privy Garden," "nagges and geldings," "two little turkey carpets motheaten for five shillings," and "a little pair of tongs" all were knocked down to Goodwife Andrewes, Goodman Albert, Mr. Cogan (the sequestrator's assistant), Goodwife Gilbert, or their neighbors.

It must have happened here too, and the evidence is in the woods. In the whole of Sissinghurst, there are now only two trees that were certainly growing here before the summer of 1644: the pollard oak in the big wood, in whose branches I once spent the best part of a day, and another down by the Hammer Brook, its fat trunk scarred by lightning, its branches hanging out over the stream. Otherwise, they have all gone, and it doesn't take much to imagine the scene, the great old oaks and beeches that the Bakers had treasured, and even named in their wills, felled unseasonably in midsummer, the huge leafy crowns slowly descending to the parkland grass, the outer limbs cushioning the fall, splintering as they came down, the bodies of the pollards laid out like shot cattle, the timber wagons taking them away to the saw-yards. In other Kentish parks, payments were made by the sequestrator to the men doing the work for Parliament's cause. And there is one further clue. A description of Sissinghurst Park in 1695 says, "The Growth of the Wood in it is most Birch, which is much in use for Birch-Wine." Birch is the great pioneer species of Wealden woods, colonizing any space vacated for it. For Sissinghurst to be covered in them in 1695 could only have meant that the oaks and beeches had been taken away fifty years before.

By July 1644, the Committee for Compounding proposed to fine Baker £5,000, "it appearing that he has been in service against parliament and has 2,500 l. a year." Negotiations continued; the fine was reduced to £3,000, but he didn't pay up and still hadn't by July 1645. His indebtedness rolled on throughout the years of the Commonwealth. As late as 1652, "on the morrow of Holy Trinity," he at last signed a mortgage on almost everything he owned in Kent: houses, barns, stables, seven watermills, forty gardens, forty orchards, 2,005 acres of arable land, seven hundred of meadow, five hundred of pasture, seven hundred of wood, and "40 acres of land covered with water"—the huge pond upstream of the furnace at Hammer Mill. Although Baker's London properties were not mentioned, "the manor of Sissinghurst" was included by name. In return, Baker received £2,760 sterling and with it paid the debt he owed the state.

Old Sir John died the follow year and his son, yet another Sir John, inherited a heavily encumbered estate. He rearranged the mortgage in 1657, and with the money restored the pale around the whole park, but Sissinghurst was now fatally burdened with its borrowings and the Bakers would never recover. This last Sir John died in about 1661, having committed the ultimate crime against his family's fortunes: he left a widow, four daughters, and no son. The girls began by living with their mother in the huge house. Any number of others, unnamed, were living in the house with them. There were thirty-eight hearths alight here on Lady Day in 1664, compared with eighty-five at Knole but only twenty-one at Penshurst. Inside the park, at the top of the lane in the fields still known as the Well Fields, there was an "old admired well," set with stones and basins, a "curative chalybeate spring" much in use for those with infections of the urinary tract. Multitudes came. There were walks laid out. "The park," it was said, had "very great plenty of Stawberys in and about it. . . . Also near-adjoining . . . is very good *Chery-gardens* and great plenty of Fruit: The best Sider is but Six pence the Bottle." The district as a whole was "much supply'd with Fish, there being much Gentry in the Parish, and many great Ponds of Fresh Fish."

It didn't last. Lady Baker "hated all the people and had the gates of the park locked to obstruct the same." The stones and basin were removed as Sissinghurst sank toward its nadir. When the Baker daughters "married into other counties," the old lady moved to her London house and Sissinghurst became half destitute and lawless. In 1673, the inhabitants of the mansion house attacked "the possessors of a wood adjacent," the reason not recorded. An arrest warrant was issued, the parish constable came to the front gate "with 16 or 20 to assist him." The Sissinghurst gang refused to come out or give up the man named on the warrant. There was a standoff, but the constable and his men could hear them inside arming with staves. "The constable and his assistants fearing mischief went away." About fourteen of Sissinghurst's inhabitants then rushed out of the gate, chased the constable, "the constable commanded the peace, yet they fell on and killed one of the assistants of the constable, and wounded others, and then retired into the house to the rest of their company." The precise individual who had committed the murder couldn't be identified, but nine of them were arrested, all found equally guilty, and all of them hanged, thus establishing the powerful precedent of the Sissinghurst House Case, by which membership in a murderous gang is considered the same as committing murder oneself.

Any question of Sissinghurst being the center of a perfect world was long gone. It is not quite certain what happened here in the early eighteenth century. A very old pauper, interviewed at Sissinghurst in the 1830s by a visiting American descendant of the Bakers, "said he remembered the last of the family coming to Church every Sunday with their guests and visitors in four coaches and four horses, long tails, etc., etc." There is no record of them. Sissinghurst and the larger Baker estate had been inherited by the four sisters, in equal shares. Each share followed a tortuous path down the different branches of the family, and although each of those four Baker girls, Anne (d. 1685), Elizabeth (d. 1705), Mary (d. 1714), and Catherine (d. 1733), returned from their husbands' estates to be buried in Cranbrook church, Sissinghurst was neglected. The buildings rotted. The park pale collapsed. The unpaid mortgage continued to climb, until by the 1750s the sum owing had reached £9,000, nearly three-quarters the value of the entire Baker estate in Kent. Sissinghurst had become a lump against which money could be borrowed. The place, in a way that might be shocking to us in the age of preservation, was allowed to fall apart. But the eighteenth-century rich lived in a profligate world. Many families in England were overhoused. Each of the Sissinghurst heirs had their own satisfactory houses elsewhere. What good was a crumbling Elizabethan mansion, only as old for them as a Victorian concrete shooting box might be for us?

The eighteenth century gave nothing to Sissinghurst. It only took away. I have often wondered what might have happened here if the Bakers' male line had not died out. Would there have been an exquisite Palladian pavilion placed on this gentle rise, surrounded by the elegances of its improved eighteenth-century park? Would Capability Brown have been brought in to dam the Hammer Brook and make a sky-reflecting lake in the valley? Would one or two Gothic eye-catchers have been built up by the pines in the wood? Maybe. And maybe Sissinghurst would have been colored not with its air of romantic abandonment but with suede-lined riches, a title, perhaps an earldom for the Bakers, money from an advantageous marriage or two in the City. Perhaps Vita, pursued in 1912 by the earl of Sissinghurst, would have turned down him and his palatial residence as something too smart, too obvious, without poetry?

In 1752, Horace Walpole was touring the sites of Kent, and on August 9 he wrote to his friend Richard Bentley:

> Yesterday, after twenty mishaps, we got to Sissinghurst to dinner. There is a park in ruins and a house in ten times greater ruins, built by Sir John Baker, Chancellor of the Exchequer to Queen Mary. You go through an arch of the stables to the house, the court of which is perfect and very beautiful. . . . This has a good apartment, and a fine gallery, a hundred and twenty feet by eighteen, which takes up one side: the wainscot is pretty and entire: the ceiling vaulted, and painted in a light genteel grotesque. The whole is built for show; for the back of the house is nothing but lath and plaster.

"Nothing but lath and plaster" is a mid-eighteenth-century view of the medieval house behind Sir Richard Baker's Elizabethan *cour d'honneur.*

Four years later, Sissinghurst entered the pit of its existence, when even the sad remains that Walpole had seen were effectively destroyed and the break with the sixteenth century was made final. The agents of the dispersed Baker estate found a means of making some money out of the old mansion. About fourteen hundred acres of the surrounding land were let for £445 to a farmer called George Tempest, but the big house was reserved from the lease and let instead to the government. Britain had embarked on a Seven Years' War with France, and on July 21, 1756, the house at Sissinghurst was leased by the Admiralty's Sick and Hurt Board as a camp for French naval prisoners.

1760s: Drawing by S. H. Grimm of the Elizabethan Tower with the prisoners'
day-sheds built as lean-tos on either side.

Up to three thousand Frenchmen were held here at any one time,
most of them common seamen. There were rooms reserved for officers
in the Tower (where their graffiti have been preserved in the plaster:
their names and both brigs and square-rigged ships in full sail), but most
officers, having given their word of honor, were allowed to live in Cranbrook, Tenterden, Sevenoaks, or Maidstone.

This broken-down and brutalized "château," as they called it—a
term then borrowed by the English; this was the moment at which
Sissinghurst House became Sissinghurst Castle—was a strange and
alien place for the French. Their letters refer to the "Chateau de Sis-
sengherst," "Sisinchers," "Chisterner," "Sinsinhars," and "Ste. Sigherts
pres Cambrouck." It was a zoo of abuse and maltreatment, the prison
that Frenchmen in other prisons were threatened with if they misbehaved. The stories coming out of Sissinghurst became so bad that in
November and December 1761 Dr. Maxwell, the commissioner for the
Sick and Hurt Board, came down for a month and held an inquiry in a
room in the great Elizabethan courtyard. From the evidence given to
that inquiry, transcribed verbatim into a long manuscript now in the
National Archives, a powerful picture emerges of the grief and suffering
that thousands of men underwent here.

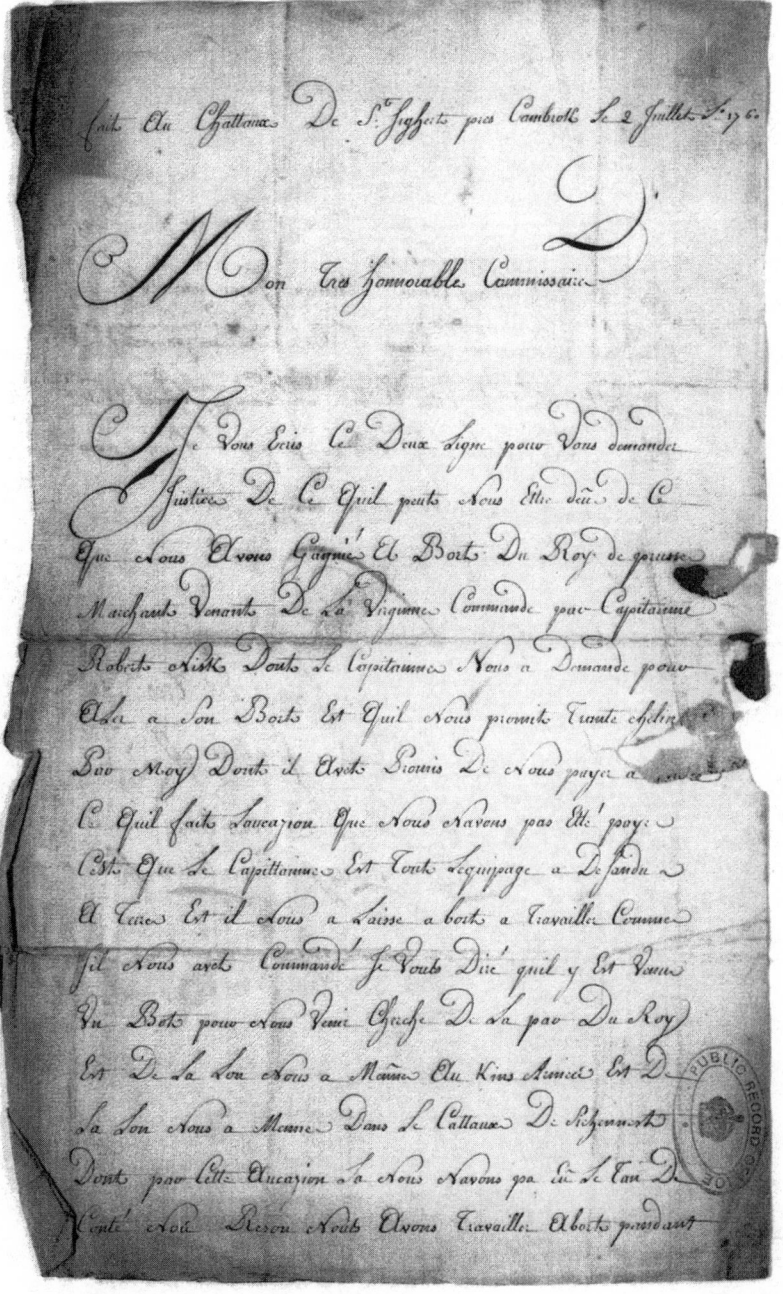

1757: French officer's letter.

The prisoners were guarded by revolving detachments, each of about 220 men, from various county militias. Supervising them on behalf of the Admiralty was a Mr. Cooke, "Agent for Prisoners of War at Sissinghurst," known to the French as "Monsieur Cok," and suffering a little from the gout. He could speak no French but communicated with the prisoners through an interpreter called François le Rat. Cooke's relationship with the army officers was usually unsatisfactory and he was generally distrusted by both guards and prisoners alike for his "Gouvernement," which according to one prisoner's complaint was "nothing less than tyrannical and capricious."

1750s: *Prison ward number and number of men billeted there, on tie beam in north wing of front range.*

The place was disgusting, with "great heaps of dirt in all the courts." The moat was "very foul and stinking," filled with all kinds of ordure and no proper means of cleaning it. The prisoners were packed into every available space on all three floors of all the buildings. They slept in hammocks strung from posts specially inserted into the rooms, converting Sissinghurst into the navy's equivalent of between-decks accommodation. The numbers of the wards and the number of men to be housed in each of them were painted up over the doors. There was no money to replace broken windows and so the prisoners blocked them up with bricks and clay to keep warm. They had coal fires but no scuttles or bunkers and so the coal lay in heaps on the floor and its dust blackened everything. Large numbers of unwashed men lived in virtually lightless and airless rooms, which Maxwell reported as "dirty and very bad smelling" and "very close, by the windows being shut up for want of casements and shutters." The rooms of Elizabethan elegance became "Bowling Alley Ward," "Long Gallery Ward," and "Great Parlour Ward." Worst of all was a room known simply as "Black Dog," and above it "Black Dog Garret," both of which were "very close, wanted air, bad smells in them."

A deeply unhappy and rather chubby twenty-three-year-old Edward Gibbon, who was here for a few days in December 1760, hated every minute of it. Sissinghurst was "a strong large old Seat, situated in the middle of a Park," with about 1,750 prisoners housed there. The daily march to and from a "miserable" Cranbrook was disgusting, the "dirt most excessive," and the other officers despicable. He was already "sick of so hateful a service, tired of companions who had neither the knowledge of scholars nor the manners of gentlemen," and was longing to begin again "to taste the pleasure of thinking." Life at Sissinghurst was "at best, not a life for a man of letters." It was "both unfit for and unworthy of me."

There is one curious sidenote in young Gibbon's diary. His detachment was at Sevenoaks on June 5, 1761. "We took a Walk to Knowles the D. of Dorset's seat, a noble pile, very much upon the plan of Sissinghurst." The Knole-Sissinghurst connection was alive in the 1560s, when Richard Baker's sister was married to Thomas Sackville; again in the mind of a particularly alert young man in the 1760s; and again two centuries later in the 1930s, when a disinherited Vita recognized Sissinghurst as the nearest to a ruined Knole she would ever come.

Sissinghurst was a world of gossip and hate, bubbling with violence, threat, and mutual loathing. Prisoners would spit in the face of militiamen, who in return would knock them down with their musket stocks. Brutal kicking and beating occurred almost daily. The lingua franca of the prison was foul abuse. Soldiers would habitually break the pipes in prisoners' mouths or smack them on the head.

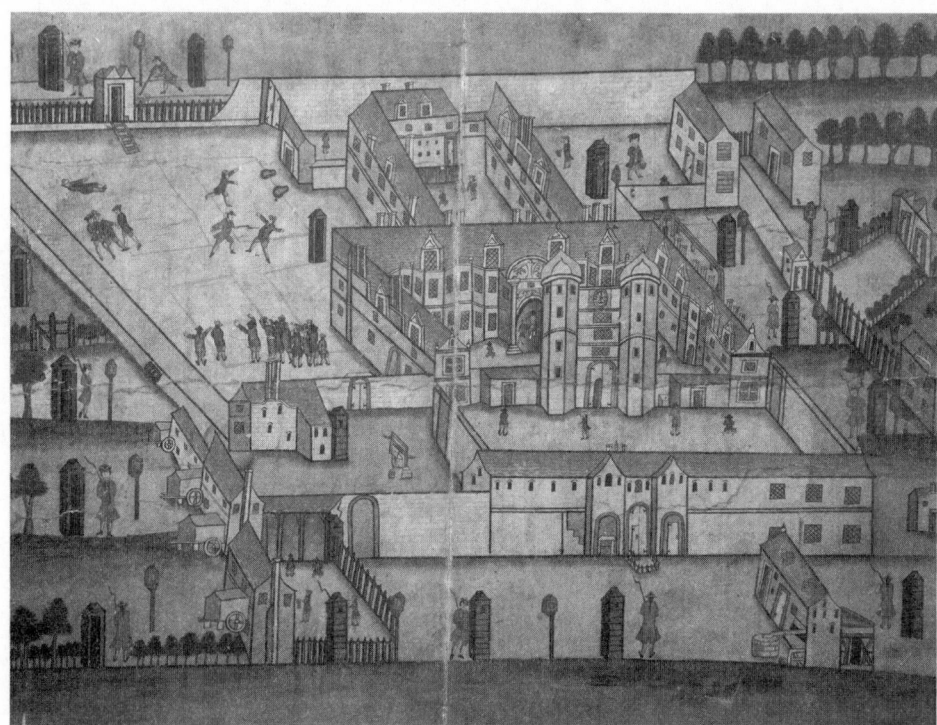

1761: *Anonymous drawing of a double murder by an English militiaman at Sissinghurst.*

Inevitably, this undertow of loathing and brutality now and then tipped over into murder. One guard, William Bassuck, was killed by a prisoner who dropped a filled pail on his head from the top of the Tower. A soldier who killed two prisoners in the garden said, when asked about it, at least according to one of the prisoners, "if he had killed more it would not have given him uneasiness." A picture recently discovered in Canada shows this incident: the militiaman firing from the far side of the moat; the two men lying dead in the garden; the crowd of outraged prisoners; the ring of sentry-boxes and braziers, a Lilliput version of a human hell.

On October 27, 1759, Mr. Cooke's assistant, Mr. Ward, and an officer of the West Kent Militia, Mr. Mortimer, were walking in the Long Gallery, on the north side of the Middle Court. It was about eleven o'clock at night, an hour after the regulations stated that all lights should be put out. They were looking across the court to "the uppermost ward of the south wing." Mortimer was convinced that the prisoners still had a light burning. Ward

spoke to Mr M and endeavoured to convince him that there were no lights. That it was the Reflection of the Lamps. Upon which we walked up & down the room three times in the Long Gallery where I said I cannot be persuaded that there have been any lights in the room this night.

Philippe Hardie, one of the sixty or seventy prisoners in the upper ward in the south wing, sleeping next to a man called Joffe from Dunkirk, was asked at the inquiry what happened. "The soldier called to them to put the candle out and there was no candle alight; as all the people were asleep nobody answered him." Mortimer claimed that the prisoners "bid him fire and be damned," but Philippe Hardie's testimony has the ring of truth:

Everybody in the room was very quiet and I was laid alongside of [Joffe]. The reflection of a lamp shone upon a window in our ward & the centinel thought there was a light in the Room & he fired & the other prisoners say now he called out 2 or 3 times but I heard nothing of that & was asleep. The ball went through his thigh as he lay asleep in his hammock across the window.

The lead ball that hit Joffe in the thigh was found in his hammock. It had gone through one thigh and flattened against the other. But terrible damage had been done in its passage:

A large hands breadth of the thigh bone [was] shattered to pieces the ball having taken an oblique direction. The wound was so near the head of the bone that amputation was impracticable. The man lived in excessive pain till the 31st then died.

Deprived of firewood, the French prisoners took Sissinghurst apart, tearing up the woodwork, "especially in a ward called The Black Dog by destroying the hammock posts and pulling up and making away with the Boards of the floor," destroying all the fittings in the chapel, parlors, and Long Gallery, taking out the inside of the stables, making two barns and four oasts unusable "by cutting out the principall beams," stripping off the paneling wherever it had survived, destroying "the Palesade fence to the Kitchen Garden with other fences & gates Destroyed," and wrecking "the best Garden, by the Wall fruite & other trees all destroyed and not even the stump of a Shrub nor Tree left."

The owner of Sissinghurst was now Edward Mann of Linton, a Baker descendant who in 1762 had bought its 1,402 acres from the other claimants for £12,982, plus £300 for the mansion house. When the war came to an end in 1763, Mann wrote to the Admiralty assessors, telling them that he was "filled with a perfect Desire of bringing our affairs

1763

An Estimate of the damage don by
the Prisoners and forces at Sisinghurst
so farr as came to our Knowledge by
a Survey taken on the tenth & eleventh
of October last

1. To 2092 foot of Glass destroyed
and gon with great damge to the
winder frames by many Jams
& Iron Barrs being gon & winders
and many Parts of Winders stoped
up with Bricks Morter or Mud   100:0:0

2. To the Chapel by destroying the Pulpett
Pewes Partition Carve work & Table
floor Ceeling and all the timber of the
Ceeling Floor   40:0:0

3. To the long Gallery by Destroying
neer two hundred yards of Wainscott
with a Rich Cut a Cetor Carved
marvel Chymny piece Broke down
and wood work greatly damaged   50:0:0

4. To the Stables by 82 foot of Reck
and Manger four Stalls gon
by Doors & Door Cases gon   20:0:0

5. To the two Barns by floors great
Doors Recks gon with many Breeches
in the Brick Walls   50:0:0

6. To the Oast House by four Oasts
being pulled down & gon & by Cutting
out the Principall Beams &   40:0:0

7. To the Great & little Halls
by destroying wainscott floor
Partitions & Ornaments   20:0:0

8. To wainscott damaged & three Rooms
up Stairs Front Door gon & one floor   11:10:0
To the Walls & Ceelings of the the
House broke Down   20:0:0

9. To Palesade fence to Kitchen
Garden with other fences & Gates
Destroyed & gon   10:0:0

1763: List drawn up by the Mann estate of damage to buildings
at the end of the Seven Years' War.

1760: *Sissinghurst "Castle"—so named for the first time in an engraving by James Peak of a drawing made by one of the militia officers.*

together to an Eclairissement." He asked initially for £361 "in compensation for the great Destruction in every Particular which such a number of Prisoners have occasioned in every part of the Buildings & Mansion House & Gardens," but soon accepted fifty pounds plus the Admiralty's "sheds and erections," which had remained here when the prisoners left.

Sissinghurst had been utterly degraded, and this is the first moment when its history just leaks into the margins of living memory. In the 1930s, Vita met a "very old" gentleman who had lived in the Castle in his boyhood. He had been a ten-year-old in the 1860s, when he met a ninety-year-old laborer, who had been about thirty in 1800, when his father-in-law (then about sixty) told him that he "had been employed not only to pull down the walls, but also to pick the foundations in 1763."

Most of the old house disappeared, probably as brick rubble used as the foundation for tracks and yards. Electronic resistivity surveys of the site have revealed next to nothing, and when drainage ditches have been cut through the lines of the old ranges, all that is revealed in their walls is dark scars of eighteenth-century earth filling the Elizabethan and medieval foundation trenches. All the fields around Sissinghurst are full of shards of tile and crumbled brick from the dismantled buildings. The value remained only in the land. The park now disappeared. The pale was never recreated and a regular, eighteenth-century field pattern was laid over the open grounds. A survey was made of the trees here in June 1763 in Sissinghurst Park, Hammer Wood by Hammer Mill, Fludgate Wood next to it, Graylins Wood near Whitsunden, and Legge Wood and Eleven Acre Wood, both near Wadd. In them, the indefatigable surveyors counted:

7981 oak trees
5012 beech trees
125 ash trees
320 chestnutt trees
3 walnutt trees
10 Sycomore trees
14493 tillers [young trees] and pollards of the above sorts

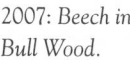

2007: *Beech in Bull Wood.*

The Sissinghurst woods had begun to make their recovery from the depredations of the Civil War and were now valued at £5,302, nearly eighteen times as much as the damaged house. Among these trees, so carefully counted, are most of the big oaks and beeches now growing at Sissinghurst.

In 1796 a lease was taken by the parish of Cranbrook on Sissinghurst Castle Farm, the idea being that the farm would provide work for those able-bodied men who would otherwise be incapable of earning their living, especially during the winter months. This Cranbrook poor-relief scheme was exceptional. The general rule at the time was to give outdoor relief as a supplement to low wages, the Speenhamland system, which had the effect not of subsidizing wages but of depressing them, causing the widespread misery of which William Cobbett was the fiercest scourge and critic. Cranbrook's hiring of Sissinghurst Castle Farm meant that housing, shelter, and food were provided for up to a hundred men at a time. The farm made a good profit, which meant that Cranbrook local taxation, the rates, did not rise too high and the desperate poverty of farm workers in other parts of southern England was avoided.

Because of the income derived from the Castle Farm, Cranbrook rates throughout the early nineteenth century were consistently running at a third and even a half lower than in surrounding parishes. Farmers in need of casual labor could hire men from this farm, paying the parish a fee according to the current level of wages. Men could come and go from Sissinghurst whenever they pleased. Between 1813 and 1818, with grain at a wartime price peak, this farm earned £1,000 profit, which was given to the parish for the poor. Even in the widespread postwar depression in the 1820s, Sissinghurst Castle Farm lost only a hundred pounds a year, a small price for its benefits as a whole. When the violent Swing Riots broke out in the 1830s and agricultural laborers burned ricks, destroyed threshing machines, and threatened and shot at employers, Cranbrook, almost alone of all the surrounding parishes, had no trouble. This farm, overseen by the group of Cranbrook men who had signed the lease, had

1820s: Pen and wash drawing by T. D. W. Dearn of the entrance gateway as it appeared when Sissinghurst was rented by Cranbrook parish as the parish farm.

done its part in maintaining some kind of social cohesion. The rest of England was in the full flood of laissez-faire market capitalism. Sissinghurst, not through any interest of the landlords, the Manns, who had by now become the earls of Cornwallis, but through the leaders of the local community, remained an island in which the poor had been treated as more than economic cogs to be used and rejected at will.

After the economy recovered in the 1830s, Sissinghurst started to pour money into Cranbrook's coffers. The Frittenden brick kilns were opened on the northern edge of the estate and there was a sawmill set up next to them, both making a profit. Between 1842 and 1847, £2,500 was credited to the parish from the farm, which was fondly called "The Old Cow," as it could be milked and milked and would always deliver. Assistance was given to Cranbrook families wishing to emigrate. Money

1828: *The Tower and a thatched*
South Cottage beyond it.

was provided for the repair of churches. Only with the downturn of the late 1840s, and an overdraft growing to £1,500, did the parish trustees decide to pull out. Having first traded their way out of that debt, in 1853 they found themselves in pocket, surrendered the lease to the Cornwallises, handed £3,622 to the parish, with which the Vestry Hall in Cranbrook was built, and considered sixty years of poor relief well done.

The buildings were in a fairly ruinous condition. The South Cottage was a thatched hovel. Both the Tower's turrets had lost their upper prospect rooms and in the 1830s were roofless. In 1839, the Mann Cornwallis estate repaired the roofs with oak-shingled conical caps, surmounted by some beautiful weathervanes marked "MC 1839."

Nevertheless, the Cornwallises were keen to get the farm back in hand. In 1853, when the farm here was still rented out to the Overseers of the Poor in Cranbrook, a report had been made on the condition of the Cornwallis estates. Of Sissinghurst, the Cornwallis trustees had written:

This is the most important farm on the estate in the Weald. We incline to the opinion that it is much more desirable to have a respectable tenant residing on the farm and farming on his own account than to have so many non-resident Trustee tenants, who could not feel the same interest in it that he would feel. The only objection to this change which presents itself, is the heavy outlay which must necessarily be incurred in erecting a good farmhouse and suitable buildings, many of the present ones being very old and inefficient for an occupation of this extent. The farm is not in so good a state as it was ten years ago, and about half of it requires draining.

When the poorhouse was closed, Sissinghurst entered a period of high Victorian farming. A dynamic and highly cultivated young man, George Neve, whose father was a land agent, managing several large aristocratic estates, was chosen as the new tenant. George had worked with his father and this was his opportunity. A big brick farmhouse, called "The Castle Residence," was built in 1854–55, a large family house approached by an asphalted carriage drive and sweep, with seven bedrooms on the second floor, a bathroom and a flushing loo, four more bedrooms above, four stalls for hunters, and two loose boxes, a harness room, and two coachhouses. The house was surrounded by lawns, shrubberies, and gardens. There was a greenhouse and a vinery, "with the remains of Sissinghurst Castle close by, which are a prominent and pleasing feature to the property and full of historic interest."

The new asphalted carriage drive, which is the present lane, was built in a long curve down from the main road to arrive at the front of the new house, where cedars, laurels, and rhododendrons were planted. Twenty-five acres of ancient woodland were cleared from in front of the house, leaving only the older trees standing in a stretch of what became elegant new parkland, "which is of excellent grazing quality and beautifully timbered with oak, chestnut, silver birch, ash and walnut." Chestnut coppice was planted throughout most of the old woodland and over some of the older fields called Roughter near the Biddenden road, turning them into woods "which produce some of the highest priced Chestnut and Ash in the district, as well as being Splendid Game Coverts." The field pattern that had been imposed on the abandoned park in the eighteenth century was regularized, some new, mainly hawthorn hedges planted and others taken out. A small stream between Large and Lodge fields was canalized. George Neve was a great advocate of dry land as a way of preventing sickness in animals, and drains were installed in most of the Sissinghurst fields. New oast houses with four kilns were built. There was stabling for ten carthorses, more for the bailiff's and shepherd's horses, and a new brick dairy. There were cow sheds, fatting lodges with pits, two chaff steaming rooms, wagon and implement sheds. The large Elizabethan brick barn had the windows that had been opened for the prisoners' hospital filled in. Huge wheat and barley stacks were made on the stack plat to the north of the barn. Every winter the threshing teams would arrive with their giant steam-driven machines and the corn in sacks was hauled up by hoists in the barn and then stored in the upper floors of the granary beside it. Beyond the new dairy, there was a range of hop pickers' huts with a cooking house beside them.

The Neves' coachman lived in the South Cottage, and eight other farm families lived in the old buildings, a bailiff in the Priest's House, others in the front range and in the Tower, where both the archways were bricked in to make a room. A gamekeeper lived in Horse Race House, which had kennels and outbuildings. Fruit trees were trained on the south wall of the great Elizabethan courtyard and a greenhouse built near the Tower.

Neve had the 278 acres of Bettenham (where the farmhouse was divided into three cottages) as well as the 478 of Castle Farm. The brick kilns were "in full working order with plenty of excellent brick earth close at hand," and next to them was the highly productive timber yard with four cottages for sawyers. The farm produced "heavy crops of hops, grass and cereals." It was even said that the finest hops in Kent were grown

Circa 1900: *Oxen at Sissinghurst.*

here. A large flock of sheep and many head of cattle were fattened on it, and there were "extensive piggeries." There were six acres of allotments on the southern side of the wood, let out to people from the village.

Payments made by the Cornwallises' agent to men at work on the Sissinghurst estate describe a world of unbridled energy and productivity. All fencing and gates were made from the wood grown here. Ladders, stepladders, and brick molds were all made in the timber yard next to the Frittenden brickworks. The brick "lodges" in which the clay for the bricks was dried before being fired were made from oak cut in the neighboring woods, roofed in the tiles dug from the neighboring brick earth, and held on the riven oak laths with pegs cleft from the same oak. Hundreds of payments are made for "hewing and sawing," including for up to five hours at a time to one "Elizabeth Eldridge." Hired-in labor worked in the woods, "setting and planting," weeding around the new chestnut plants, picking up nuts at a shilling an hour, ditching, digging, carrying manure, "letting off water" from the rides in the woods, brushing the roads, cleaning the carts after they had come out of the thick clay, making bridges over the streams. In all this multifarious work, there was one constant: the men and women who did it were paid a pittance.

It was, amazingly, a farm still worked largely by oxen, creatures that would remain in harness here until the First World War. To feed them, 110 acres of the farm were given over to grass, including the Park. Arable covered 108 acres, hops were grown on 59 acres and then carted in their giant sacking pockets to Cranbrook railway station and from there to London. There were 13 acres of orchard and 265 of wood. When the Neves had some time off, they fished for trout in the Hammer Brook and hunted deer with the Mid-Kent Stag Hounds, which met here every winter. There is not even the faintest suggestion that Sissinghurst, as it arrived in the twentieth century, was an abandoned or declining place. It was a living monument to farming excellence, to Victorian enterprise, and to all the sustained and sustaining virtues of "imbarning, stacking and foddering out." The ruins of the Elizabethan house stood there not as the focus for nostalgia but as a kind of memory, full of half-mythical stories. The Neves' children used to dig in their garden for the secret passage Bloody Baker was meant to have built from here to Cranbrook. Frederick William Neve, one of George's sons, listened agog as he heard "a tradition handed down among the peasantry that when Queen Mary came to the castle, she alighted from her horse and the footprints which she made are still there. Even when ploughed over they would return. However, as flagstones cover the ground, there is no way of testing the truth." The first postcards of Sissinghurst were made. One or two tourists used to come and for a few pence would be shown the top of the Tower, its room full of carved Tudor heads, and, intriguingly, its museum. A note written by Vita survives among my father's papers:

A curious old couple came to Sissinghurst in the spring of 1942, to visit the garden. The woman told me she had been a midwife in Cranbrook many years earlier & had often been up the towers. She asked me what had become of the things from the "museum" that used to be at the top of the tower, and mentioned that there was a ceinture de chasteté there. I must have looked surprised, for she explained "What the gentleman locks the lady into when he goes away." She said her daughter was one of Epstein's favourite models.

When the Sissinghurst Castle Estate was sold by the Cornwallises at auction on June 25, 1903, in Maidstone, in twenty-one lots, it was advertised as "an unusually fine sporting property in this lovely part of Kent," on which "the estate has been well farmed & looked after for a long period." The 1,083 acres of Sissinghurst, including a great deal of arable land, meadow, pasture, and wood that no longer belongs to it, went for £16,500 to the Cheeseman brothers, one of whom, Barton, came to live here in the farmhouse. In 1925, he left and the castle and farm were sold to a sixty-eight-year-old coal and feed merchant, William Wilmshurst, a rich man, who was already dying of cancer. Against the wishes of his son and heir, he wanted to spend his last years doing something worthwhile and had decided, after driving round Kent and Sussex, to pour his money into the ruins of Sissinghurst Castle. His nephew, John Wilmshurst, lived in the South Cottage and ran the farm, while his niece, Dorothy, was living only a mile away, married to the farmer who had bought Bettenham four years earlier, Captain Ossie Beale.

Wilmshurst died in 1927 before he could do anything for the Castle ruins, and his son, also called William, who had thought his father's plans absurd and romantic, decided to sell the whole place. Ossie Beale started to rent the Sissinghurst fields on the Bettenham side, but England was just tipping into an agricultural depression and Sissinghurst sat on the market unsold for more than two years, increasingly glum. The farm started to slide away from its Victorian condition. Then one day in April 1930, Ossie's brother Donald, who was a land agent, brought two women over from Sevenoaks to look at the place, a pair of aristocratic women poets: Vita Sackville-West and Dottie Wellesley, her lover, to whom four years earlier she had dedicated her long pastoral poem "The Land." My thirteen-year-old father came with them, appalled at the mess. Vita fell "flat in love with it." By May 6, she had bought Sissinghurst, its lands, woods, and buildings, less for the overbrimming excellence of its farm than for what the agents' particulars described as "picturesque ruins in grounds."

CHAPTER *10*

Acceptance

QUITE UNEXPECTEDLY, James Stearns, the last man to have been the resident farmer at Sissinghurst, died at the end of February 2007. He was on the way back from South Africa with his wife, Pat. Their children had given them three weeks of holiday as a fortieth wedding anniversary present. He was sixty-five.

I went to see Pat on the morning she returned from the airport. A packed cluster of cars in the driveway of the farmhouse and frost in the puddles. Her family was all there in the sitting room and the hall. The whole of George Neve's Victorian house was busy with them, and a feeling of sweetness and gentleness filled it. We had coffee and biscuits, in a strange and heightened party, sitting on the sofas, everyone bright in the bruised air, people coming and going, the friends and neighbors, all of us suddenly allowed an intimacy we had never had. Pat was pale and brave, sitting expectant in the center. James's mother, Mary Stearns, was there, her cheeks flushed, and his sister Linda and his daughter Catherine: these four strong, capable women who had surrounded James and sustained him in his lifetime. I hugged Pat and kissed her and we talked about his death. They had been side by side in the airplane on the runway when he died. Pat had just told him to put his seat belt on, she looked away, heard him cough a little, looked back, and he had gone. They had been so happy on the holiday. There had been no buildup to this death. It was just a sudden removal, a hole cut in their lives. It felt as if the family had been stabbed, or attacked in the street, and had gathered here now to dress the wounds. Mary Stearns held my hand as she spoke to me. Hurt and affection were so close to the surface that morning, they were like a scent hanging in the rooms.

I thought as I went back home of the long talk I'd had with James two years before about the farm and its history. He had told me how everything in his life had been bound to this place. His grandfather, Ossie Beale, stood at the foundations. As a young man, Oswald had his own farm in Sussex at Hadlow Down, and at the beginning of the First World War he had enlisted as a trooper in the Sussex Yeomanry. But his own father, Louis, a great, waistcoated, bearded patriarch, who was running the Beales's construction and property business in Tunbridge Wells, had taken him out to dinner, told him to go to Sandhurst and get himself a commission. So it was that Ossie fought the war as a commissioned officer in the Bedfordshire and Hertfordshire Regiment, the Beds and Herts, at the Somme, at Passchendaele, in Italy, and then on General Ironside's staff during the Murmansk expedition, returning as Captain Beale in 1919, a veteran, with the Military Cross and the Croix de Guerre and a shrapnel wound on his forehead. His admiring father gave him £17,000 to buy the farm at Bettenham in 1921, and the family had moved in: a lovely but drafty and earth-floored medieval house, surrounded by a moat—disgusting because the drains ran into it; two hundred acres of good valley land; hop gardens; some stables and huge, marquee-sized barns; a herd of beautiful, milky Guernseys. Every one of the Beales loved it there.

James told me this over his dining room table in the Sissinghurst Castle farmhouse, in his deep, reverberating voice, while his hangdog, rather lugubrious eyes looked into mine now and then to confirm that I was getting the picture. This was the other Sissinghurst. To begin with, the farming went well. Captain Beale rented the eastern half of Sissing-

Circa 1910: *Ossie Beale as a young man.*

hurst Castle Farm, up to the Sissinghurst moat, planting an expensive new hop garden in Lodge Field, managing it with expertise and tailor-like precision. Everything was orderly and the whole place breathed well-being. Vita immediately took to him, charmed by his gentlemanly, buccaneering manner and charming him in return. Both, from their different sides, liked the antiquity, the half-formal almost-courtship of their neighbor/landlord relations. She loved his knowledge and he loved her romance and perhaps her aristocratic allure, that inexplicable se-ductiveness she could summon at will. He was a self-consciously won-derful man, a showman and a commanding figure. As his party trick for his grandchildren he would blow cigar smoke out through a hole—a childhood defect—just below the bridge of his nose, like a smiling dragon in a tweed jacket. His daughter Mary called him her "BM"—the Blooming Marvel—and between him and Vita the relationship was one of long-sustained mutual flattery and delight.

This happy time was not to last. In the late 1920s farming started to slip into a catastrophic depression. Every year the milk had been sold locally, delivered by van, the potatoes were sold, sheep and cattle came and went to Ashford and occasionally Biddenden markets, the apples

1950s: *Ossie Beale in the Frogmead hop garden.*

were packed and shipped to London, the hops picked and dried and sent to London in their giant pockets, first by wagon on the road to Cranbrook station, and from there to the brewers in London. Every year the produce going out was a guarantee of the year to come.

Mary Stearns can still remember the late autumn moment in her teens, at some time in the late 1920s, when one day at Bettenham they all heard and then saw a train of wagons coming back rumbling down the lane toward the farm. On them was the whole of the Bettenham hop harvest returning from London unsold. The market had failed them. There was a glut of hops. Supply far outstripped demand. All the work and investment in the hop gardens that year, all the setting up and stringing of the poles, the manuring, weeding, spraying, picking, carting, drying, packing, and dispatch: all had gone to waste. The hops were worth nothing. The wagons were unloaded, the pockets taken out onto the land, slit open, and the precious contents spread as a mulch on the fields.

The Beales only just got through the Depression and emerged from it financially damaged. In 1936, after Vita's mother had died and left her a fortune, she bought Bettenham from them, the debts were paid off with the purchase price, and Captain Beale took on the whole of Bettenham and Sissinghurst Castle Farm, now as Vita's tenant. With some reluctance among his womenfolk, he moved the family up to the Victorian farmhouse at Sissinghurst (at Vita's suggestion) and left Bettenham behind. Their capital had largely disappeared, but in Ossie's hands the whole joint farm nevertheless became glowingly beautiful, perhaps never more beautiful in its history: the Guernseys down at Bettenham, the dairy shorthorns up at Sissinghurst; hops; apples, pears, and cherries; blackcurrants and potatoes; a large flock of sheep; peas and beans, wheat, barley, and oats for milling and cattle feed; kale, turnips, rape, and mangolds or chard; fifty acres of meadow; men and women at work, working horses and the first tractors arriving, a kind of bright, rich, ancient modernity. Vita had added Brissenden Farm (in 1940) and Little Bettenham (a year later) to the estate. And Captain Beale was riding high, presiding over the county, becoming chairman of Ashford cattle market, a justice of the peace (with Vita), and a governor of Wye Agricultural College, from where one or two students always came to live and work here.

During the war Mary had married Stanley Stearns, a Canadian pilot with Coastal Command, who after the war and a spell training pilots in Canada came to work here in partnership with her father. The Stearnses lived at Bettenham and the Beales lived in Sissinghurst Castle Farm. Vita and Harold were in the Castle itself, Jack Copper and the cook, Mrs. Hayter, lived in parts of the front range, and a cowman and the head gardener were in new cottages built beyond the oast houses. There were other cottages in the village, where other gardeners lived, and still more attached to Bettenham.

Ossie Beale, called the Captain by the farm staff and students,

1940s: *Cattle show on the Plain.*

presided over this beautiful and multifarious kingdom until his death in 1957. In 1952 the Sissinghurst shorthorns were sold and the Bettenham Guernseys moved up here, but apart from that there was no shrinking of the enterprise. New orchards were planted, new machinery bought, and after Stanley Stearns took over, much the same was true. He too was a go-ahead farmer, bought a new efficient hop-stripping machine that made most of the hop pickers unnecessary, and became chairman of the Kent National Farmers' Union.

So when, I asked James, had it all begun to unravel? First, he said, when Nigel, my father, was forced to sell Bettenham in 1963 to pay his mother's death duties. The Stearnses had to surrender the tenancy there (for which my father paid them £6,000) and the size of their farmed area shrank by almost half. That was a body blow. The Stearnses should have bought it themselves, James said, but the capital wasn't there. The Bettenham house and land were sold separately and for the first time since the Dark Ages that unity was broken. Then, in 1967, James's father died suddenly and young—"he was a smoker, sixty cigs a day." James in partnership with his uncle John Beale took the farm over. John was a distinguished virologist, scientific director of the Wellcome Research Laboratories in London, and at the weekends he did the book work for the farm. James was the hands-on farmer. The business was laden "with quite a bit of debt and no assets." I asked James why he had taken it on. "Because I loved it," he said. "I always loved farming. And I loved it here." There were seven men working on the farm, looking after a flock of sheep, the Guernseys, ten acres of hops, two orchards, and the big arable fields on the eastern end of the farm. A capital injection from Pat's father, who was a big vegetable grower at Offham near West Malling, paid off the overdraft, but it was not long before the first disaster struck. In 1967, the hops in Frogmead became infected with verticillian wilt, an ineradicable fungal disease, and the hops, always the most treacherous of crops, expensive to grow and threatening low prices in a high-yielding year, lost the Stearnses more than they could afford. James pulled them out in the following spring.

1960s: *James Stearns.*

The Guernsey herd also seemed wrong. James and his father had started a move toward more productive Friesians in the early sixties, but the Milk Marketing Board had insisted that each farm stick with a single breed. So James kept the Guernseys, even though he never felt particularly drawn to the life of a dairy farmer, until they too stopped making financial sense and finally left the farm in 1980. His father-in-law was an expert in vegetable growing, and under his encouragement James started with Brussels sprouts and lettuces in 1968, labor-intensive crops that involved management of the gangs of pickers, but nothing on the farm was singing.

"Lack of capital was beginning to strangle us," James said. There was no financial cushion, nor assets to borrow against, nor any sense that they could easily weather a crisis. The debts were looming larger. From 1968 onward, the family was running the tea room for the visitors in the now redundant oast house. Mary was making her famous apple cake, and the wonderful unpasteurized cream straight from the Guernsey herd lay at the heart of the teas. In 1971 Pat started up a farm shop, supplied from the wholesale vegetable market at Covent Garden in London, and they began doing lunches. All of these were buoyancy aids: without them, the small farm, with no ability to make large capital improvements, and with a debt burden on its shoulders, could not possibly have kept afloat.

Then the hammer fell: in 1982, the National Trust, itself looking for income to maintain an increasingly expensive property, told the Stearnses they wanted to run the tea room themselves. Two years later the transfer was made. Now James and Pat were faced with the hard fact: the farm had become unviable. Though 1984 had been an extraordinary bumper year for grain, still it was no good. They were "getting deeper into real debt" and James was living night after night with racking anxiety, the feeling that everything he loved was dissolving around him. He hung on until Christmas 1989. "'We're bust,' I said to Pat.

'I don't know what to do.'" By then only the bed-and-breakfast business that Pat was now running in the farmhouse was going well. They struggled on with the farm for another decade. All the work on it was now done under contract by outsiders. No one was employed here. Finally, in 1999, it came to an end. James surrendered the farm and the Trust gave the family a fourteen-year tenancy on the farmhouse. No other farmer came in. Sissinghurst was divided up and let to four separate farm businesses, whose main focus was elsewhere. It was the saddest possible end to the three generations and eighty-eight years that the Beales and Stearnses had been at Sissinghurst.

James's life had coincided with the worst years the farm had seen for centuries. No one had suffered the decline of Sissinghurst as much as he had. He had experienced the deepest change in the ways of farming, not as a business phenomenon, a technological or market shift, but as something of a personal and private crucifixion. Once, before James died, Pat Stearns heard me giving a talk at a charity lunch in Tenterden, when I had spoken about what I wanted to see happen on the farm here. She came up to me afterward and said gently and kindly, "That was interesting, Adam, but I don't think you know just how difficult it was." I could only say to her then, as I do now, that I hope I was at least trying to understand.

The question remained whether this story could be reversed. Could the farm ever return to the rich, mixed condition it had enjoyed until the 1960s?

On March 16, 2007, James's funeral was held in Cranbrook church. The pews can fit five hundred, but the crowds for James were so large that lines of people stood at the back to hear his friends pay their tributes. One described him as a "yeoman," a word, with its roots in the Sissinghurst earth, that brought tears to my eyes, for its irony, for its taunting understanding that James had been a yeoman at a time when yeomen were not wanted or their qualities understood. I stared at the small stone pediment fixed up on the wall in front of me, brought here in the 1830s from the remains of Elizabethan Sissinghurst. Others talked of his kindness, his warmth and jokiness, his generosity, the way in which he was loved by everyone who knew him, his love of Kent and Sissinghurst. We sang "Jerusalem" and "I Vow to Thee My Country." His mother, wife, sister, and daughter were there to mourn him like four queens. I thought of him as an oak in the wood, which had fallen and left a gap, a big present absence where the crown had been, something rooted now down and gone.

1560s: *Pediment from Sir Richard Baker's great courtyard at Sissinghurst, now in Cranbrook church.*

IN APRIL 2007, THE SOIL ASSOCIATION delivered its final report. We had met and talked through it often throughout the winter and spring and we had come up with something that looked quite like Sissinghurst in its glory days under Captain Beale. There was to be a suckler herd of Sussex beef cattle, and a flock of Romney ewes. Most of the farm would be grass and there'd be fifty acres of crops. Cow Field was to have its vegetable patch of two and a half acres. Twenty-five acres of mixed fruit orchard would have grazing under the trees. There would be chickens in mobile houses. All of this needed a capital investment of just over £300,000. After five years, there would be a small working profit.

We imagined that this second time around, our proposals would look as if we were on the money. We weren't. In May, the plan was rejected for a second time. Unaffordable. Yet another report, by yet more consultants, delivered in July 2007, concluded that the whole idea was impracticable unless it were part of a bigger enterprise. We had spent yet another year trying to get this right and it was still as dead as it had been the previous summer.

Pat Stearns had in the end decided, after talking to her children and her friends, that she could no longer live in the great battleship of the Castle farmhouse. It is a Victorian brute of a thing, expensive to heat and laborious to clean. She and James had run a successful B&B business there for more than twenty-five years. People came back year after year, every time booking their next season's visit before they left. At the height of the summer you could never get in. It was a sad day, but Pat could no longer think of running the six-bedroom business on her own. What this meant for Sissinghurst, though, was that a house for the farmer and more significantly a bed-and-breakfast business for the farmer's wife or partner had suddenly become available. The farm business no longer had to stand on its own. Tied to a bed-and-breakfast, it was surely a viable proposition. It is the greatest irony that this opportunity should have occurred because James Stearns died. I hope it is not too sentimental to think that if the farm at Sissinghurst does work in the future it is because his death allowed it to.

These elements seemed at last to be pointing in the right direction. A candle flame flickered, if only just. Jonathan Light asked me to come to the meeting of the NT Regional Committee at Sissinghurst on August 9 to talk about my "vision"—a word that by now had acquired something of an ironic tinge.

I stood at one end of their table and talked to them. The farm scheme was fighting for its life. We could, I said, reduce the ambition, set up a partnership with local growers, and end up at Sissinghurst with a superficial gesture toward the original idea. It would be highly compromised. The heart would have been taken out of it, because the essence of the idea was "an intimately close connection between food, people and landscape."

Do you know those moments in meetings when you are more fired up than everyone else around you? When you notice a sudden balloon of your own passion come wobbling out over the table and hang there as a form of radiant embarrassment? While people shuffle in their chairs and look at their papers? This was one of those moments.

But I was going on. The other option was to increase takings in the restaurant. Sell more of what we grow and/or charge more for what we make. Don't be idealistic about it: be entrepreneurial about it. The sums were pretty straightforward. The restaurant turned over £600,000 a year. About half of that was on prepared food. A 10 percent rise in that half of the revenue would deliver an extra £30,000 a year. The projected shortfall was in the region of £75,000 a year. Half the solution to the problem lay in the market. And there was another figure: the Chatsworth combined farm shop and restaurant turns over £5 million a year and makes a £1-million-a-year contribution to the Chatsworth estate. I had been to talk to them about it and the key word was *processing*: not leeks but leek pie, not apples but apple cake. If you add the value, you get the profit.

I have no idea if these Regional Committee meetings usually have speeches of this kind made to them. Maybe not, but after so long and after so much hope denied, I was in a state of high frustration.

Don't abandon the ideal, I said to them, because the ideal is the only thing worth having, but go slowly and build a ramp toward it. But don't kick it back again. There were only a certain number of times you could fell a scheme like this and expect it to come bouncing back as before. If they inserted another year into this process, the air would come leaking slowly out of the balloon, a long, slow wheeze, and nothing would change. Or at least other places would change and Sissinghurst would only have to catch up later.

I would like to have seen me, to see just how Billy Graham-ish this was. As so often in this process, I looked for the nods around the table, for the skepticism to ease. I didn't dare look at Jonathan Light, who was sitting next to me. I can't think this is what he expected me to say.

> Why was only the whole idea worth doing? If we go for a dilute version of this scheme, reliant on other local growers, Sissinghurst-lite, there would be nothing to shout about. "We buy our raspberries from within a ten-mile radius." "Our lamb comes from the southeast of England." "Our salmon is not from Nagasaki." That is not a message for which anyone nowadays is prepared to pay more. The word "local" is well on its way to overused exhaustion.

> But if we can say, "Here, for a small premium, is lunch for fifty thousand people a year from 250 acres of farmland at Sissinghurst," that is a story to tell.

The battle lines were clear. You either thought that there was nothing to be done against the large-scale, globalizing forces of international commodity agriculture, or you stood out against it, found other ways of establishing a relationship with the land, which were not "romantic," but attentive to a modern appetite for real food from enriched places. By establishing something here that was full of hope and optimism, it could generate its own market. The farm at Sissinghurst could, like the garden itself, become something to which people would want to come, and from which they would want to buy. If you think you can't do anything except the homogenized, the cost cutting, and the mediocre, it's true: you can't. You can only if you think you can.

✦ ✦ ✦

JONATHAN LIGHT'S RESPONSE to the new situation was to gather everyone together and make us find a solution. The original timetable was now shot. We could not start hiring people to run a project that had not been given the go-ahead. If the orchards and new hedges were ever to exist, they would have to wait a year. Everything would slip, but a slipped something was better than a nothing, so we all went along with it. The old tenants were each given an extra year on the ground. But there had been a curious shift in atmosphere. We still had a hundred and one things to agree on. There were some horrible gaps in the budget and yet somehow, now, without anyone quite saying so, it was understood that this idea would not be allowed to fail again. A Scottish fisherman I knew used to claim that he could tell whether the tide was rising or falling by the different sounds that waves made during the ebb or the flood. There was something of that here in the autumn of 2007: I felt, without being able to put my finger on it, that, for all the negative signals, our boats were somehow just lifting up off the sand.

On December 4, 2007, Sally, Jonathan, and Sue Saville all went to the National Trust headquarters in Swindon to present the final proposals, and that afternoon Sally rang me from her mobile. "It's a yes," she said. We had the go-ahead. We had five years to get it right.

I went out into the Cow Field and stared into the dark of the evening, up along the line of the old drove to Canterbury, across Sissinghurst's wet and lovely fields, and wondered what would become of them. Would this scene in 2020 or 2030 be a model of delicious productiveness, of the land as its hundreds of owners would have recognized it? I thought and hoped so. I could people this place now with layer on layer of different ghosts. I could bring to mind that long flickering film of its bogs and woods, meadows and orchards, streams and lakes, its herds, flocks, and draft animals and the ten thousand years of birdsong that had been sung in these hedges and skies. The phrase "an unfinished history" ran on in my mind. That was surely the point: nothing was over. The land at Sissinghurst was no longer staring at a sterile and redundant fate. It would be more than just an adjunct and backdrop to a famous garden. Sissinghurst would be a place that fed off its own richness again. None of it would be easy. But now, here, in the cold and dark, looking to the north, with my coat wrapped around my chin, I thought I saw coming toward me the future of which I had long dreamed.

CHAPTER *11*

Admiration

A T THE END OF THE SEASON at Sissinghurst, the gardeners always find spots on the lawns where visitors have stood and gazed at a particularly seductive rose or luscious wisteria, and under their feet the grass has withered and the lawn gone slightly bald. They call these "admiration patches," and they need to be aerated and revived each autumn. There is no doubt that in the history of Sissinghurst the period from my grandparents' arrival in 1930 until Vita's death in 1962 is one of those exaggeratedly looked-at and slightly worn patches, the most famous moment in ten thousand years of Sissinghurst's existence.

The story of their arrival and life at Sissinghurst has been told over and over again, in private and public. This fame was nearly all due to my father's persistence in the 1960s, '70s, and '80s. An element of it was commerce. He knew in his parents' story there were valuable publishing properties. He knew, too, that the National Trust was anxious that when Vita and Harold died, the interest in Sissinghurst would wane and its financial basis would collapse.

The world of Bloomsbury in the 1960s was, if anything, a little old hat. Virginia Woolf was not yet the icon of modern feminism she would become. Lytton Strachey, Duncan Grant, and all the lesser stars of the

Bloomsbury firmament—including, at its very edges, Vita and Harold—were yesterday's story: too old to be interesting, not old enough to be interesting again.

My father became, in the last forty years of his life, Sissinghurst's custodian, librarian, archivist, publicist, and entrepreneur. All through the peak of the Bloomsbury boom, he carried on an enormous and global correspondence with scholars and fans. He edited his father's diaries and letters in three fat volumes, sponsored two different histories of the garden and its history, helped and encouraged separate biographies of each of his parents, and, as the culmination of this campaign, wrote *Portrait of a Marriage*, published in 1973 simultaneously on both sides of the Atlantic. It told the story of Vita and Harold's many love affairs, almost exclusively homosexual, and sent shivers of outraged delight around the world. You could tell, each year, where the latest foreign editions had appeared, as first American and French, then German, Dutch and Danish, Latvian and Russian, Hungarian, Greek, Turkish, and, finally, Japanese and Korean enthusiasts for Sissinghurst and its literary-lesbian-hortico-aristocratic amalgam arrived at the gate to drink at the shrine. My sisters and I used to stand there trying to spot the territories my father's publishing campaign had recently conquered.

But if this was canny, it was not cynical. It was also a form of honoring his parents' memory. Nothing in his life mattered more to him than them, and Sissinghurst became in effect a portrait of their marriage. They framed his life and he remained their perpetual son, bound to them both, but in polar-opposite ways. His relationship with his father was one of overwhelming love and admiration. Harold played with him, told him stories, drew him pictures, empathized with him as he made his way into the world, understood his nascent homosexuality, urging him to keep it in perspective, and always pressing on him the central virtues of a civilized life: tolerance, kindness, energy, civility, integrity. They discussed everything all the time. "He always claimed," my father wrote of him, "that it was impossible for a father to transmit experience, but in fact he did so, for his advice was always practical, and by understanding the exact nuances of our dilemmas, he dissipated them." My father felt he lived not in his father's shadow but in his light.

Toward the end of his life, my father sold nearly all of his parents' letters to American universities, but before he died, he told me that if I were to sell anything, as he imagined I might, the one thing he would like to remain at Sissinghurst forever was the file of letters that his father had written to him and his brother Ben during the war. It is a thick typewritten folder that contains what is, in effect, a manual of fatherhood: of love, anxiety for his children, a flattering ease in the telling of news and the testing of opinions, a fascination for the world, a brilliant play across anything that amused, stirred, or worried him, in his life or theirs, written from the House of Commons where he was an MP or from the Ministry of Information, where for a time he was a junior minister in Churchill's government, to the battlefields of North Africa and Italy, page after page drenched in a form of love that was so strong it could be easy, funny, courteous, dignified, articulate, and challenging without ever losing its undernote of deep and passionate affection. My father kept this file in his bedroom until he died.

With his mother, it was different. She had neglected him and his brother when they were children, leaving them for months on end when away with lovers or friends; and when, in the second half of her life, she returned from her adventuring, to embed herself at Sissinghurst, she was absent there too, in the Tower, and when in the Tower in the world of poetry, from which her children felt—and were—entirely excluded. Whenever my father wrote about her, that sense of exclusion, almost of expulsion, was the dominant note. She "withdrew into preferred solitude." Poetry was "her secret life, the life of the tower, into which we never attempted to penetrate." He was constantly anxious that he might wound her. There was a "gap between her and us. It had been there since we were babies." If she talked to them or wrote to them, her tone was "constrained." She "thought herself a failure as a mother, but it was as much our fault as hers. We never made the necessary effort to know her well."

This double emotional inheritance, of warmth and cold, transmitted through my father, has soaked into Sissinghurst. Its image has become fixed in a binary vision of the twentieth century here. Harold was classical, Vita romantic. Harold was kind and engaged, Vita distant and unintelligible. Harold was clever, Vita passionate. Harold was civility, Vita poetry. Harold my father knew, Vita he didn't. Harold he loved, Vita he didn't. These polarities became our governing myth.

I knew the story of my grandparents' lives from the moment I was conscious. My father used to stand on the dais at one end of the Big Room and tell it to visitors while I stood at his side. The climax would always be that, after his death, "Adam, and Adam's Adam, and Adam's Adam's Adam" would live here, far on into the unforeseeable future, words that would make me glow with significance and squirm with embarrassment while the people stared from three steps below us on the polished oak floor.

The family mythology swirled around us, planets orbiting above our heads in ever wider and more distant circles. There was a Nicolson element, to do with generation after generation of public servants and military men, backed by layer on layer of Edinburgh lawyers, and going on beyond them, mistily, to chieftains of the clan in Skye and Assynt in the far northwest of Scotland. But the Nicolson story was not at the heart of Sissinghurst. It was never important enough. Two coats of arms stood on either side of the entrance arch: three Baker swans on the right and the checkers and bars of the Sackville-Wests on the left. It was Vita who had the money, who bought and owned Sissinghurst, who conducted negotiations with Captain Beale, the farm tenant, whose flag flew over the Tower, whose room in the Tower silently oversaw Sissinghurst, and whose spirit infused the place. Under the Tower a memorial stone put up after she died remembers her as the person "who made this garden." Harold is not mentioned.

She dominated the present and behind her stretched an inheritance of pure glamour. Her mother, Victoria Sackville, had persuaded Sir John Murray Scott, the vast, five-foot-waisted, lonely owner of the Wallace Collection, to leave her half of it in his will. The legacy was contested by his relations ("dumpy, dull and middle class," according to my father), but as soon as Vita Sackville established her claim, in a spectacular court case, she sold the collection en bloc to a Paris dealer, adding £270,000 to the £150,000 in cash Scott had left her too. These figures can be multiplied by at least fifty for their modern equivalents. Vita would inherit most of it; it became the fund on which Sissinghurst floated for Vita's life. Her mother's mother, Pepita, had been a Spanish gypsy dancer, whose hair was so long that it dragged on the floor behind her, with whom her grandfather, Lord Sackville, had fallen in love after seeing her dance onstage. Behind them lay receding avenues of Sackvilles going back toward Restoration, Cavalier, and Elizabethan heroes, all set in the huge gray Kentish palace of Knole, the house in which Vita had been brought up and which, if she had been a boy, she would have inherited. Against this bouillabaisse of a story, the Nicolson aspect, the element of middle-class normality and sanity, was thin fare.

Vita had been lonely as a child. She had looked with a skeptical eye at the Edwardian indulgences of her mother's friends, fell in love with poetry as a girl, and more than that with Knole and with the romance of its stories. She was wooed by the great heirs of Edwardian England, could have had dukedoms and county-covering estates for the asking, but never stooped to that. She refused the giant houses offered her by Lord Lascelles (Harewood) and Lord Granby (Haddon Hall and Belvoir), largely perhaps because Knole was greater than either, not in the gilded richness of its rooms, but in something less articulate: the pale gray simplicity of its ragstone walls; its succession of courtyards and the buried secrets they promised; the way you could push into Knole, uncovering layer after layer, one court folding out from another, linked by intricate route-ways, through flagged back halls and into other high,

Circa 1900: *Young Vita Sackville-West dressed as a basket of wisteria.*

narrow spaces, where the windows of the surrounding galleries looked down blankly from above, suddenly coming by chance at the foot of a stair on a cupboard full of gilded porcelain or the delicious eighteenth-century statue of a duke's mistress, nude and prone on her velvet blanket, her body resting on cushions as luscious as herself.

Knole is more maze than house, a private coral reef of accumulated riches, where under its four acres of roof, and within layers of encrustation, its long galleries are filled with the pictures still hanging in the order in which they were inventoried in the seventeenth century, furnished by successive Sackville lords chamberlain, who brought down to Knole everything rejected by each change of fashion at court. It is the most beautiful beach in England, thick with the successive tidelines of English taste. It would be difficult to imagine a more powerful stimulus to the imagination than this: Knole, loneliness, the flamenco brilliance of the Spanish-gypsy-dancing gene, dusty brocades, the looming portraits, the charm and volatility of her seductive, plutophile, intemperate mother, the mulch of Englishness, the badge of illegitimacy only a generation back, a sense of herself as the heir to this slow, deep river of fading beauty, something that poured over and through her as if she were more weir than heir.

As a young woman, Vita added to all this a love of Italy and the jeweled life of the Renaissance, the scents and tastes of the Mediterranean world. Benozzo Gozzoli, Venetian colors, cistus and rosemary, almond and apricot blossom all combined to intoxicate her as a teenage girl. She began to feel in herself what she thought of as the fire of her own Spanish blood, mixed with Kentish earth, and began to sense even in her earliest poems her own self to be strung between these poles. Nothing in her was ever parochial or limited, but that exoticism, and a willful streak of selfishness and dominance, played over a deep and almost stagnant bed of Kentish rootedness. Richness and melancholy joined hands across her own inner divide.

Instead of one of the grandees of aristocratic England, she married a young third secretary in the Foreign Office, who came, in his own description, from a family of "impecunious high civil servants." He was a matching combination of contradictory talents: high-minded, with a belief in the central role public service should play in a man's life; homosexual, with an almost unassuageable appetite for clever and beautiful young men; a brilliantly witty and delighted describer of the world around him; multilingual, passionately internationalist, in love with the civilizations of Greece and France; and above all filled with curiosity for anything that life might bring. Only one man in a thousand is a bore, he told my father, and my father quoted repeatedly to me, and he is interesting because he is one man in a thousand.

Again and again my father would tell me when I was young about his father's comparison of his life and career to an alpine meadow, spotted and lit with flowers, and how preferable that was to a single crop of maize or lucerne. But this multiplicity, and the love of the shimmering surface, was always to be allied to work, love, and loyalty. Harold longed for rootedness himself. "I wanted to feel autochthonous, the son of some hereditary soil," he wrote. These desires and interests, and this appetite for a life that combined wide horizons with a sense of enriched belonging, were what made their marriage. They felt, immediately, mutual. When he and Vita were married, at Knole in 1913, and lived first in Constantinople, where Harold was attached to the embassy, and then at Long Barn, a cottage outside Sevenoaks, which they called their "little mud pie" and could have fitted inside one of Knole's courtyards, they thought of each other as playmates, self-consciously innocent, young and happy.

All of these threads would, in time, find their way into Sissinghurst, but after the end of the Great War, two devastating events changed this happy, pretty picture of their early lives. The effects of both could have been foreseen; neither was; both left them changed; and both became, in opposite ways, shaping influences at Sissinghurst.

The first was Vita's long love affair and elopement in 1918–19 with Violet Trefusis, the daughter of Alice Keppel, Edward VII's mistress. It began in "a mad and irresponsible summer," as Vita described its early phases, "of moonlit nights, and infinite escapades, and passionate letters, and music, and poetry. Things were not tragic for us then, because although we cared passionately we didn't care deeply." Violet, according to Victoria Glendinning, was "a damaged and damaging young woman"; to Harold "some fierce orchid—glimmering and stinking in the recesses of life, throwing cadaverous sweetness on the morning's breeze." She undoubtedly wanted to destroy Vita's marriage. Vita was more equivocal and, in letter after grief-stricken letter, wrote piteously of the love she had for a husband she claimed to be deserting.

1918: *Vita with her parents, Ben, and Nigel.*

In 1920, as the affair's fire was dimming, Vita wrote a long manuscript account of it, which she kept in a Gladstone bag, stamped with the gold letters V.N. It remained hidden first in her sitting room at Long Barn and then in her turret room in the Tower at Sissinghurst for the

Circa 1919: *Vita at the height of her love affair with Violet Trefusis.*

rest of her life. It was never shown to anyone. When she died in 1962, my father found the Gladstone bag in that turret. It was locked and the key was missing, so he cut the leather with a razor and reached inside, taking the manuscript to her desk. He didn't stand up until he had read its forty thousand words. When it was finally published in 1973, after Violet and Harold had also died, it formed the central element of *Portrait of a Marriage*, a title in which he packed the pain and grief of this affair in the cushioning tissue paper of his parents' lifelong, often-declared love for each other.

I remember with great clarity the moment the book came out. He had written to me at school to warn me of the coming scandal. I now know, from his own papers, how anxious he was. The prospect of its publication left him "terrified by the reproach I might draw on myself."

He felt guilty,

knowing that even if it was true that Vita wanted it published, Hadji [as all the family called Harold] would have deplored it. He was the figure that haunted me throughout. I argued that it was a confession which only a son could handle with delicacy and love, but this was an excuse. I wasn't doing it out of love, but to set a new style in biography, of total honesty, to make a stir, earn me money, show that I was capable of taking a risk—not only with my reputation but with Vita's.

He had justified it, he wrote in his own self-reproaching memoir, written twenty years later, as "a eulogy of marriage, [which] had lessons for other people who found themselves lesbians and homosexuals, but could still have a very happy marriage. It might 'help' people, I wrote, but this was special pleading. I was finding excuses for my guilt. That guilt has still not dissolved."

Violet Trefusis's sister, to whom Nigel sent the typescript, called it a "distasteful book." "It seems incredible to me," she wrote to him, "that while professing to revere your mother's memory, you are prepared to publicise for profit details of her infatuations of over half a century ago." Lord Sackville, who "had affection and great admiration for your mother," told Nigel that "these feelings have been tarnished by your book." Admiration poured in from much of the world, but none of it ever quite washed away his own sense of betrayal. When the serialization of the book started to run in the *Sunday Times*, he could not bring himself to look at it. "Ben knew," Nigel wrote in his memoir, "that my love for Vita was very shallow, his shallower."

I was back at Sissinghurst the day the papers came with the reviews in them. He had been told that Bernard Levin had reviewed the book in the *Sunday Times*. The paper lay on the kitchen table unopened between us. My father finally steeled himself to look at it and turned to the review section. He leant over the pages with both elbows on the table and his head in his hands, reading between the protective grid of his fingers. Levin had fixed on what he saw as the narcissism and self-indulgence behind this story of late, luscious, moneyed romanticism, the urge of the wild "gypsy" spirit to break free of the tedium of a civil servant husband, of children and normality. The skewering sentences, on which Levin fixed, were these:

> I saw Violet twice more. Once in my own house in London; she looked ill and changed; and once in the early morning at her mother's house, where I went to say goodbye on my way to the station. There was a dreary slut scrubbing the doorstep, for it was very early, and I stepped in over the soapy pail, and saw Violet in the morning room. Then I went to Paris alone.

Levin said my father should have burned the manuscript. Rebecca West said the same. Cyril Connolly had been friendly about the book in private but in his *Observer* review was cold. After reading them all, my father went upstairs without a word. My sisters and I read with some delight the copy of *Private Eye* that ran a spoof introduction to the book. Under a large picture of an Edwardian country-house party, "Nigel Sackville-Nicolson" wrote that he had published this account of his mother's homosexuality only "after long and careful consultation with my family, my dearest friends and my bank manager." It left his reputation enlarged but, in some quarters, damaged, and it made him £80,000.

Violet, Vita had written, very rarely came to stay with her at Long Barn, their house near Sevenoaks. Whenever she did,

> the antagonism between her and the house was ludicrous and pain-ful. The country would seem deliberately to drape itself in tender-ness and content, and she, feeling the place to be an enemy, would turn yet more fierce, yet more restless, while I stood bewildered and uncertain between the personification of my two lives.

My house, my garden, my fields, and Harold, those were the silent ones, that pleaded only by their own merits of purity, simplicity, and faith; and on the other hand stood Violet, fighting wildly for me, seeming sometimes harsh and scornful, and riding roughshod over those gentle defenceless things.

Engagement with the draped tenderness of the Weald, the mud-pie life, competed in Vita with something larger, unsweet, and more domineering. The traumatic affair, "a vortex of unhappiness," had revealed to her in the starkest possible form the contesting elements of her own personality. That polarized view of herself, both domineering and tender, both private and theatrical, both rotted and filled with a love of the exotic, would in time come to shape Sissinghurst.

The second transforming event of their lives was the death of Vita's father in January 1928. It was the moment when Knole passed into the hands of her uncle Charlie, when the fact of dispossession was finally confirmed. The house and its lands had in the nineteenth century belonged to two of her great-aunts. There had never been a question of women not being able to inherit Knole. But Vita, who possessed it in a way more deeply than anyone ever had, was now finally denied it.

On May 16 that year, as she wrote to Harold, now in Berlin,

I allowed myself a torture-treat tonight. I went up to Knole after dark and wandered about the garden. It was a very queer and poignant experience, so queer and so poignant I should almost have fainted had I met anybody. . . . I had the sensation of having the place so completely to myself that I might have been the only person alive in the world, and not the world of today, mark you, but the world of at least 300 years ago. . . . Darling Hadji, I may be looney but there is some kind of umbilical cord that ties me to Knole.

At the end of May 1928 she heard that Charlie, the new Lord Sackville, and his American wife were moving into Knole and were thinking of selling some of the great paintings and furniture she most treasured, a dismantling of her store of memories. She went there, had lunch with them, and came home in tears, almost blinded by them and scarcely able to drive, with the rain streaming down the windscreen outside.

It was in the light of this dispossession that the cottage at Long Barn no longer seemed enough. In November 1929, in a flush of excitement, they heard that the moated stone keep of Bodiam Castle was on the market. They thought for a moment that they might buy it, that each of the four of them—Vita, Harold, Ben, and Nigel—could occupy one of the corner towers, meeting occasionally for a ham sandwich in the central hall, a model of Nicolson family life to which they all apparently quite happily subscribed, but at £30,000 it was out of their range.

The search for a substitute Knole was already under way when in March the next year they heard that the fields next to Long Barn were to be turned into a battery chicken farm. In April 1930, with the poet Dottie Wellesley, Vita came to Sissinghurst for the first time. They found the ruin, dripping with wet. It bore every mark of its long history, a place of broken grandeur, looking, in a curious way, like a ruined Knole, with a tower and a succession of courts, filled with the ghosts of Sackville ancestors and rubbish where life might have been. It was crying out for redemption, an opportunity to make a garden that drew on the sense of its own abandoned past. Perhaps its fragmentary and broken state made it more satisfying than Knole. A ruin, in these circumstances, was better than anything gilded and complete. The disintegrated Sissinghurst could stand in for a ruined inheritance.

The sales particulars described the splendid Victorian farmhouse—the "excellent family residence and grounds," "well clothed with choice creepers, approached by a Carriage Drive and Sweep," ten bedrooms, "well matured grounds with lawns and rhododendrons"—the five hundred acres of wood and land, and, almost as an afterthought, "the Towers of Sissing-hurst Castle in the background." It was, of course, that background to which Vita and Harold were drawn: gaunt, partly unroofed, damp, and bleak. They wavered. Harold, on April 13, after a second look, considered it "big broken down, and sodden," but Vita had the money, and it was her choice. They bought it for £12,375. There was no electricity, no running water, no drains, no heating, and scarcely a fireplace that worked. One or two of the windows had glass in. But this was the invitation: to pour their energies into redemption of the past.

It was here in 1931, in her room on the first floor, that Vita wrote the poem that she called simply "Sissinghurst." It was the best thing, Harold thought, she ever wrote, and she dedicated it to Virginia Woolf.

1930: Harold in front of Sissinghurst on the day he first saw it.

Far more than Vita's garden writing ever could, the poem addresses the core of Sissinghurst. It is a place apart:

> Buried in time and sleep,
> So drowsy, overgrown,
> That here the moss is green upon the stone,
> And lichen stains the keep.

Time has almost stopped. A kind of enriched stagnancy colors the place and her vision of it. Sissinghurst, like the depths of its darkened moat, becomes a pool in which Vita can feel both ecstatically alive and at the same time suspended from the real world:

> For here, where days and years have lost their number,
> I let a plummet down in lieu of date,

1932: Harold, Nigel, Vita, and Ben under the Tower.

And lose myself within a slumber,
Submerged, elate.

Those last two words are the essence of Vita's Sissinghurst, a freedom found in a deep absorption with place, land, and the sense of a treasured past, a past that was better than the present, drenched into these bricks and this soil.

There was a chance here to revitalize a once great but deeply neglected place, to take a ruin and make it flower. Again and again, whenever Vita wrote about Sissinghurst, the atmosphere she summoned was of that embedded history, a certain rich slowness, even a druggedness, as if evening, when colors are soft and thickened, were its natural and fullest condition:

> The heavy golden sunshine enriched the old brick with a kind
> of patina, and made the tower cast a long shadow across the
> grass, like the finger of a gigantic sundial veering slowly with the
> sun. Everything was hushed and drowsy and silent, but for the
> coo of the white pigeons sitting alone together on the roof. . . .
> They climbed the seventy-six steps of her tower and stood on the
> leaden flat, leaning their elbows on the parapet, and looking out
> in silence over the fields, the woods, the hop gardens, and the
> lake down in the hollow from which a faint mist was rising.

The garden became, inevitably, a reflection of its makers. The received idea is that it was a marriage of sensibilities: a certain classical elegance and even austerity in the planning by Harold; a rich and romantic profusion in the planting, mostly by Vita, what she called the "cram, cram, cram, every chink and cranny" method, the verve of "exaggeration, big groups, big masses." All that is true, even if not in quite so schematic a way. Often it was Vita who advocated a simplicity and straightforwardness in design; often it was Harold who wanted a more

1934: *Harold and Vita in her workroom in the Tower.*

baroque and theatrical effect. Letters from many of Harold's passing lovers, now preserved along with the rest of his papers at Balliol but never published by my father, describe him as masculine and assertive, a manly man, with his yacht, his pipe, and his familiarity with the powerful and the great. His reputation among those who lived and worked at Sissinghurst was for brusque coldness and indifference. It was Vita who used to come and sit on the kitchen table in the farmhouse and talk to the children, who was always amused by the jokes and joshing of the men who worked on the farm or in the garden. She always used to come to the birthday parties of the young Stearnses in Bettenham. Harold was away in London much of the time, only to be spotted leaving for or arriving from the station in his dark blue pinstripes. The distant and reserved Vita in the Tower, always calling herself Vita Sackville-West and never Mrs. Nicolson, seems largely to be a product of my father's emphasis on it. In fact she was known at Sissinghurst only as Mrs. Nicolson or, after Harold was knighted for his biography of George V, as Lady Nicolson. Most of her books in the Tower are initialed "VN." "V. M. Nicolson" was how she described herself to the War Agriculture Committee. And although Nigel rarely went to her room in the Tower, many others did, spent long hours there with her, talking deep into the night. Jim Lees-Milne, Harold's friend, lover, and biographer, remembered a bewitching, dusky evening talking up there:

> There were no reservations of any kind. No topics were barred. Her curiosity about and understanding of human nature in all its aspects were limitless. Her sympathy with every human frailty and predicament was all embracing. This was the Vita I knew and most dearly loved. As dusk faded into night I watched the outline of her noble head against the chequered Tudor casements of the tower, would watch the tip of her cigarette from a long holder glow fiery red as she drew upon it, with constant but imperceptible inhalations so that her profile—always her profile

of drooping eyelid, straight nose and soft rounded chin—would emerge from the darkness as in a momentary vision. I would smell, when I could no longer see, the cloud of Cypriot tobacco peculiarly her own; and listen to that deep slightly quavering, gently swelling voice, broken by eddies of short sharp laughter. "Oh do tell me what happened next." Then I understood what this unique woman's love meant to Harold.

Even in the way the garden developed, the received picture is not quite true. Many of Harold's plans for Sissinghurst, including a wall of busts of himself and his friends, loggias and "caves," are far from the picture of the cool, Mozartian rationalist struggling to impose order on Vita's bubbling chaos. In the early days he suggested vast flower beds to fill the Upper Courtyard—not the cool green pools of lawn that are there today—and a Versailles-style fountain occupying the Rondel in the Rose Garden. It was often Vita who had to slim down his grandiose fantasies. The story and its interactions are subtler than the myth often allows.

The relationship of exact form to luxuriant planting is now almost a cliché of twentieth-century garden design. Sissinghurst's planterliness, its love affair with the Mediterranean, with spring bulbs and roses, with yew, brick, stone, and grass—all of this is simply the lingua franca of twentieth-century gardening. Much of it was there in Vita and Harold's first garden at Long Barn. And it has mistakes. The color of the new brick walls, despite an enormous amount of care taken over them, is not good, too brown and too dead, never glowing. Even the curved wall at the west end of the Rose Garden is a little pretentious. The small north-facing Delos they never got right. Harold's additions to the Priest's House and the South Cottage are a little lumpen. This is not an exercise in perfection. The Yew Walk is too near the Tower and the two rows of yews are too near each other. Nor is the walk aligned properly with the paths in the Rose Garden, even though my father always claimed that was his fault. Hadji had asked him to place a marker in the Rose Garden that would exactly extend the line of the yews. The poor boy placed it about a yard and a half wrong, the new Rose Garden path was laid, and the kink in the alignment remains there to this day.

Does any of this matter? Of course not. The genius of Sissinghurst's design—Harold disciplined by Vita—is in its self-deprecation, its lack of egoism, its courtesy in playing second fiddle to the plants, the place, the surrounding country and its deeper meanings.

1932: Sissinghurst from the northeast. The lawns, the Cottage Garden, one side of the Yew Walk, and the plan of what would become the White Garden are already laid out. Vita's Rolls-Royce is parked outside the front and vegetables are growing both in Delos and in what would become the Rose Garden.

The garden at Sissinghurst was known and loved by a small band of enthusiasts from the 1930s onward. *Country Life* had run a long illustrated article about it over three consecutive issues in September 1942. In 1946, Vita herself had appeared on the cover "in the garden of her home, Sissinghurst Castle, Kent," wording that implies that the Vita-Sissinghurst connection still needed explaining, even to a *Country Life* audience. It was only in the 1970s, with the coming of the heritage boom, the Bloomsbury boom, and the *Portrait of a Marriage* boom, that Sissinghurst became the English garden par excellence.

Not that it doesn't deserve its fame. I am sure the reason that Sissinghurst continues to stand apart from its many near-contemporaries is the way it is slipped so discreetly into the ruins of its site, its interfolding of building and garden, garden and farm, farm and country. The garden, as a design, merely fills the frame that the place provided for it. It is subsidiary and subtle, no more than the dancing partner for an existing ancientness. It has sometimes seemed to me as if the fullness of the planting in the garden is merely drawing up the stories that are soaked into Sissinghurst's bones. Harold's design does not compete with that. As Jane Brown pointed out, there are no elegant drooping curves at wall ends, no rich Italian stone frames to openings, no niches of plum-colored brickwork to enliven the Elizabethan pink. A garden was not imposed on Sissinghurst; it seems as if Sissinghurst was allowed to have its garden.

The bones of what they did were outlined extraordinarily quickly: by 1932 what is now the White Garden, the Tower Lawn, the Spring Garden, the Cottage Garden, the Yew Walk, and the Nuttery had all been laid out. The hedges and trees that would in time give the garden its form were already largely planted. By the end of that decade, the new walls closing off the Rose Garden and the north side of the Upper Courtyard had been built and the orchard designed.

Innocence had no place here; there was to be sophistication in the ruin. Rarities and subtleties came from the very beginning. Harold collected foxgloves from the wood in an old pram and by accident brought up bluebell bulbs with them. They would have preferred to make the paths of York stone as they now are, but there wasn't enough money, so paving-stone-sized slabs of rough concrete were cast on-site. What statues they bought were cheap. Some have already disintegrated and been replaced with copies. Only what they inherited from Vita's mother after her death in 1936—the bronze and lead urns, the statue of the Bacchante now in the Spring Garden, the bench at the head of the Moat Walk designed by Lutyens—was of undeniable quality. The beautiful stoneware pot in the center of the White Garden, a seventeenth-century Chinese oil or ginger jar, had been bought by Harold in Cairo for ten pounds.

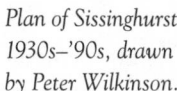

Plan of Sissinghurst 1930s–'90s, drawn by Peter Wilkinson.

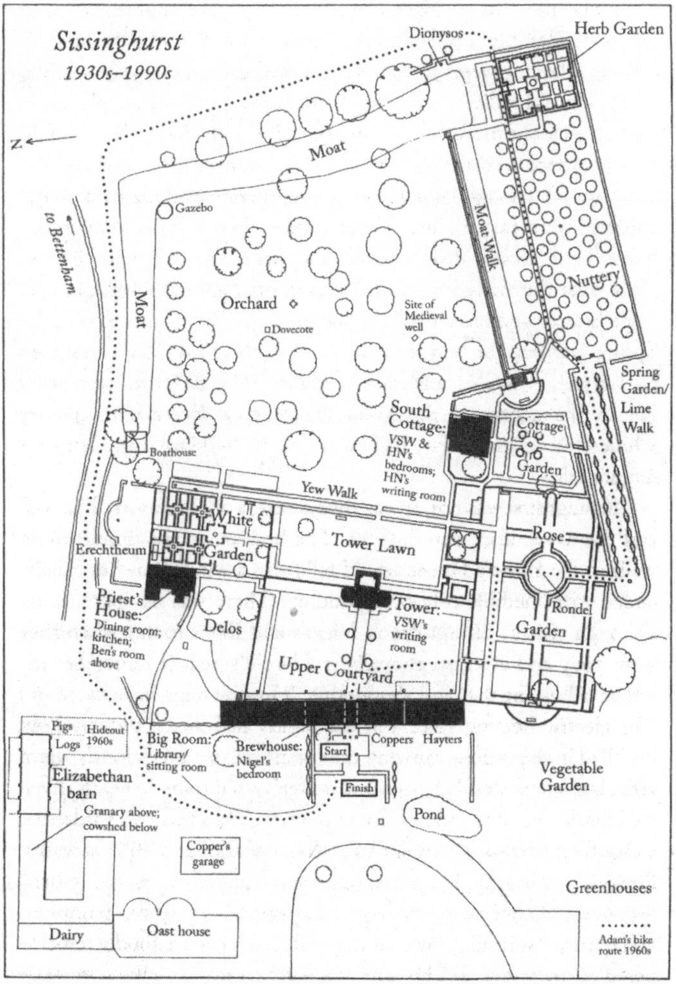

Sissinghurst
1930s–1990s

Sissinghurst was not, it was always said, a winter resort. The cold and the discomfort were intense. The hessian on the dining room walls in the Priest's House would billow in a wind. Lunches usually ended with inedible roly-poly pudding. There was no spare room, although visitors often slept in Nigel's and Ben's rooms when they were away and even occasionally in Harold's bed. (I remember my father telling me that and shuddering: "How he must have hated it!") The electric heating system in the library had unaccountably been installed in the ceiling, creating the conditions for a deliciously warm attic, but a persistently frozen and scarcely used room beneath.

Even so, Harold and Vita did not live in poverty. They had two gardeners, a chauffeur, a cook, a lady's maid, two secretaries, and other servants. Grapes, peaches, apples, pears, raspberries, gooseberries, cucumbers, tomatoes, mangetouts, cabbage, eggplants, squashes, pumpkins, and quinces were all grown for their table. Scenes are fondly remembered of the butler and his wife, the kitchen maid, walking gingerly across the winter garden, trays in front of them, from the kitchen in the Priest's House through the snow-encrusted White Garden, leaving their tracks across the Lower Courtyard, through the Yew Walk, and to the South Cottage, the only surviving part of the great Elizabethan courtyard, where Vita was lying ill in bed, waiting for her lunch or supper. In wartime it was worse. Vita wrote to Leonard Woolf in January 1940:

> Dear Leonard,
> I ought to have answered your letter long ago, but both the boys came home for 24 hours leave and immediately took to their beds with 'flu. You may imagine that Sissinghurst is at no time an ideal place for invalids, but when it means carrying trays, hot water bottles and other requirements through snow-drifts some sixteen times a day it is really hell. Then George got it; then I got it; then Mac [her secretary] got it. Nigel lost his

voice. I lost my voice. Pipes froze; lavatories ceased to function;
snow came through the roof and dripped on to my bed.
So perhaps you will forgive the delay.

Something of the atmosphere in the early Sissinghurst emerges in
a letter from Vita to Harold describing a day in April 1936:

> *How people can say life is dull in the country beats me.*
> *Take the last 24 hours here. An extremely drunken man had left*
> *his pony to be tried in the mowing machine. So it was put in the*
> *mowing machine; I watched; all seemed satisfactory; I went*
> *away. So did the mowing machine. Kennelly [the gardener] sent*
> *it away without saying a word to me or to Copper [the chauffeur-*
> *handyman] who is responsible for it. Copper arrived in my room*
> *and abused Kennelly. I went and cursed Kennelly, who indeed*
> *was in the wrong. In the evening at about 9, I was told that*
> *Punnett [the builder] wanted to see me. I went out. He was in*
> *tears, having just found his old father drowned in the engine*
> *tank, and a note written to himself saying it was suicide.*
>
> *Next morning, ie today, George [the manservant] came to*
> *fetch me: Copper would like to speak to me. I found Copper in*
> *the garden room covered in blood with a great gash in his head.*
> *Kennelly had come into the garage and knocked him down*
> *without any warning. He had fallen unconscious, and had come*
> *round to find Kennelly throwing buckets of water over him.*
> *He had then tried to strangle Kennelly, and they had only been*
> *separated by the arrival of Mrs Copper. So I sent Copper to the*
> *doctor in George's car, and meanwhile sent for the police.*
> *Accompanied by the policeman I went out in search of Kennelly,*
> *whom we found very frightened and white. He was ordered to go*
> *and pack his things and leave at once. So that was that and we*
> *are now without a gardener.*

1950s: *Vita talks to a visitor in the Cottage Garden.*

They first opened the garden to the public for two days in 1938, the entrance fee sixpence in an old tobacco tin, if you noticed it, on an old card table in the entrance arch. There must have been some pent-up demand: eight hundred people came that day. Vita would happily meet and chat to the visitors who accosted her. Harold could be ruder: "A dreadful woman bursts in upon us," he wrote in his diary of an unexpected photographer from *Picture Post*. "I am very firm. But Viti with her warm-heartedness is weak. She calls it 'being polite.' Anyhow I refuse to be photographed, and go off and weed. I am weeding away, grunting under a forsythia, when I realise she is behind me with her camera. All she can have photographed was a large grey-flannel bottom."

The family had little to do with the farm. Captain Beale was the farmer, and Vita would negotiate rents with him, or object to his planting ugly crops (which meant everything except wheat or barley), and there was an orchard in the present car park. East Enders came down in scores for the hop harvest, and Vita, who, according to my father, "thought their squalor romantic," would go down in the evenings to join their campfires. My father "went with her once and they gave us evil-smelling and tasting mugs of tea. Dutifully I drank her mug as well as mine, for she hated any tea, and seeing her mug empty she said 'Oh I must have spilled my tea' and they gave her another which surreptitiously I drank too."

The Nicolsons were never really a landed family. They had left much of the Sackville grandeur behind. "Granpapa Sackville left us his Purdy guns," my father wrote, "which Vita encouraged Ben to use, but we did only once, when Hadji took one of them, saw a rabbit sitting still on the wood-path, aimed, fired, missed, rabbit didn't move, missed again, then it loped off, and we laughed with a delight that I still remember. After that the guns were given to Copper, and he sold them after Vita's death."

The war interrupted progress, and for six years Sissinghurst roughened and thickened. Hay crops were taken off the lawns. Weeds invaded the beds and haystacks were made in the orchard. Vita extended her ownership of the surrounding land, buying Bettenham and Brissenden, trying to buy Hammer Mill, but at £12,000 it was too expensive. Captain Beale organized the Home Guard and a watch was kept on the tower for German parachutists. But the cycle of the year continued; the lumbering wagons brought up the cordwood for her fires; the "classic monotony" of the rural life persisted, heightened and even made perfect by the threat hanging over it. In the autumn of 1940, they watched the fighters in the Battle of Britain, cutting white patterns against the blue of the summer sky, tumbling silently overhead like butterflies. One night, unable to sleep, Vita

> went down to the lake where the black water gave me a sense of deepest peace . . . the moon gave no reflection into the darkened waters. The only things which gleamed and glowed were the water lilies, whitely resting on the black pool. Taking the boat out, I cut the milky stalks of the lilies in the moonlight and as I did so drifting aeroplanes appeared over the lake, chased by the angular beams of searchlights, now lost, now found again; now roaring out now silent, traceable only by their green and red lights sliding between the stars. A fox barked at them, like something in a fable. I tried to compose the fable for myself, something which would combine the fox, the lilies, and the white bodies of the young men up there aloft, but nothing neat would come to me.

Jack Vass, the head gardener and mainstay of Sissinghurst from 1939 onward, volunteered for the RAF in 1941, saying to Vita as he left, "Look after the hedges. We can get the rest back later." Dutifully, if a little amateurishly, Harold and Vita clipped the yews and pleached the limes until he returned. Vita knew she couldn't make Sissinghurst without him. One year he planted twelve thousand Dutch bulbs, and in 1946 she prayed to her diary:

> Oh dear kind God, please let Vass live strong and healthy until he is eighty at least, and never let him be tempted away to anyone else's garden. His keenness is so endless, and nothing is too much trouble. Besides he's so good looking, so decorative.

1950s: *Harold weeds the paving in the Lime Walk.*

Her long-running gardening column in the *Observer* from 1947 until 1961 subtly and even surreptitiously, without actually naming Sissinghurst, advertised the garden to the wider world. It was something she longed to put on show. Vita was enthusiastic when the BBC wanted to make a Sissinghurst documentary in the mid-fifties. Harold was not keen on "exposing my intimate affections to the public gaze." But when both of them were first conceiving of the White Garden—and it is scarcely ever remembered that the planting was as much Harold's as Vita's idea—it was with a view to what it would look like to the public. "I believe that when we scrap the delphiniums," he wrote to her on July 5, 1949, "we shall find the grey and white garden very beautiful. . . . I want the garden as a whole to be superb in 1951 for the British Fair or Festival, with heaps of overseas visitors, and many will come down by car."

Vass finally left in 1957, after he and Vita had argued over something to do with the Sissinghurst Flower Show. He was succeeded by other stopgap gardeners, but Sissinghurst entered a new phase with the arrival in October 1959 of Pam Schwerdt and Sibylle Kreutzberger. They remained joint head gardeners until 1990.

The Sissinghurst they found on their arrival was rough and untended. When Vita interviewed them for the job, she had a hole in her breeches that she held together with her thumb and finger. Vita was in the habit of digging up the odd plant while a visitor was with her and offering it to them, leaving a hole in the flower beds. The glasshouses were full of scraggy and rather shameful plants. In the White Garden, the bricks on the wet ground squelched when you walked on them and water squirted up your trouser leg. The fig trees in the Rose Garden were occupying three-quarters of the flower beds, with no room for flowers. Sibylle Kreutzberger remembers Vita and Harold setting off for a winter cruise in late 1959 and leaving the two new gardeners to tackle the pruning:

> We hacked away for weeks while she was away. There used to be a winter secretary who came in and sent Vita's post off to wherever they'd gone to. One day this secretary came round the corner and the whole Rose Garden was strewn with branches the thickness of your thigh. "I do hope Lady Nicolson hasn't got second sight," she said.

Circa 1959: *Harold, Vita, and the German shepherd Rollo on the Tower steps.*

As Harold had predicted, Vita's entire inherited fortune poured into the creation and maintenance of Sissinghurst. Even when ill, she continued until 1961 writing her articles for the *Observer* because she needed the income. Only in her last years did she have to start selling her possessions at auction, some silver and a pair of the bronze Bagatelle urns, of which six now remain in the garden.

When Vita died in June 1962, she knew that she had created something of lasting value. "We have done our best," she wrote to Harold in November 1961, "and made a garden where none was." He survived her by six years, sad and lonely. Visitors would see him sitting on the Tower lawn with the tears running down his cheeks. My father was "awed by his desolation," but when Harold died in 1968, my father also collapsed in tears of a depth he had never known.

FOR A WEEK OR TWO AFTER VITA DIED in the summer of 1962, my father tried to use her room on the first floor of the Tower as his own. But he was haunted. "I could not endure it. I ceased to be myself: I became a ghost of her." Ever since, it has remained as she left it, carefully curated by the National Trust, packed away in a thousand leaves of tissue paper every winter, carefully revealed every spring, so that visitors can peer in through the metal grille that now fills the doorway, allowing one to look but not to touch.

My father had been in there only half a dozen times in thirty years, and it is now a shrine, a preserved ensemble, drenched in a peculiar faded, organic tobacco brown, "the verdure brown," as Vita called it, of a tapestry or an autumn wood. One morning the other day I sat and worked for a few hours at her desk when the garden was closed. Vita's Sissinghurst remains more present in that room than anywhere outside it. A French blue-brown tapestry, of a pool in a garden, where a pair of swans drifts in the water and oranges hang from the trees in pots, lines the wall in front of me. Looking at it, I write down the words "a curved arcade of shadowed trees" and feel the Vita-ism creeping up on me, the ghost, another generation on. On the rough oak desk itself there are ink rings where a bottle tipped or was spilled. There is a photograph of Virginia Woolf, her lover, that long saluki face from which the person, it seems, has withdrawn half an inch below the surface, and is apparent only in the heavy, tented eyes. "The human contact others can achieve is not for such as her," as Ethel Smyth described Virginia to Vita.

Opposite her, there is a photograph of Harold by Karsh, with a cigarette in one hand, a pencil in the other, his curly hair oiled back and on his face half a smile, more in the eyes than the mouth, as if about to speak, the person not sunk into the face, but barely contained within it.

Circa 1960: *Vita looking into her copy of* Knole and the Sackvilles, *which she had published in 1922.*

This room is an assembled world. In the drawer of the desk there are amber beads, a screwdriver, a Moroccan dagger in its sheath, a book of matches and some envelopes, a label saying "Potentilla Nitida," and a dried seed pod like a small artichoke. There is nothing thin or refined. Everything is richly itself: the eighteenth-century leather-bound memoirs of Mademoiselle de Montpensier stand beside a selection from Landor. Sticks of sealing wax lie with some pens in a Mexican earthenware tray. There is a small alabaster pot and some tarnished gilt scales on which letters can be weighed. Everything is rich and faded, a fraying of stuff that was once valuable and is now merely treasured. Nothing here was ever renewed. It arrived and, as soon as it arrived, like a picked flower laid on a desk, it began to fade. Vita allowed her possessions to age, silks to wear, wood to darken, terra-cotta to chip and fail. "Her possessions must grow old with her," my father wrote. "She must be surrounded by evidence of time." It was a vision and an aesthetic of gradual withdrawal, the bass line of music in which the high notes were the growing and flowering of the garden around her. In here was the lower register, a kind of melancholy, a saddened music. Sissinghurst as a whole, as Jane Brown wrote, also became one of the "crumbling shrines of the ancient garden gods of Florence and Rome."

It is a more reflective, slower, and deeper place than much of modern Sissinghurst can really allow. On the morning I worked there, trying to understand this place by absorption, osmotically, one of the gardeners, Peter Fifield, was mowing the lawn, and the burr of the mower's engine and the smell of the grass came up the spiral Tower stairs. I realized, as I never had before, that nowhere has quite the relationship to Sissinghurst that this room does: central and presiding, the onion layers of it spreading out from here, across the garden and the other buildings, the farmyard and the farmhouse, the closer fields, to the woods and the shadowed trenches of the streams. This Tower room is the gravitational middle of all of that but it is also hidden and enfolded, buried in the layers of the place like its heart, a presiding secrecy.

October 1959: *Letter from Vita to Harold.*

Inventories have been taken here, and the Trust has carefully numbered every object, book, and paper. But you can read this room as more than a catalog of objects. It is a form of self-portrait. There is a layer of imperial richness here: a chipped lapis tile on which a vase can sit.

And another, on the other table, a brown and amber medieval floor tile, made of English clay. On the bookshelf next to her desk, there is *The Rhymers Lexicon*, in which in pencil on the title page she has written, "a rhymer, that's what I am," and in which many words are ticked as used and not to be used again. Some are added: *puerile* between *peristyle* and *reconcile*; *cruelle* between *coracle* and *demoiselle*.

In a Venetian notebook there is a letter from Freya Stark, describing the olives and lemon orchards of the Mediterranean scene then spread before her eyes, and a long list, stretching over thirty years, of the books she lent to her children, to her cousin Eddy and uncle Charlie, to Dottie Wellesley and other lovers, even to her mother. There is a letter written by a woman who loved her, from 17 Montpelier St., SW7, undated:

> *Thank you for a very lovely day. I shall long remember the rain sliding on the panes, the chanting fire and your voice coming from a long distance as if suddenly you were speaking to me across the years. An echo—or a warning—I shall probably never know—but thank you for everything*
> *Madeleine*

There are duplicate order books from the great nurseries for hyacinths, Roman hyacinths, jonquils and narcissi, for tulips, and crocuses, for *Iris reticulata*, and a hundred dark fritillaries. In a secret drawer in one of the wooden cabinets, there is an ivory paper knife in the shape of a tiny shoe. Vita's grandfather had it made when Pepita, his mistress, died, having the ivory cut to the shape and size of the sole of one of her dancing shoes. Beside it, a small coral brooch is pinned to a photograph of Pepita surrounded by her children. There are photographs here of Victoria's brother's children and grandchildren, Vita's lost Spanish cousins.

All the English poets are in her writing room, but in the small turret room off it are her gardening books, books of literary criticism and biographies of the poets, Frazer's *Golden Bough*, Bergson's *Le Rire*, and a shelf of Elizabethan history. Above them is a complete run of Havelock Ellis's *Studies in the Psychology of Sex*, initialed "VN Long Barn" and with an inscription on the flyleaf from Verlaine in the hand of Violet Trefusis:

> *On est fier quelquefois*
> *Quand on se compare.*

Beside it, in *Sex and Character* by Otto Weininger ("VN Polperro July 1918"), Vita underlined, "Men who are merely intellectual are insincere. All that they care about is that their work should glitter and sparkle like a well cut stone."

Tucked high in one of the rather damp shelves in the turret I found the proofs of her poem "The Garden," which she composed here, at this desk, through the war years, and which was the last poem she wrote. It was her final claim on poetry, in which she had once felt secure, but even then sensed slipping from her. I read it, with the April cold in my fingers and the mower outside, as the thudding ringing of the bell came down from above on the hour. I wanted to redeem what she had written, to find the Sissinghurst music here, but, strangely, and for no want of trying, I could not make her poetry take hold. It lacks the final, unanswerable authority of real poetry. There is an emptiness to the rhetoric and it does not get you by the heart, or the throat. Its lines seem always to be more interested in their form, their appearance, than in what they might mean. Vita's misfortune was that she was so much greater as a gardener than as a poet. In the end, everything she wrote was nothing compared to what she did in this place. "Gardener," she calls out at one point in "The Garden," "poet unaware / Use your seeds like words." Perhaps in those few words there was a moment of knowledge and recognition.

A life and its griefs are soaked into the fabric of this room. At the foot of one of the bookcases, I found a calfskin attaché case. In it was a note in pencil from my father: "These objects and papers were found on VSW's desk when she died." They were mostly the stuff of everyday life, interrupted by illness—she had cancer—and death. Some little notebooks, with lists of what to pack, sachets of photographs of the donkey Abdul, Harold, and various women I could not identify. An engagement diary, with dates stretching on into the summer of 1962 beyond her death. A seed packet of Sutton's wallflowers, "Persian Carpet," 5s. A small note saying "Foie de veau veneziana" and "Sultanas in apple pie." A quote from Xenophon: "There is nothing that does not gain in beauty when set out in order," and a poem by Thom Gunn cut out of the New Statesman. But alongside those daily, transitory things, two others remained from her long-distant past, kept here, not in some hidden uninspected repository of a filing cabinet or a drawer but on her present desk, as much to hand as the photographs of Virginia or Harold. First, a letter from my father to his, written in December 1925 when my father was eight and his father had gone to the embassy in Tehran for two years.

> Darling Daddy,
> Last night I felt so sad about you being so long and far away and I cryed a bit. Oh Daddy I do miss you, it is horrid to think of you all those thousands of miles away, and two years is a long time to wait for a person whome one loves very much which I do you. I love you more than very.
> Gogy [his French governess] has litten the fire in your little sitting room, and I am writing on your desk.
> I hope I will no longer be sad about you,
> Your loving,
> Niggs

That letter is the only sign of her children in this room. Alongside it, still on her desk nearly forty years after it was written, was its opposite, something a few years older, evidence of another kind of love. Nigel's little letter is in pencil, carefully corrected by Goggy, neatly tucked into a small, neatly addressed envelope. This other thing is rapidly and even wildly written in heavy black ink in short hurried lines on the back of the telegram forms of the Hotel Windsor in Monte Carlo. It is a poem in French, written by Violet Trefusis at the end of those "four wild and radiant months" between December 1918 and March 1919 when Vita, dressed as Julian, the wounded soldier hero, had lived her life of ecstatic freedom away from the bonds of bourgeois normality, from Harold and the children. But this poem, the passion of its writing still apparent, comes at the end of all that, the moment, or at least one of them, when Vita rejected her most dangerous lover. It is Violet's admission of defeat, when Vita made her choice for Harold and her family. It marks the moment, one could say, when Sissinghurst became possible. "*Adieu Mon Ange,*" Violet had written,

> *Si triste échange*
> *Tant pis pour moi.*

Sissinghurst itself is the monument to the choice Vita made.

CHAPTER *12*

Renewal

THE DECISION TO GO AHEAD with the farm project had been made in December 2007. It seemed for a time as if all was set. Advertisements were put in relevant papers for a project manager; for a vegetable grower and a deputy; and for a farmer. Early in 2008 we had a string of open days on which candidates came to Sissing-hurst for their interviews and to be walked round in the cold and the wind. It was exciting. Here at last, living in flesh and blood, were some of the people who were going to make the change.

The first to join was the new project manager. Tom Lupton is a tall, big-voiced man, Oxford-educated, with a long history of land management in the tropics, a hunger for order, and eyebrows that jump at each emphasis in a sentence. It was like having the engineer on the Aswan dam supervise the building of your pond. Why was he doing it? Certainly not for the National Trust salary. More because it was "an ideal thing to get involved with. It was an idea with a very holistic view, doing things I have spent all my life doing, using land to improve people's lives at the same time as protecting the environment, and done by an organization which takes a long-term view. It was a marriage of all those things."

May 2008: *Tom Lupton, the Sissinghurst Farm project manager,*
at Whitegate Farm, Sissinghurst.

Next was the vegetable grower. The ad in *Horticulture Week* came
out in February 2008. Amy Covey, a twenty-three-year-old, with a big-
teeth smile and a blonde, tanned presence as buoyant and English as her
name, was working in a private garden in the Midlands. She was young
to take it on, but we all felt when she came for an interview and we
showed her the bleak unplowed, wind-exposed stretch of ground that
was going to be her vegetable garden that her sense of enthusiasm and
capability, her wonderful undauntedness, was just what Sissinghurst
needed.

Third in this flow of new blood was to be the new farmer. But here
it went wrong. A farming couple was chosen, but after months of nego-
tiation with the Trust, no agreement on the details of the tenancy could
be reached and they withdrew. It was the first sign that the sailing might
not be all entirely plain.

May 2008: Amy Covey, *the vegetable grower, in the new veg garden in Cow Field.*

There were some marvelous and optimistic developments. A three-and-a-half-acre vegetable plot was laid out in nine different segments, the crops to rotate through it year by year. Peter Dear, the National Trust warden, had it manured, drained, plowed, fenced, gated, and hedged. An extra segment was added for the children of Frittenden school to grow their own veg. The site for the polytunnels was set up behind a screening layer of oak trees. Irrigation was put in. Plans were made for the drained-off water to be collected in a pond in Lower Tassells and then pumped back up to the top of the site where it could reused to irrigate the crops. Peter and a party of volunteers made windbreak panels from the wood, using chestnut poles and sliver-thick chestnut slices that he wove between the uprights. Birch tops and hazels were cut for the peas and beans to climb. Peter drew up a plan for the whole farm in which all the hedges, gates, and stiles were carefully and exactly detailed.

I loved it all. Suddenly, new life was springing up out of the inert Sissinghurst ground. It was slightly rough at the edges. Despite some

May 2008: *Peter Dear, National Trust warden at Sissinghurst, with the newly installed irrigation pipe in the vegetable garden.*

ferreting earlier in the year, the rabbits wrought mayhem with the early plantings and the beds had to be surrounded by low green electric fencing. Black plastic mulch marked out each strip of veg. The soil was not as good as we all had hoped and the vegetable gardeners had pushed grapefruit-sized lumps of clay to one side so that they could get each bed half-level. The sown lines were a little wobbly and there was an ad hoc feeling to the garden, but it was this handmade quality of the vegetable garden that touched me. Not for decades had someone attended to this ground in this way. The paths worn between the rows by the boots of the gardeners and their volunteers; the picnic tables for the Frittenden children; and the *Handbook of Organic Gardening* left on the tea-shed table: all were marks of a new relationship to this place. They were the signs of Sissinghurst joining the modern world, the same movement that had reinvigorated allotments across the country, that understood the deep pleasures and rewards of growing your own, that loved the local in the most real way it could. This new presence of people out on the ground—bodies in the fields—was exactly what I had dreamed of four years before: land not as background, as wallpaper or flattened "tranquillity zone" to walk your dogs in, but the thing itself, engaged with by real people, the plants sown in it bursting into a third dimension, the soil the living source of everything that mattered.

Sarah drew up a planting list of what the veg garden could and should grow, a cornucopia menu that stretched across the months and years. Intensely productive but not labor-intensive salads, herbs, leafy greens, chard, spinach, zucchini, and beans. Alongside them all the veg that taste much more delicious if they have just been picked: tomatoes, carrots, and sugar snaps (peas themselves were thought to be too labor-intensive for the kitchen—too much shelling for not enough product). Third were the "unbuyables"—unusual herbs such as lovage, the edible flowers, red Brussels sprouts, stripy pink-and-white beetroot, as well as yellow and purple French beans. All of them, as Sarah said, "for flavor, style, and panache." Kale, leeks, and purple sprouting broccoli, "the hungry gap crops," would grow through the winter and be harvested in March and April when the restaurant opened for the season. Raspberries, blackberries, gooseberries, and red- and blackcurrants were planted in long lines between the nine sections of the garden, both to provide windbreaks and to give the plot a visual structure. Forty new volunteers were recruited to help work there and in the polytunnels.

Tom, Peter, and Amy drew up plans for the new orchard. A third of it was to be filled with ninety big old-fashioned apple trees (mainly juicing varieties so that the apples could be collected from the ground and no one would have to climb high in the trees to pick them). Most of the rest, just over three acres, was to be smaller modern trees, fifteen hundred of them, no more than eight feet tall, for easy picking and tons of fruit. Plums, apples, pears, and a few cherries: a vision of blossom and fruiting heaven. I had the idea of putting thirty acres of hay meadow back into Frogmead along the banks of the Hammer Brook and meadow experts came to advise. Peter was designing wet patches for birds and

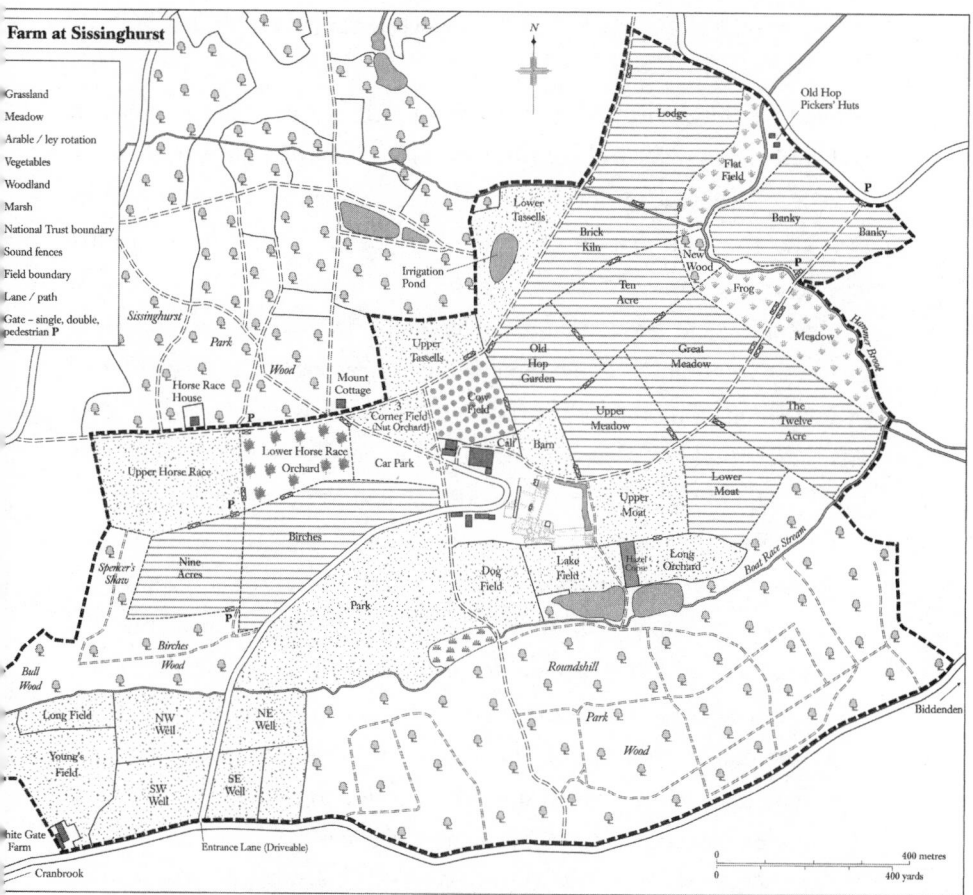

The farm at Sissinghurst, map by Peter Wilkinson on the basis of a drawing by Peter Dear, integrating the new ideas for the farm landscape.

dragonflies along the streams and a new rough wood to extend the habitat for nightingales and warblers. We bought some new disease-resistant elms to place around the landscape as the great towering tree-presences of the future. Architects redesigned the farmhouse as a modern B&B.

Everywhere you looked, all through the spring and summer of 2008, change was under way. More people, new people, new structures, new land uses, new relationships. All these changes were exciting, but it also felt like a long, slow earthquake heaving up under a stable and intricately defined place. Inevitably, the stress and grief began to tell.

Difficulties, tensions, and rows started to break out. There were tears and snubbings, huffs and confrontations. No one had quite understood how deeply these ideas for the place, and all its emphasis on reinvigoration and the reanimation of the landscape, would disturb the people who lived and worked here.

People were getting angry, offended, offensive, and dismissive. I talked to Tom Lupton about what was going wrong. He is the definition of a wise dog, and one of the problems, he said, was that I had not properly understood how deeply attached other people were to Sissinghurst. I had assumed I was the only person to whom it meant a great deal.

There is a lot of emotion tied up in this project. From you, of course. You have obviously staked a lot of emotion in it. But that's true of a lot of people who live and work here. Sissinghurst is not like going into the supermarket. People come here and very quickly form emotional bonds. They love it. It feeds many individual needs, which are very difficult to get fed in many places these days. Sissinghurst spoon-feeds it to people. As you walk from the car park, you are given these wonderful, sensuous experiences. In through the gateway, the tower, you wander into the garden. It's beautiful but it's obviously been beautiful for a long time. That is very reassuring and very comforting. It's a refuge but it does a bit more than that. I can't believe that many people don't leave here feeling better. It's a recharging point and for people who work here it has an increasing value to them the more they are steeped in it. You, Adam, need to be aware how many other people have loved being here.

It was well said and I heard it clearly. I asked Sam Butler, the National Trust visitor services manager, about this too. Why were people so attached to Sissinghurst? Was it just a tranquillity balm? I had always thought of it as a place that should have life and vitality, that should feel enriched by the things going on here, by a sense of a living landscape, not an embalmed one. Sam gave me a skeptical look.

I know you would like to bring the farm up close around the garden so that there was more of a contrast. I can see that, but I quite like the feminine, soft, National Trust sanitization. I quite like that because that is where I am comfortable, but what you are proposing is much more masculine and that's unknown territory. I am not sure how I am going to respond to that.

Really? Was a sanitized, blanded-out soft zone really what was needed?

I like it and most of our visitors like it. It makes it accessible and for those who don't know the countryside, who need their hands held, it gives them a comfort zone so that they can access the country without it being too threatening.

How was she feeling about the whole transformation? A week or two before, at a meeting, she had suddenly colored up at something I said.

It was like a slap in the face. I had been listening to you and Tom and I suddenly realized that this place was going to change forever in the way I felt about it. It didn't matter whether it was good or bad. I knew it was different and that for me was a loss, because I have been tied to this place for such a long time.

We have visitors who come here every Saturday morning to read their papers in the orchard, who have come here maybe with a partner or a husband or a wife or a child they have lost and they come here to reflect as well as to enjoy the flowers and the views and the vistas. And you know we must look after those people too.

All this was an education for me, almost the first time I had ever listened to the stories other people at Sissinghurst were telling me.

The real pinchpoint, though, was the restaurant. It was vital that the restaurant change to reflect what was happening in the wider land-scape. It would make little sense to set up all these connections between land, place, and people if the restaurant continued to produce food much as before. Sarah, who was the author of prize-winning gardening and cookery books and had a decade's experience of growing and cook-ing vegetables for her gardening school in Sussex, if no knowledge of running a large-scale catering operation, took on the task of introduc-ing the restaurant to these new hyperlocal sources of produce. She tried to persuade the managers and chefs to adopt a new responsiveness to the food coming in off the field. For months, over these questions, there was an agonized nonmeeting of minds.

Both sides felt deeply unappreciated by the other. Ginny Coombes, the restaurant manager, who has been generating quantities of cash for Sissinghurst year after year, felt bruised by the whole process.

There is no appreciation of how far we have come, or of what we have taken on. A lot of ideas have been thrown at us and it isn't easy. We are moving in the right direction and we are doing a lot already with local and seasonal. That's my mantra! It is some-thing the Trust has been working towards for years. And we are improving year on year. Someone needs to say, "Listen to the staff, they run it, they know what they are doing. We want to help you improve what you have got already." But we don't feel that anyone is saying that.

It was never going to be easy. For chefs and restaurant managers used to high-pressure, high-volume production of meals for hundreds of visitors, often in less than perfect circumstances, all our talk of "the dignity of vegetables" was not even funny. Mutual frustrations erupted. Sarah pursued her gospel: vegetables are cheaper to grow than meat, better for the environment, better for you, utterly delicious when they are so fresh, and make you feel good when you know exactly where they have come from. And Ginny said, "Look, do you know what it is like in here on a busy day?"

When you came to me three years ago and said, "What about growing our own veg here?" I thought that would be a wonderful thing. But it has all got so overcomplicated. I love what Sarah does at Perch Hill and I listened. That is all fine when you have fifty people to feed. When you have got a thousand people a day, they want choice.

Early in June 2008, to get some understanding of what Ginny and her staff were having to deal with, Sarah and I worked in the restaurant for two days, she in the kitchen, I on the tables, behind the counter, and doing the washing up.

Seeing it all from the other side was pure reality check. The customer demand was relentless and the need to shave costs unbending. The building—a restaurant inserted into an old granary-cum-cow-shed—is badly laid out. For the staff it is often unbearably hot as wafts of hot air come from the industrial dishwasher, the heated counters, or the ovens. The clearing-away system does not help the waiters and there is a lot of double handling. The queue for a pot of coffee gets muddled with the queue for the hot dishes. Space behind the counter is cramped and, where different routes cross, inconvenient. Everybody works unrelentingly hard and remains cheerfully nice to each other through the heat and harassing customers. And everybody ends the day exhausted.

I felt I had been in a trawler for eight hours. Only when one of the visitors said, "This must be such a nice place to work," did I very nearly ask him if he had just landed from Mars.

Of course this restaurant finds it difficult to embrace any change. An irregular supply of vegetables from the plot, in variable volumes, is going to need an elastic frame of mind. Working in this tight and difficult environment allows no room for elasticity. I asked Ginny about this. "People here don't see our side of it, our passion for it, the work and energy we put in here," she said.

> I know you saw it the other day, how drained people are at the end of a working day. But nobody gives us credit for it. And nobody knows exactly what is needed. It is all big ideas, everybody thinks they know better than us. We are taking on board the advice that everyone seems to be giving us, but give us time.

It was in truth a culture clash between Sarah and the NT restaurant staff. There was an assumption on their side that Sarah was promoting her own private agenda, when she felt she was ushering in part of the food culture that had been the lingua franca of food writing, restaurants, and shops on both sides of the Atlantic for the last twenty years. An emotional and resolute refusal to entertain most of her ideas made her feel as if she was banging her head against a wall. Parts of the National Trust wanted her to contribute, others didn't. "All I am trying to do is modernize the restaurant in its attitude to fresh produce, to simplicity as the modern way. They think I am trying to extend my empire. And the organization can't back me up because they have to support their staff. But you don't have to wave goodbye to flowers and texture and freshness and goodness just because you are providing two hundred meals a day."

Late that summer, Sarah and I went to a meeting in London with Sue Wilkinson, the NT's director of marketing. She told us, in effect, that the place Sarah was trying to take the restaurant was not the place the NT wanted to go. The local food managers had said that "the expectation of the general public was the "hot two-course meal," and the chef at Sissinghurst had reiterated that: "This is a standard fish and meat and three vegetables place. It always has been and always will be." Sarah had arranged for Peter Weeden, head chef at the Paternoster Chophouse, a London restaurant that specializes in modern, fresh, seasonal food, to be brought in as a consultant, but his contributions were rejected. "Maybe Sissinghurst is not ready for that much change," he said when he left. When Sissinghurst volunteers were asked about suggested changes to the restaurant menus, one said, "Just because Vita went to Persia and ate some curry or whatever they eat there, I don't think people would really want that experience here." And another: "I don't think you come to Sissinghurst wanting Chinese meals. I'm sure that's not people's expectations." A man I had never met said to me at the garden gate, "It all depends on whether people prefer olive oil and vinaigrette to bangers and mash. And if it's bangers and mash, you're going to have egg all over your face, aren't you, Mr. Nicolson?" I said I didn't think he had quite understood the whole picture.

Much of what Sarah was suggesting—a freer, looser, richer, more internationalist line—was not only part of the modern mainstream but came from the roots of modern Sissinghurst. That cut no ice. An almost purely conservative sense of "we know best" carried the day. In the autumn of 2008, Sarah took a step back. The Food Group at which she had tried to persuade and show the National Trust catering staff what she had in mind was disbanded. It was agreed that she should provide the restaurant with the recipe for a single dish a month, which they would trial. Her relations with the restaurant manager and chef should from now on be exclusively through the National Trust hierarchy.

At the same time, I was also suffering my defeats. I had been asked by the property manager to devise a new, historically based approach for the area immediately outside the garden, between the car park, the ticket office, and the front gate. Over the previous thirty years, it had been managed in a bland, corporate, golf-course style of large swathes of mown grass with ornamental trees. This was the first part of Sissinghurst to be seen by visitors and to my mind it gave all the wrong signals. I wanted it to be more rural, to give a sense that this was a garden in a farm, that Kent itself not suburbia lapped at the garden walls. But the head gardener did not see the point I was making, or at least did not agree with it, and told me that she and the property manager alone should decide how it was managed. The grass would be allowed to grow a little longer around the edges but essentially the area should remain unchanged. The Trust hierarchy supported her and the ideas I had been asked to provide were dropped.

By the autumn of 2008, things were looking glum: no farmer; little change in the restaurant; no change in the immediate surroundings of the garden. Then it got worse: although the veg garden was going organic, the conversion of the farm to an organic system was delayed three years; the tenancies of the bed-and-breakfast and of the farm were separated, as it was thought unlikely that a single couple would be able to do both. As the farm was so small, this meant that the farm would not have a dedicated farmer of its own but would again become part of a larger enterprise. I felt that the idea I had originally proposed was suffering death by a thousand cuts, that the all-important connections between farm, food, restaurant, bed-and-breakfast, garden, history, land, and people were all being neatly snipped one by one. And if the connections were cut, where was the idea?

Fiona Reynolds, the director-general and chief executive of the Trust, came down to see me and told me that I needed to look at things more optimistically, that it was damaging to morale only to look on the downside and that I was "an old romantic." After she left, I thought about that phrase and realized that what, from the outside, looked like romanticism seemed to me like a belief that only something done *wholly* was valuable. The wholly done thing is also—literally—attractive, something that by its exception from the norm draws people in. People don't come to Sissinghurst because it is quite like everywhere else, shaped by the tastes and expectations of everywhere else, but because it is exceptionally itself. That should be the aim and goal of what was done here now. It might be the motto for this entire project. Nor is that goal merely romantic in the derogatory sense. As a result of the publicity surrounding the publication of this book in England in the autumn of 2008, an extra fifteen thousand visitors came to Sissinghurst in those months, spending an average of ten pounds each. They were drawn by the idea that something courageously different from the norm was being done here. At the beginning of the beautiful and sunny 2009 season, visitor numbers at all National Trust properties were up on average 30 percent. Sissinghurst, largely as a result of a BBC television series about the project, filmed over the course of 2008 and broadcast in February and March 2009, was up 73 percent. If nothing else, romanticism is good box office. Vita and Harold saw that. And the wholly done thing, driven to fulfill itself by a powerful and commanding sense of its own value, will always be at the root of the beautiful landscape, the beautiful painting, or the beautiful piece of music. Beauty is not based on consensus. Beauty would be impossible without exceptionalism, a denial of the average. It stands out for its own conception of itself. That is not the only ingredient, but it is certainly a necessary part of it.

After Fiona had left, and under her prompting, I made a list of what was good here. There was a lot. The new orchard had been laid out and marked with chestnut stakes from the wood. Six hundred and thirty-six young fruit trees (cookers, early eaters and cider apples, greengages and Victoria plums, three different sorts of cherry, with a range of fruiting season, and delicious Doyenne du Comice pears, as well as Concorde and Conference pears for cooking) were planted as soon as the weather allowed. Almost a mile of new hedges on the old lines were marked out across the big arable fields, and as soon as the ground dried, the new ditches alongside them were dug and thousands of hedgeplants

June 2008: *Amy Covey, vegetable grower, and Sarah Raven, my wife, with the first salads from the veg garden.*

planted. New water troughs, piped water, and new fencing were all put into the permanent pasture. Thirty-five acres of a new streamside hay meadow (on Frogmead, probably a meadow for about a thousand years until it became a hop garden in the 1860s), two new pieces of scrubby woodland, ideal for nightingales and willow-warblers, and a new "scrape," a slightly dished boggy patch by a stream, were designed as a dragonfly and wader heaven. On January 1, 2009, the vegetable garden had gone into organic conversion, under the auspices of the Soil Association. New advertisements for the farmer and the B&B, although separate, would at least refer to each other, so that the chance remained that farm and farmhouse would be reconnected. There was a presumption that in 2012–13 the farm would go into organic conversion.

This was the inventory of where, early in 2009, the project stood in relation to its original intentions:

INTENTION 2005	OUTCOME 2009
Meadows	*Yes, bigger than envisaged*
Orchards	*Yes, and more planned*
Nut orchard	*Yes, if small*
Beef cattle	*Yes*
Sheep	*Yes*
Vegetable garden	*Yes, a great success*
Volunteers on the land	*Yes*
Smaller fields	*Yes, and others planned*
New woods	*Yes*
New wetlands	*Yes*
New hedges on old lines	*Yes, and others planned*
Farm supply to restaurant	*Yes, from veg garden, planned from farm*
Restaurant to reflect farm	*Yes, partly, but a way to go*
Pigs	*A good possibility*
Chickens	*A good possibility*
Organic system	*Planned, but some hesitations in the air*
Farmer as resident	*A possibility*
B&B as integrated part of farm	*A possibility*
Dairy cattle	*No (but a micro-dairy remains possible)*
Hop garden	*No*
Redesign of garden surroundings	*Not in detail but the atmosphere is changed*
"A place exceptionally itself"	*Coming on. . . .*

A *future orchard.*

It was a mixed picture, but the feeling here was that spring was one of enormous optimism, that the landscape around Sissinghurst was one of possibility. There had not been a snap change, nor should there have been, but something was under way that five years later had the chance of being as deeply and integratedly wonderful as any romantic could wish. An old friend of my father's, who had known this place all his life, wrote to me after he had seen what was beginning here and said, "It's as if we have all been blind for the last 40 years." That recognition was enough for me.

ONE IMPORTANT QUESTION REMAINS UNADDRESSED: does this project have any significance beyond itself? Partly, my answer is no. These ideas are about this place, this ecology, human and natural, this particular set of connections between people and place. And that particularity is its virtue.

But the question recurs. Is it not just a private indulgence, an exercise in the unreal, attempting to impose on the real world ideas that belong in a dream or onstage? Is it a masque, a replaying of "The Shepherd's Paradise"? Or an attempt to "turn the clock back," as people have often said, a nostalgic and unreal longing for something that no longer exists?

I passionately believe that it is none of those things, and I will make my case here, but these are questions and criticisms that need answering. Three people have put versions of them to me recently, two in public, the other in private.

First, the journalist Simon Jenkins, now chairman of the National Trust, produced a hybrid objection. On the platform of a meeting we shared in Oxford he said (in a perfectly friendly way) that in promoting these ideas, I was "acting out a combination of an eighteenth-century squire and a hippie." The motives behind this project were both doo-lally idealist and deeply prebourgeois and preindustrial conservative. "Adam has an agrarian vision, wants to return Sissinghurst to the conditions of his childhood in the 1960s. Why should the National Trust do that? Other people, who *work* there, are just as attached to the highly successful Sissinghurst of the 1980s or 1990s. Why should Adam's vision of a dream world have priority over any other? Why is his childhood important?"

The second public objection took one of these elements—the squire line—and played it harder. Charles Moore, a prominent right-wing columnist, neoliberal, and Thatcherite, who was at school and university with me and has been my friend for forty years, saw the Sissinghurst project as little but snob drama. He had watched the beginning of the TV series and reviewed the first program. "It's the lower middle classes who own England," he wrote in the *Daily Telegraph*, but Sarah and I apparently did not like them. Instead, we had a vision of a world that we controlled.

What emerges at once is that the staff at Sissinghurst do not like what Adam and Sarah want. The chef thinks her idea of lots of home-grown vegetables and less meat might be fine for London, where people like being "conned," but will never do here.

The head-gardener is told by Sarah that she has just destroyed a romantic little corner of the garden in her desire to make everything "too perfect." Perfection, she says through gritted teeth, is exactly what she is trained to provide.

It does not take long to see that the clash is irreconcilable. What she and Adam cannot say—but clearly feel—is that the Sissinghurst restaurant is frightfully common. Even when redone, the floor is too shiny, and there is too much vinegar in the beetroot. The staff use words like "condiments," which make the Nicolsons wince.

The stalwart staff at Sissinghurst hate mess, worry about how to run the place efficiently, and feel unappreciated by the couple. Related to the question of class is one of ownership. To whom does Sissinghurst belong? In law, of course, it belongs to the National Trust. It is a hopeless, soul-destroying quest to try to own what you cannot, and one feels enormous sympathy with the poor, despised Sissinghurst workers. Why should they have all this emotional and dynastic baggage dumped on them? This series illustrates the great argument about who owns England. The answer is, the lower middle classes, the people Kipling called "the sons of Martha." One's romantic streak may regret this but, in the modern world, our life, liberty and property depend on it.

The first effect of this article was to irritate everyone who works at Sissinghurst. Lower middle class? Who was Charles Moore? And who was he calling the "sons of Martha"? Who did he think he was? I was blackened by association, for being his friend. But what could I say in response? There was no way I was dumping emotional or dynastic baggage on anyone. I had been to hundreds of meetings to avoid any dumping. I didn't want to become any kind of squire here. I had always recognized that none of us would be living here without the National Trust. We lived in an extraordinarily privileged situation. My motive was not any form of control but of partnership. I did not feel that I had any rights over the direction of things at Sissinghurst because of my genes. The only possible justification for raising these ideas was that I had known this place a long time, had thought a great deal about it and the relationships that lay at the root of it, and had researched its story carefully. Future directions would benefit from deep roots. Of course we did not despise the people who worked here, nor was I trying to own what I could not. Charles Moore labeled Sarah and me as nostalgic snobs, but I cannot think of a single thing we have done that could justify that.

Simon Jenkins had said hippie-squire; Charles Moore had said squire; Oliver Walston said hippie. He is a barley baron, owns a two-thousand-acre intensive arable farm in Cambridgeshire, entirely dependent on chemical fertilizers and pesticides, feeding wheat and oilseed rape into the international commodity markets, and over several decades has been steadily subsidized by the European Union to the tune of some £200,000 a year. When he was a boy eighty people worked on his land. Now he has two employees who drive the giant tractors and the very large Klaas combine harvester (which drinks £700 worth of diesel a day). His job of managing them and the farm, he says, takes up 15 percent of his time. Much of the rest of it he spends in his charming house in Fleurie, in the Beaujolais, writing brilliant, candid articles for the press that are designed to inflame environmentalists.

In April 2009, I asked him to come to Sissinghurst to look at what we were doing. I also asked Patrick Holden. He is both an organic dairy and carrot farmer in the far west of Wales and director of the Soil Association, Britain's leading organic organization. I asked them both how this tiny farm project stood in relation to the world.

On one thing they were agreed: in global terms, a crisis was approaching. For Patrick, it was

> the biggest crisis there has ever been. We are the binge generation. We have consumed half of everything that the planet ever laid down in one lifetime and now we have got to prepare the planet for our children. Agriculture has been spending beyond its means for more than a hundred years, treating environmental capital as if it were income. Fossil fuels, minerals, phosphates, water, soil fertility, human skills capital—all that collective capital, much of it laid down by centuries of relatively sustainable farming, has been used up in the last hundred years. We now have an industrial agricultural system which crudely uses ten calories of fossil fuel energy to grow one calorie of food. That is not sustainable and it will only go on as long as there is any environmental capital to exploit. The problem we face is that we have nearly used up the store. *And* we have exponential world population growth *and* climate change which is going to shrink the area in which agriculture is possible. The crisis will come in fifteen years if we are lucky. We cannot go on as we have been.

Oliver Walston's answer was to quote Richard Nixon's secretary of agriculture, Earl "Rusty" Butz, the 1970s advocate of "Get Big or Get Out" farming: "Before we go back to organic agriculture, somebody is going to have to decide what fifty million people we are going to let starve." Every acre of Walston's farm grows fifteen tons of wheat every decade. No organic farmer could approach a quarter of that yield. That is the wheat problem. If there are going to be nine and a half billion people in the world in 2050, they will need wheat to be grown by efficient, Walston-style chemical and industrial methods. Any other form of farming can be no more than a niche, to satisfy rich, middle-class customers who are keen on wildlife. "I am interested in sustaining human beings," Oliver said. "Patrick is interested in sustaining an agricultural system."

He admitted, though, that his type of farming was not sustainable. Finite reserves of phosphate, potash, and fuel mean that it cannot continue into the future. His answer is what greens call a "techno-fix." Science has come up with solutions in the past. There is no reason to doubt it will again.

Patrick reminds me of the man who in 1875 would have been sitting here and he would have been saying the future for London was in danger. His voice would quiver with passion and integrity. "At the present rate," he would say, "in my lifetime you won't be able to walk down Regent Street because it will be knee-high in horse shit." How was he to know, poor man, about the internal combustion engine?

For Patrick, the nub of the crisis is in the relationship of energy and fertility. The coming shortages of fossil fuels will need us "to switch from the energy capital laid down over the last 150 million years to operating within current solar energy input. And the biggest single change is the switch to generating fertility from solar energy within the farming system. Of course we will need tractors and there will be techno-fixes to fuel them. But we won't be able to power the growing itself by artificial fertilizer because natural gas is going to run out and the amount of energy required to fix a ton of nitrogen fertilizer is enormous."

Patrick described a revolution in the farmed landscape of Britain and the rest of the industrialized world. Cereal production will halve. And as half of all the grain grown in the industrialized world is fed to animals in sheds, most of that form of agriculture will also disappear. It will be the end of intensive poultry and pigs. Dairy cows will return to what they were before the 1960s, not relying on grain but eating grass, "dual purpose"—i.e., dairy calves will make good beef animals. Human diet will have to change. There will be a lot less white meat, although this is not a vegetarian system. In a sustainably farmed Britain, half the land area will be in clover or grass or permanent pasture, and the best way to harvest that phase of the rotation is with cattle and sheep. There will be a great deal of red meat and dairy products, as well as grass-fed poultry and pigs fed on swill and grass. "This is not a question of choice," Patrick said. "We have got no choice."

"Last time this happened," Walston said, "was before the industrial revolution. Most people ate the kind of diet which any dietician would now say was outrageous. It wasn't the good old days. No lovely meat pasties. They had awful food and they died very young."

His hopes were pinned on a new kind of genetically modified wheat, which has genes from a nitrogen-fixing bean implanted in it so that as the wheat plant grows, it derives its own nitrogen fertilizer from the air. No need for any artificial fertilizer, no need for any break-crops. It could be GM nitro-wheat year after year, feeding the world.

I asked him whether, accepting his argument for the moment that only chemical farming could feed the world (even if, paradoxically, he said there was no visible future for chemical farming), there was not a case for a version of farming that attended to other things (nature, landscape, beauty) in certain places where those things mattered. He talked about a plague of locusts in Ethiopia. "How do you kill a locust organically? You can't. In the third world that is the reality. But it doesn't matter in Kent?"

Does that degrade the organic idea in Kent? I asked.

"Yes, it does. It is like saying, 'Let's all drive Bentleys.' If you want to drive a Bentley, great. But don't for God's sake tell me, 'Let's all drive Bentleys,' because it is an impossibility."

The question for me was how to connect any of this giant global agenda to any of the intuitive desires and ideals I had for Sissinghurst. Was there no way in which the plans for Sissinghurst could be seen as more than a first-world luxury, the twenty-first-century Petit Trianon? Was everything I believed about it finally trivial, a form of exterior decor? What about local meaning, I asked them, the particularity of doing particular things in particular places? Did that have no role in their thinking?

Patrick of course thought it did. "The old idea was if you wanted to solve the world's food problems, get a bunch of global leaders together, they will hatch a plan, the G20, trillions of whatever, they will do it top-down and things will be all right. But the really interesting thing is what the bottom-up components of that top-down plan will be. I am thinking about that, driven by selfish motives, because unless I make the necessary preparations on my own farm in Wales, when the crunch comes, the food crunch, I am scared that my business will collapse."

Oliver answered in terms of the market. "If I were running Sissing-hurst now, I would be growing organic food for the restaurant. The punters can afford it, they will appreciate it, and so you should go for it. If I opened a restaurant in Grosvenor Square, I would do the same. If I opened a restaurant in the poorest parts of northern England, I am not sure I would."

PATRICK: You have to assume some trigger event, a trade dispute, an act of terrorism, a conflict, a sudden shortage of energy. I get back to my farm. I lose my diesel and then the grid goes down. That is the scenario I have to work to. I have to work out a resilience plan. I need renewable energy to drive my tractors. I have to make sure if I can't buy grain from England, or seeds and straw from England or even, as I did in the past, South American protein, I can carry on farming. I am three years in, have plans for a wind turbine, a methane digester, and so on. I need to be in the position where if there is a sudden breakdown in power I can carry on farming. At the moment my farm wouldn't last twelve hours. The farms uses no chemicals or imported fertilizers but still it is incredibly vulnerable to interruptions in the centralized, globalized input system.

OLIVER: Patrick is a pessimist and I am an optimist. Everything he says is based on the idea that we're going to hell in a
handcart. What I am doing at the moment *is* unsustainable, as
was horse-drawn transport. But I am not preparing for nuclear
war. Patrick has the gall to talk about bottom up. Patrick's bottom appears to be the poorest Whole Foods customer there is.
Forget the bottom up. You are talking about nine-tenths of the
way to the top up.

This, then, was one version of the question: the Sissinghurst
scheme was either Bentley-driving self-delusion or, in its tight producer-
consumer loops and its concern for more than mere production, a necessary component of the only farming system that would be viable in
the energy-poor future. Perhaps it is both. Will the Bentley mysteriously
transmute into the only form of transport we can afford?

But it was obviously much more than that. I had read something
written by Ivan Illich, the 1970s alternative-life guru. He had described
what he called "the interior degradation of our lives under the effects of
hyper-specialization, mechanization, and generalized marketization."
Instead he proposed what he called "a civilization of conviviality." I put
those phrases to them both and Patrick talked about the need for a balance, a correspondence between "interior and exterior cultivation. . . .
Neither industrialized farming nor the industrialization of organic
farming is capturing what the world needs at the moment. Any approach to the land has to connect up to motive and to the human
condition":

> If I don't become the change, starting with my own farm, we are
> all in trouble. That is not demoralizing. It is inspiring and moti-
> vating. It is inspiring my family. A million little cells of resilience
> constitute our response to this threat and Sissinghurst is one of

them. It is an attempt, in a tiny microcosmic way, to reestablish some of the connections between inner and outer cultivation which have been broken by industrialized farming. There are an awful lot of people in denial about this and Oliver is one of them. You need to ask him whether the incredible technical and financial success on his farm has come at a price. And what is that price? Why does he escape from East Anglia to his cottage in the Beaujolais? Is it because he yearns for a culture alive with people?

Oliver talked about the changes he had seen since the 1950s, the disappearance of so many farming jobs, the loss of wildlife on his farm, the way in which his son if he were to take the farm on (worth £10 million at current prices, the real gain) would have nothing to do unless he became a tractor driver. Those were real losses, but in no way did he look back to lost halcyon days. They weren't.

Manual labor was the norm, lifting heavy sacks resulted in frequent back injuries, and working in dusty conditions damaged the lungs. The combine driver in the harvest still sat outside and wore a handkerchief round his face in a forlorn attempt to stop the dust. Wages were insulting, hours were long and holidays short. And above all the farm workers invariably lived in tied cottages—from which, in theory at least, they could be evicted at the whim of the farmer. This period, it should be remembered, is today usually referred to—by the commuter who insists on organic food and lives in what had once been a tied cottage—as "the good old days." Like hell it was.

And for Patrick, finally, the real loss, the loss that had to be made up, was in human and cultural value:

We have deskilled in one generation, lost people who want to work in agriculture. The average age in farming is nearly sixty. Most people think a job in farming is absolutely not cool, with low social, economic, and cultural status. But here is something. All my children have got jobs in food or farming. Not because I encouraged them to, because I haven't. I am sure the reason is that the farming system I practice is more interesting culturally. My son and his wife, after leaving highly paid jobs in London, are now making cheese on the family farm in Pembrokeshire. My daughter is growing vegetables for the National Trust, having been to university in London, tried and left London jobs. And that pattern of reconnection, of reacquiring the cultural, emotional, and social skills that come with the growing life, that is what this huge challenge is all about.

So either (the gospel according to Patrick): we have to make the change, we ought to make it, and we would like it if we did make it. Sissinghurst is a beacon, somewhere that can signal the virtues of those changes widely in the world.

Or (according to Oliver): we must not make the change, we cannot afford to make it, we must trust that a techno-solution will emerge, and we must accept the cultural and environmental losses that industrial farming imposes as part of necessity itself. Sissinghurst is an irrelevance.

The positions are clear enough, but it is difficult to see any resolution of them. In my own mind, simply as a life choice, I am entirely on the side of those like Patrick who say that for our own good, let alone the future's, we must choose the better ideal, not to remain clamped into the sterility of a moribund global production system, but each of us bubbling up into one of Patrick's million little cells of resilience.

✦ ✦ ✦

Summer 2008: *Growing beans and peas in the new vegetable garden.*

WENDELL BERRY, THE KENTUCKY FARMER AND POET, has a potent phrase for the assertion and dominance of agribusiness and the destruction of the American family farm: "the unsettling of America." The foundations of the culture have been eroded by the industrialization of food and by the emptying of rural landscapes. We are living in an unsettled world. As long ago as 1993, as Berry has pointed out, the U.S. Census Bureau decided no longer to count as a separate category people who lived on farms. They had become statistically insignificant.

The same story can be told all across the United Kingdom. Oliver Walston's trajectory in East Anglia from eight farm workers in the 1950s to 2.15 now (including himself) is symptomatic. Ten million European farmers have left the land since the 1950s. Even Sissinghurst's neighbor farm, Brissenden, which in 2009 constituted one thousand arable acres farmed by Robert Lewis with the help of a single employee, had in the recent past been part of fourteen different farms (Bettenham, Brissenden, Catherine Wheel, Church Farm, Beale Farm, Commenden, Hammer Mill Farm, East Olney, West Olney, Park Farm in Biddenden, Whitsunden, Buckhurst, Ponds Farm, and Street Farm). Nearly all those farmsteads are medieval; some go back to the Dark Ages. None of them now, except Brissenden, is connected to the land. A world that was almost continuous for fifteen hundred years disappeared in the 1970s and '80s. The fate of Sissinghurst, described in these pages, was common.

Robert Lewis told me something of the Brissenden story. He is a strong, bluff man, although a little shy, with a way of looking at you from a distance, with an evaluating pause, not a seeker of the limelight, but direct, without side, happy to plow his own furrow and to work hard for the goals he identified long ago: a planned approach, a systematic outcome, efficiency, self-reliance. "I have always got on with things quietly. It has served me better." He came to Brissenden from Essex in 1974, as farm manager for the landowners, Thomas and Margery James. Professor James was a lawyer at King's College London and Margery had been a botanist at Kew. They had in mind, from the 1960s onward, to make a landholding in Kent that would be viable in the modern world.

Gradually, from the 1960s through to the '80s, the Jameses expanded their farm, always folding the profit into new acquisitions. It had begun with Bettenham and Brissenden, the two farms my father sold them in 1963. When Robert arrived, it was still a bundle of small, ill-drained fields, nothing but "cow pats and water grass," he says, "derelict dairy farms which we were welding together to make a single unit." It was a challenge he relished. He was twenty-seven then, away from his own county, surrounded by farming neighbors who were "difficult" with him. "Some were better than others. But the point is we were doing something and most of them were sitting on their hands. There was a fair bit of jealousy." Perhaps they were waiting for the whole enterprise to "go tits up," as stock farmers say. But it didn't and Robert rationalized the stretch of country that increasingly fell into his hands. He took out hedges, made some enormous fields, one of them nearly half a mile long, put in drainage, demolished and moved many buildings, laid a lot of concrete, got rid of any animals in what had been almost entirely cattle and meadow country, and started turning in rich and rewarding yields of wheat, barley, oats, rape, and beans. In those corners too wet to drain, he planted thousands of trees, plantations in which his beloved night-ingales, mistle thrushes, nuthatches, wrens, woodpeckers, treecreepers, and grey wagtails all now gather.

"The locals complained a lot," he says, "but it has been an un-qualified success. The farm is in better heart than when it was found." It had been heavily infested with black grass and wild oats. That has been largely dealt with. Over one hundred acres are now in an environmental scheme of one kind or another. "It is all you could do with it. The soil is silty, better than the sand up at Sissinghurst, but you couldn't begin to farm it organically. It is not easy ground. It is not even girls' ground. Everybody says they have the worst land in England, but this is hungry, low in potash and phosphate. You would be very pushed to do anything different here."

To someone of my persuasion, the Brissenden story is a tragedy. There is of course no doubting the good intentions of Robert Lewis or the Jameses. They were pursuing a goal of "improvement" when con-fronted with a place that looked as if it had failed. But it too is a version of failure. Robert told me how the soft wheat he now grows here gets trucked in lorries to the big container port at Tilbury, pumped into the holds of giant bulk carriers, and shipped to Dubai and other parts far-ther east to make chapatis. No sense of local provenance, nor of local habits, has survived the great transformation. The landscape of his vast fields is, despite the green corners and edges, fiercely denuded. He farms with extreme care; there is almost no sign of herbicide spray drifting beyond the farmed area. The whole place is neat beyond belief. In the springtime, there are plenty of wildflowers, buttons of primroses, cuckoopint, and wood anemones, on the farm. But the bulk and heart of it is dreary, charmless, delocalized. The vast fields might be anywhere. No sense of the past has survived the rationalization. Any idea of it being a place with a history and memories has been suppressed. Its past is no longer legible and the form of the land does not speak. Perhaps it murmurs, muffled. When walking on one of the footpaths that still crisscross it (and which Robert meticulously clears and signposts) I only want to leave, to find myself in the country I know. From every yard you can read only distant markets, global supplies. No one is here. Nothing comes from here and nothing is destined for here. There is no cycle, only inputs and outputs. Compared with the meadows and hedges, the small fields and intimate landscapes, the cherry orchards and field ponds of those few Low Weald farms that have survived largely unchanged, this is desecration. The truth is—and Robert knows this—I hate it.

When a German coconut plantation was created on Samoa in the 1880s, next to the house in which Robert Louis Stevenson was living, he saw in it

> no bush, no soul stirring; only acres of empty sward, miles of cocoa-nut alley: a desert of food. For the Samoan, there is something barbaric, unhandsome, and absurd in the idea of thus growing food only to send it from the land and sell it. A man at home who should turn all Yorkshire into one wheatfield, and annually burn his harvest on the altar of Mumbo-Jumbo, might impress ourselves not much otherwise. The nearest villages have suffered most; they see over the hedge the lands of their ancestors waving with useless cocoa-palms.

A desert of food is what I see in Brissenden and all the millions of acres like it. And there is something absurd in it too. When I asked Robert what proportion of his profit on these acres was represented by the subsidy he receives from the European Union, the Single Farm

Payment, he looked at me and said, "All of it?" That fact, and the whole place, is an offering on the altar of Mumbo-Jumbo.

IN THE LANGUAGE INSTINCT, Steven Pinker, now a professor of psychology at Harvard, very carefully describes how language is rich in redundancy. We don't need to say half the things we do. We consistently say a great deal more than need requires. The most obvious wastage, as Pinker points out, is in the vowels. We can leave vowels out of the picture and still make our meaning clear. Yxx mxy fxnd thxs sxrprxsxng, bxt yxx cxn rxxd thxs sxntxncx xnd xndxrstxnd xt, cxn't yxx? Sntcs lk ths cn stll, n fct, b ndrstd, lthgh ths s rthr mr dffclt nd slghtl slwr thn th sntnc wth th xs whr th vwls shld b.

You can read it but it's not English, and tht tght-lppd, clppd wy f tlkng sounds a little mad. It's not human. The natural human manner is voluble, assertive, openmouthed, vowelly, and oversupplied with signals. That communicative generosity is a sign of humanity itself, a form of biophilia, the love of vitality itself. The ever-present but strictly unnecessary vowels are, it turns out, symptoms of a much more general phenomenon. We surround ourselves with a thick meaning blanket, a pelt of significance. We don't spit sharp little pellets of predigested information at each other like sharp-beaked, defensive, aggressive owls. We lounge together in the same meaning bath. Redundancy, an oversupply of meaning, and a certain inefficiency are the defining qualities of a humane life.

This is an intriguing idea. For something of human and cultural value to be communicated, something more than that has to be cultivated at the same time. The stripped-down meaning, the thing made efficient, the thing reduced to essentials, has lost something essential in the process. Fuzz is more accurate than core. There is no such thing as a core meaning and a précis always lies because meaning is spread throughout whatever appears contingent or nearly irrelevant. Imprecision is the first requirement of understanding. Clarity obscures the nature of what it hopes to clarify.

The landscape is also a language. If you don't want change to involve loss of meaning, the key question is: what about the vowels? What about the soft, subtle, pervasive, and evasive, apparently inessential things that make so much of what is important but that can't be measured, or not easily? What about the darkness of the sky at night, the bendiness of the lanes, the nature and form of the hedges, the precise form of the latches with which the gates open and close, the ways in which the orchard trees are pruned, the habits and colors of the local cows, the hereness of any particular here?

Summer 2009: *New hedges and ditches, planted and dug on the old lines, divide up the Sissinghurst arable fields.*

There is a difference between Sssnghrst or even Sxssxnghxrst, loca-
tions whose meaning can be understood but that read like components
of a formula or marks on a despatch docket, and Sissinghurst, a rounded
being, which I have always thought of as entirely female, like a sister
turned into a place, a fully syllabled, generous description of home.

If we only attend to the consonants, and reduce a place to its efficient functions, if we make the operation of a stretch of country financially and technologically efficient, if we make it singular and pointed,
rather than multiple and rounded, then a good environment—that is, a
good place in which to live—will have been damaged. You might even
say that the more unimportant something seems, the more important it
is. Redundancy is all. Compare a place you love with somewhere no one
could possibly love, perhaps one of those stretches of mown grass on the
outside of an intersection, a curved region that looked good on the road
engineer's plan but in reality is a piece of curved vacuity. One seems like
a place and the other no more than a place where a place should be.
And the difference between them lies in a certain unnecessary complexity, a bobbled scurf of things, the trace of the past, the embedded
quirk, the wrinkle in a face, the burble of a particular family's or a particular person's lack of clarity.

It is the distinction between a landscape and a place. Landscape is
an idea but place is a sense. Landscape requires a prospect, a surveying
eye, even a controlling and appropriating eye, place an embeddedness, a
skin experience, a kind of fleshy, sense-rich thickness. The only way to
enjoy summer in England, according to Horace Walpole, was "to have it
framed and glazed in a comfortable room." That is the landscape view.
Coleridge in 1802 saw the Cumbrian waterfall called Moss Force in full
spate, churning through its

> prison of rock, as if it turned the corners not from mechanic
> force, but with foreknowledge, like a fierce and skilful driver.
> Great masses of water, one after another, that in twilight one

might have feelingly compared them to a vast crowd of huge white bears, rushing one over the other against the wind—their long white hair shattering abroad in the wind.

That is an understanding of place. A landscape is seen; a place is experienced and known. And so the key the qualities of place may perhaps be complexity, multifariousness, hidden corners, both closeness and closedness. A place rather than a landscape allows the folding of individual energies and passions into its forms. It must in other words be full of the potential for change and development, for a sense that its potential might be fulfilled. A landscape is stilled, perfected, and inert.

We do not live in a great art gallery where objects stand exposed and isolated. The beauty of the places we love is webbed, interfolded, everything connected to everything else in a multidimensional grid over the extent of place and the depth of time. There are, inevitably, a thousand ways in which this idea of connectedness can make its presence felt in the real world. Take for example, as a barometer of intent, the place of the hedgehog, as a symbol of the sort of landscape this book is arguing for.

Nobody knows very much about the hedgehogs—how many there are, where they are, how many are needed for a viable population, how they cope with modern life, or, in a country teeming with foxes and badgers, their natural predators. But one thing now is certain: the hedgehogs of Britain are dying out at a rate of about a fifth of the population every four years. By 2025, they will be gone.

Does it matter? I think so. The hedgehog has always been the embodiment of something subtle and tender in the landscape. It is not a flamboyant creature, but quiet, nocturnal, and discreet. Even though it has a great sense of smell, it is not, on the whole, very clever. One owner tried to teach his hedgehog a simple lesson—open the red door for lunch—four thousand times. It never understood.

They doze in long summer grass where strimmers chop them up. They get tangled up in tennis nets. They die inside expanded polystyrene cups. The hedgehog smells something delicious left in the bottom of the cup, pushes its snout in to lick up the remains, and then finds the cup stuck to its prickles. Many have been found dead with yogurt pots and ice-cream containers clamped to their faces.

The hedgehog, in other words, seems to inhabit something of the underside of life, its existence largely hidden, its dignity silently preserved. It is an animal often persecuted (and eaten) but that has always appealed to those not attracted by the flash or cleverness of life.

They have been protected from hunting since 1981, although not, bizarrely, from torture when alive, which is easily done if you are that way inclined, as they are so easy to catch. But they are dying now in a less obvious way. The prospect of their loss seems dreadful, partly, I think, because the hedgehog should be seen as the symbol of a kind of world, or even of a certain frame of mind: self-absorbed, private, snuffling through the landscape, self-protective, neither very dynamic nor sharp but dignified and curiously important.

That understanding lies behind Philip Larkin's famous poem about a terrible moment of destruction in June 1979, when pushing his mower, a Qualcast Commodore, around his Hull garden:

> The mower stalled, twice; kneeling, I found
> A hedgehog jammed up against the blades,
> Killed. It had been in the long grass.
> I had seen it before, and even fed it, once.
> Now I had mauled its unobtrusive world
> Unmendably.

This discretion of the hedgehog is not just literary or sentimental: a kind of patient unobtrusiveness is its central characteristic. What the biologists call the hedgehog's "generalism," its lack of slick speciality, the way it noses for beetles, caterpillars, earwigs, and worms, sometimes eating frogs, baby mice, eggs, and chicks, its happy existence at the bottom of hedges and in people's back gardens, its inability to cope with very large, chemically denuded arable fields—in other words, its fondness for the private, the scruffy, and the marginal—all make it a measure of the state of the landscape's health as a whole. If a place isn't good for hedgehogs, it isn't good for anything else. That is what Larkin's poem is about: the Qualcast Commodore destroys the world of unobtrusiveness. Larkin never used the mower again.

The British Hedgehog Preservation Society has said that the hedgehog is "a useful chap to have around." Only in England would the conservation of wild mammals be discussed in these terms, but "a useful chap to have around" sounds strangely like what a hedgehog's rather modest description of itself might be. It might be that the removal of hedges has removed the hedgehogs' foraging habitat. It may be that the use of chemicals on arable fields has probably killed most of the insect prey and perhaps had a deleterious effect on the hedgehog's own metabolism. All this tidying up, the radical simplification of systems and the breaking of connections between elements that could and should be joined: all these are literally fatal for the hedgehogs. They love the gaps between things, the interstices, the rough brambly places, places to hide in the daytime or in winter. But the hedgehogs are still dying. Quite silently, an unobtrusive world is being mauled and, because it is largely invisible, nothing much is being said about it. The same could probably be said for the mole and, astonishingly, the bee. Farmland birds, let alone farmland snails and other invertebrates, are all on the same path. As a result these creatures, the barometer creatures, are, in our lifetimes, in danger of ending up as little more than memories.

This book is perhaps an argument and plea for the virtues of idiosyncrasy of which the hedgehog is the emblem. At its roots, idiosyncrasy means a "private commixture," a coming together of qualities that are characteristic of that thing alone. Idiosyncrasies are symptoms of the richness in things that are wholly themselves, and those are the reservoirs of value.

✦ ✦ ✦

THERE IS ANOTHER EUROPEAN FARMING STORY, recently described by the English anthropologist Jeffrey Pratt, that can be laid alongside this tale of the destruction of places and the dissociation of land from lives. It may be one model for the future. Until the 1990s, Tuscany, the beautiful hilly part of central Italy north of Rome, was considered backward in the world of agriculture. A particular history was deeply embedded there, and had shaped both the landscape and the culture of the people who lived in it. Since the Middle Ages, most of the land was owned by urban landlords. Rural tenants farmed it, sharing the profits with their urban masters. A steady flow of food was delivered to urban markets and an intimate web of relations bound together town and country. But the system kept the small farmers radically poor and each tenant family could focus on little more than subsistence for itself. The market did not penetrate their lives. So each farm was an entirely mixed enterprise: cattle, sheep, pigs, rabbits, chickens, pigeons, a patch of woodland for fuel and some arable land on which wheat, barley, oats, maize, beans, and hay to feed the oxen were all grown. Each farm had a tiny vineyard and terraced olive groves, figs, walnuts, almonds, and many fruit trees, as well as the all-important kitchen gardens. The diet was based on wine, olive oil, bread, and vegetables, enhanced now and then by cured meats and fruit preserves.

This deeply mixed farming created the Tuscan landscape, both a symptom of and a response to endemic and irremovable poverty. Only after 1945, led by the heroic political efforts of the Communists, did the impoverished sharecroppers claim a greater say in their lives, a greater share of the profits from their work, and finally ownership of the farms they had always thought of as their own. Efforts were then made to shift Tuscany onto a more industrialized path—fewer farms, fewer (richer) workers, fewer products—but largely they failed. Tuscany was too conservative to change. People were too bound to what they were. Many people left the land, but still by the mid-1960s, the average farm was little more than seventy acres. By the 1980s, the region had hit a crisis. Tuscan cereal farms were too small to supply the great Italian pasta makers and industrial bakeries, and the animal enterprises could not compete with large farms farther north in Europe.

Then, to the rescue, the most unexpected of saviors: tourism. New airports at Pisa and Florence, *autostrade*, bed-and-breakfasts in farms, and a rush of second-home owners, mostly Swiss, German, and English, combined to create a new "agritourism," as it is called in Italy, valuing the very things that the industrializing movement had tried to eradicate. All the delicious Tuscan meats, cheeses, wine, olive oil, and the polycultural landscape from which they emerged (combined with a large number of derelict stone houses) created a new market for a forgotten world. Twenty million tourists, eleven million of them foreigners, now visit Tuscany each year, sustaining a new version of the Tuscan life that had looked as if it was disappearing. Tourists can generate—or at least recreate and perpetuate—the kind of life and landscapes they love. So today in Tuscany, less than a quarter of all farms growing olive oil specialize in it. The vast majority of olives are grown on a domestic scale for domestic purposes, and two-thirds of the oil is sold by the farm that grows and makes it. The Tuscan regional government insists on local schools and local hospitals buying local produce and consistently promotes what they call "the Tuscan model": small farms; delicious food; many different sorts of food; good marketing networks; policies that see the environment and the agricultural landscape as assets not obstacles. "Tuscany has won the bet," as one regional government official said to Jeffrey Pratt. "In the past 'rurality' had a negative connotation, today 'rural' means good."

Maybe Tuscany is an anomaly. The remains of an overrigid, antiquated landscape and way of life just happened to fit neatly into the patterns of consumption that emerged in rich European countries in the late twentieth century. Maybe tourism is inherently vulnerable to the shortages in fossil fuels that are around the corner. And maybe the new Tuscany is not quite all it is said to be. In many Tuscan towns and villages, the tourist is nowadays all too aware that he is the motor of the economy, that what he has come to see is only there because he has come to see it.

In the balance, though, one can put an enormous amount of collective well-being, not only in those of us who have enjoyed Tuscany for decades, but of towns and villages once decrepit now glowing with health and wealth, and more than that with a sense that Tuscany has not abandoned its past. It is no Brissenden, it is not irrelevant to the thoughts of the government or their census takers. It has embraced a version of its past and transmuted it into a viable present. First the market and then government policy have reanimated a landscape in which the connections between the social, environmental, productive, aesthetic, historical, and sensuous dimensions of the world are seen in relation to one another, as the interlocking elements of a "territory," a place.

Perhaps Sissinghurst is a little Tuscany: somewhere in which the best desires of people coming to see it can generate the kinds of life and beauty they want to find there, not as an imposition from elsewhere, but drawing those things from a past that might otherwise have been abandoned. It is more difficult here because the food culture has long been dead and the appeals of intensive, delocalized agriculture have long been powerful. But one of the motives for writing this book is to say, Don't Forget! A better version is within living memory and still within reach.

The question of scale is important here. Science has in the last two hundred years discovered scales of space and time that we, as untutored human beings, can know nothing of. We live in units of space and time that are molded to us as organisms, in minutes, days, and years, not microseconds or geological eons; in yards and miles, not nanometers or light-years. Those body-scales represent the level at which things make the best sense to us. The unknowable source and the invisible destination are both profoundly disturbing. Sources and destinations that are seen and known are among the most settling of all human experiences. And so the creation of the rich place, the home landscape, animated by apparent and mutually fertilizing systems, in which the linkages are clear, represents a level of complexity that is perhaps the most satisfying thing on earth, the experience of the embedded life. It makes for a legible world in which understanding is intimate, shared, and cyclical.

In a beautiful passage from *Consilience*, the Harvard entomologist and philosopher Edward O. Wilson expressed it like this:

> We are confined to a razor-thin biosphere within which a thousand imaginable hells are possible but only one paradise. What we idealize in nature and seek to recreate is the peculiar physical and biotic environment that cradled the human species. The human body and mind are precisely adapted to this world, notwithstanding its trials and dangers, and that is why we think it beautiful. All species gravitate to the environment in which their genes were assembled. There lies survival for humanity, and there lies mental peace, as prescribed by our genes.

But, as he goes on, humanity has a competing self-image, one in which man has been "set free to modify Earth's surface to create a world better than the one our ancestors knew." That of course is the Walston view, the principal drive since the Renaissance, which sees itself as the more robust and worldly but is in fact, as Professor Wilson portrays it (and as Patrick Holden's search for renewed "resilience" implies), increasingly fragile. Natural ecosystems are designed for robustness and resilience, to absorb shocks. But the human environment depends on an ever-lengthening chain of technological fixes. Each

> is a prosthesis, an artificial device dependent on advanced expertise and intense continuing management. The environment,

increasingly rigged and strutted to meet the new demands, turns ever more delicate. It requires constant attention from increasingly sophisticated technology.

The disappearance of fossil fuels and artificial fertilizer will not only make conventional chemical farming impossible. It will remove both the distant markets and the distant sources of energy, seeds, and nutrients. Localism won't be a choice in that future world, it will be a necessity, and the necessity will feel good.

IN MAKING THESE SUGGESTIONS FOR SISSINGHURST I realize I have in mind something of enormous proportions, an invitation to something else, virtually forgotten and distinct from the air of management in which modern Sissinghurst, and everywhere like it, tends to live. I have been reading the sorts of books that I haven't read for decades, above all *The White Goddess*, that mysterious, passionate, and incomprehensible compendium in which Robert Graves tried in the 1940s to grasp the fragments of the old female nature deity, displaced four thousand years ago by the male gods, and which has survived now only in the margins of the civilized world. His book is a vast broken maze of inspiration and speculation, an attempt to address a forgotten understanding. *The White Goddess* is clouded with its own difficulties but for all that is driven for hundreds of pages by an adoration of the ancient powers of the turning world, the vibrancy and unforgivingness of nature, the source of poetry and being. Graves's goddess is huge and potent, not a sweet thing but "with the moon between her hip bones and crowned with ears of corn." She is capable of sweetness and cruelty, like the nature of the year itself. He used an ancient Irish song to describe her:

> I am a flood: *across a plain,*
> I am a wind: *on a deep lake,*

I am a hawk: *above a cliff,*
I am a thorn: *beneath a nail,*
I am a wonder: *among flowers,*
I am a wizard: *who but I*
Sets the cool head aflame with smoke?

I had long known that I could see this figure, bedraggled and in rags, walking the rain-soaked Kentish fields, and when I read the poem Graves had set at the head of his book, I took heart from it. "I am gifted," he had written,

> *even in November*
> *Rawest of seasons, with so huge a sense*
> *Of her nakedly worn magnificence*
> *I forget cruelty and past betrayal.*

Her nakedly worn magnificence: Graves at least had an understanding that nature, however battered, might again take the world in its arms; or at least that nature's broken and enormous condition might in some way be healed and restored in these fields. That, in another form of language, is what Edward Wilson, Patrick Holden, the Tuscans, and perhaps even Steven Pinker understood: that we are all dealing with a great and enveloping mystery.

LAST NIGHT WITH SOME FRIENDS I went out into the fields and we listened to a single nightingale in the scurfy wood, beginning its song again and again, each time a new variant on what had come before, as if nothing inherited or borrowed was worth considering. Every snatch of its song was unfinished, an experiment in gurgle-beauty. You wanted him to go on but he didn't, always stopping when the song was half made. We listened, standing in the warm wind, waiting for the next raid on inventiveness. Every part of that bird's mind was restless,

on and on, never settling on a known formula, an unending, self-renewing addiction to the new, to another way of doing it, and then
another, all in the service of a listening mate and the survival of genes.
That is the nightingale's irony: his brilliantly variable song is indistinguishable from his father's or his son's. Invention is nothing but the
badge of his race. It is as if new and old in him were indistinguishable.
That is the nightingale lesson: inventing the new is his form of repeat-
ing the past.

Is that the model here? Is that how we should do it too? I have
been making some radio programs about Homer and his landscapes.
Reading the *Odyssey* now, at the end of this Sissinghurst story, brings
something home to me. People think of it as the great poem of adven-
ture and mystery, of a man traveling to strange worlds beyond the
horizon, of the threat and challenge of the sea. That is true, but it is
only half of it. The second part, as long as the other, is devoted to
something else: Odysseus's homecoming to Ithaca and his ferocious
desire, in the middle of his life, after twenty years away, to reform the
place he finds, to steer it back onto a path it abandoned many years
before. Homer certainly knew about homecoming. Odysseus thinks
that all he need do is recreate the order he remembers from his youth,
to cleanse the place of everything wrong that has grown up in the
meantime and reestablish a kind of purity and simplicity over which
he can preside. I hear the echoes of what I have done. "Nowhere is
sweeter," Homer says, as Odysseus bends to kiss the green turf of
Ithaca, "than a man's own country." That is what we might like to
think, but the truth is harder. Nowhere is the desire for sweetness
stronger than in a man's own country and nowhere is it more difficult
to achieve.

Odysseus soon realizes that home is not safe or steady. If he is to
reestablish the order he remembers, he has to use all sorts of cunning
and persuasion, and in the end even that is not enough. His longed-for
sweetness clashes with the realities of imposing it on a place that has

changed. The resolution the poem comes to is terrifying: Odysseus slaughters every one of the young men who have been living in his house and corrupting it. He leaves the palace littered with their bodies and his own skin slobbered with their guts—his thighs, Homer says at the end of the killing, are "shining" with their blood—and then, with the help of his son, strings up the girls those men have been sleeping with, their legs kicking out, the poem says, like little birds that have been looking for a roost but have found themselves caught in a hidden snare. Odysseus thinks of it as a cleansing, a return to goodness, but the poem knows that the desire for sweetness has ended only in horror and mayhem. He thinks that order can be imposed by will; the poem knows that the vision of perfection brings war into a house and leaves it broken and bloodied.

It is a sobering drama, an anti-Arcadia, with a deep lesson: singular visions do not work; only by consensus and accommodation can the good world be made; returning wanderers do not have all the answers; and anything that is to be done in your own Ithaca can only be done by understanding other people's needs and their unfamiliar desires. Complexity, multiplicity is all, and clarified solutions come at a brutal price.

So the nightingale has it. Newness is not a new quality. Ingenuity and inventiveness are central parts of life, human and nonhuman. Stay loose, it says; don't rigidify; accept that you have inherited from the past many beautiful and varied ways of being. And once you know that, sing your song, which attends to the present, and is even a hymn to the present, to the long sense of possibility that has the past buried inside it. Elegy, which is a longing for an abandoned past, is not enough. Elegy, in fact, may do terrible Odyssean damage. It feeds off regret, and even though regret is beautiful and moving, it gives nothing to the future. Regret is a curmudgeon with a way of stringing up the innocent girls. This story, then, is a lyric, a song to what might be, not a longing for what has been.

✦ ✦ ✦

AMONG THE THOUSANDS OF DOCUMENTS in the files of the Kent County Archives in Maidstone, there are two giant vellum pages, stitched together along the bottom edge with vellum strips and carrying the seals and signatures of eleven different individuals. Each page is over two feet wide and eighteen inches high, and both are covered from top to bottom in the tiny, exact, but very clear handwriting of the clerk who drew them up.

The document looks as if it might be medieval, or perhaps the translation of something medieval, written on a burnished sheepskin, with the vast Gothic headline "This Indenture Tripartite" painted across the top. It is in fact less than two hundred years old, an agreement made in May 1811 between Sir Horatio Mann, Edward Mann's nephew, from whom he had inherited the ownership of Sissinghurst, and a set of eight individuals, described as "Yeomen of Cranbrook," who were renewing their lease on renting the farm here. It is both an ancient thing, dripping in its medieval inheritance, looking like a treaty drawn up after Agincourt, and a modern one, an arrangement for the welfare officers in Cranbrook, which is what these men were, to rent the farm so that the poor of the parish could live and work there and support themselves: a job creation scheme of a modern and enlightened kind.

When I first read this document, something else came bowling toward me. This lease, in its attention to the details of the land and the habits by which it was managed, was a voice from the old world. But it was also a summons to do things like it again. It was shaped by the attitudes that I felt Sissinghurst needed, a level of care and understanding that the late twentieth century had almost entirely abandoned. People had always accused me of "wanting to turn the clock back." It was a phrase that seemed wide of the mark to me, dependent on the idea that the passage of time was a singular and univalent process, that the present needed to leave the past behind. I was not interested in turning the clock either backward or forward. I simply wanted to make the place as good as it could be.

The indenture, with its wavy upper edge, was a lease for twenty-one years, renewing another that the Cranbrook yeomen had made a few years earlier. They were now to pay £318 a year as rent, in four equal quarters, in January, April, July, and October. The land they were renting at Sissinghurst, called simply "Sissinghurst Farm," was "by estimation 342 acres and a half," in thirty-seven different parcels of arable, meadow, and pastureland. The grass in the meadow was allowed to grow for hay; the pasture was to be grazed all year. There were eight acres of hops and extensive woodland.

All hedges had to be preserved "from the bite and spoil of cattle." If any fruit trees died or were blown down, "other good and young fruit trees of the same or better sort" had to be set in their place. Hedges had to be laid (every nine years) and good ditches made alongside them. They had to keep the buildings in good repair and pay for the window glass, leadwork, straw for any thatching, and the carriage of materials. Mann's steward agreed to provide out of the rent enough rough timber, brick, tiles, lime, and iron for the work to be done.

This has a modern ring to it, a negotiated sharing out of tasks and costs. But in relationship to the land there was something much deeper, to do with a vision of cyclicality and self-sufficiency that seemed both extraordinarily and deeply primitive, laying down rules for this place that embodied almost total self-sustenance, and a form of clarion call for us.

First of all, the tenants were not allowed to carry away from the farm any of the farm's own produce. Any hay, straw, fodder, unthreshed grain, compost, manure, or dung "which now is or shall at any time during the said term grow arise or be made upon or from or by means of the said demised premises" had to stay there. Sissinghurst's fertility had to be kept at Sissinghurst because its long-term viability as a farm relied on those nutrients remaining to be recycled into the ground. The tenants "shall and will there imbarn stack and fodder out all such hay Straw and Fodder." They were to see that the compost, manure, or dung "shall and will in a good husbandlike manner [be] laid spread and bestowed in and upon those parts of the land which seem most to need it." This is something the lease repeats insistently. "They shall and will constantly during the said term use plough sow manure mend farm and occupy the said demised lands and premises in a good tenantlike manner and according to the custom of the country in which the same are situate. And so as to ameliorate and to improve and not impoverish the same." I thought, when I read those words, that they should be set up on a carved board at the entrance to the barn. I realized that they encapsulated, two centuries ago, exactly what I hoped for from my modern farm-and-restaurant scheme, which was having such difficulties finding its way to reality. This sense of self-enrichment was exactly what I had been stumbling after.

Here was a template for what we could do, for another way of looking at this place, which ran deep into its roots. It was essentially a cyclical vision. It did not imagine that next year would be very different from this, nor was it an exercise in progress. It felt for the health of the land in a way that understood it as a body, with all the implications of that organic analogy. It was not a fantasy of wholeness, but a working system, tied to earnings, rents, money, and returns. It understood about the need for money on both sides, and the careful regulation of costs and responsibilities, but it did not single out money over all other aspects. It understood that money was one outcome, not the only one. And it understood that the land could only give what was put in. It was a picture of constancy and interrelatedness, not in any Wordsworthian ecstasy of revelation or understanding, but in a lease, a formal document made between the baronet and the yeomen of Cranbrook, drawn up by the lawyers. There, preserved in the county archives, was an invitation to the future. It was a world based on cud. A love of cud—that slow, delicious, juicy recycling of the nutritious thing—was what Sissinghurst needed. This was its unfinished history, its folding of the past into the future in the way that a cook stirs sugar into a cake.

What is it, then, that makes for beauty in a farmed place, that makes it stand out and apart from the beauty of the wild? It is at least in part a recognition of its fruitfulness, of the earth there being prepared to give some sustenance to the people who work it and work with it. But in each field, here or anywhere fields have lasted some time, there is something more than that. Each field is a small world, a particular vision, a definite history, cut off from the others and from the waste beyond them. Each is a history of care, as much as a person, or a tended animal. A field holds its own stories inside its boundaries and its essence is that the natural and the cultural have been allowed and even encouraged to come to an accommodation there. The field in that way is an act of symbiosis, the product of a human contract with the natural. In a field we are neither alien nor omnipotent. Fields belong to us but there are things beyond us in them. We shape them, make them, control them, name them, hedge them, gate them, plow them, mow them, reap them, and plow them again, but they are not what we are. They are our partners. Or at least that is their ideal condition. Industrialized farming is often painful and disturbing because it involves the breaking of that contract and the chemical reduction of partner to slave. It doesn't need to be like that. It has usually, in human history, not been like that. The good farm is witness to a concordance between the human and the natural, a mutuality, as Wendell Berry has written about his own farmland, in which "every move / Answers what is still."

I think that the farmed landscape is the most beautiful thing the human race has ever made. There is no need to be parochial about this: the great temperate belt, below the great forest and above the great desert, the humanobiosphere, girdling the earth, humanizing it, is the great human habitat, the monument to symbiosis, to human and natural interpenetration. Is that human-devised skin wrapped around the earth no more than a product of an economic desire to survive, to get the food in? Surely not. More than the wilderness, it is our world, essentially cooperative and the great testament to what we are.

My particular problem at Sissinghurst—that I am both in it and excluded from it, that it is mine and not mine, that it has me by the heart but there is no possession there, that in some ways it is a source of life and meaning and in others a trap—all of this is only a heightened version of what our general relationship to place always has to be. We are all dispossessed. We are mortal, the earth is not ours, and we are transient passengers, even parasites on it. And so almost by definition we must do things on it and with it that stand to be good in the long term. In my own mind, I have arrived at a particular phrase: the honorable landscape. Honor is the only thing that survives death. Honor is the denial of self and time. Honor understands about the virtue of the broad compass, of taking account as much as possible of what matters. Honor is not singular. It stands outside the claims of the ego, the desire to exploit, dominate, or spoil. It understands about mutuality and the folding in of contradictory desires into a single variegated but integrated

I do my part in the new orchard.

whole. It is a social and moral quality, founded on a self-renewing respect for the reality of others. It may be a hopelessly antiquated formulation, but that in the end is what I am interested in here.

I AM LEAVING THIS STORY when it is quite unfinished. There are a thousand and one steps still to take. I sit on the step of the barn at Sissinghurst and look at the clouds streaming away in front of me to the northeast. That is what the future looks like too: avenues of bubbled possibility. The future here seems just as long as the past that extends behind it. Everything that Vita and Harold responded to when they came here nearly eighty years ago is still alive, but I also remember what John Berger wrote in *Pig Earth*: "The past is never behind. It is always to the side." That is true. The past is everywhere around me, coexistent with present and future, soaked into this soil but not sterilizing it. There is no hierarchy. Past, present, and future are all equally coexistent and Sissinghurst is becoming a place that responds to all three. And through that reconnection Sissinghurst will once again reacquire, I hope, a sense of its own middle, a confidence that it can turn to its own resources and find untold riches there. It will become, in the best possible sense of the word, its own place. That is the word to which this book has been devoted: place as the roomiest of containers for human meaning; place as the medium in which natural and cultural, inherited and invented, individual and communal can all fuse and fertilize. I don't remember anything in my own life that has made me look at the world with such a surge of optimism and hope.

1950s: Captain Beale with his ewes on the Bettenham meadows.

Acknowledgments

THE LENGTH OF THIS LIST OF ACKNOWLEDGMENTS IS itself a sign of how many layers of thought and direction go into running a place like Sissinghurst. It is a deeply complicated business.

First, I must thank the four people without whom the farm project at Sissinghurst would never have happened: Sally Bushell, the National Trust's property manager; Jonathan Light, until recently the area manager; Sue Saville, regional director in the southeast; and Fiona Reynolds, director-general of the Trust. Sissinghurst owes them all untold thanks.

Beyond them, I would like to thank everyone in the National Trust who has given me and Sissinghurst their help and expertise over the last few years, in particular David Adshead, Jane Arnott, Mike Buffin, Tony Burton, Tim Butler, Sue Clement, Michelle Cleverley, Andy Copestake, Ivo Dawnay, Ed Diestelkamp, Jane Fletcher, Louisa Freeman-Owen, Harry Goring, Sue Herdman, Rob Jarman, Lynne Kemp, Sue Knevett, Rob Macklin, Maggie Morgan, Simon Murray, Peter Nixon, Matthew Oates, Dottie Owens, William and Merry Proby, Stuart Richards, Richard Saville, Emma Slocombe, Sarah Staniforth, Caroline Thackray, Sue Wilkinson, and Richard Wheeler.

The changes this book describes have not been easy and I am immensely grateful to everyone working at Sissinghurst for tolerating the disruptions they have caused, especially to Claire Abery, Stephen Barnett, Maddie Bell, Di Bennett, Sam Butler, Ginny Coombes, Amy Covey, Alexis Datta, Emma Davies, Peter Dear, Stacey Deaves, Sue East, Peter Fifield,

Gavin Fuller, Anita Goodwin, Jo Jones, Matthew Law, Tom Lupton, Daniel Mead, Clemmie Mendes, Philip and Joy Norton, Lynda Pearce, Tim Prior, Heather Reece, David Reynolds, Victoria Roberts, Sarah Roots, Jacqui Ruthven, Jean Shill, Wendy and Tony Tremenheere, Sue Watson, Barbara White, Maggie White, Caroline Wilding, Nathanael Wilkins, and Michelle Woodcock.

Mary Stearns, Brian and Linda Clifford, and Pat, Catherine, and the late James Stearns are all members of a family that has been at Sissinghurst since the 1920s. They have helped me enormously with their time, memories, insights, and the loan of precious photographs and documents.

My own family has been encouragement itself, none more than my wife, Sarah Raven, who from the beginning has poured untold amounts of energy and time into the farm project; my sisters Juliet and Rebecca Nicolson; my children, Tom, William, Ben, Rosie, and Molly Nicolson; my cousins Vanessa Nicolson and Robert Sackville-West; my nieces Flora and Clemmie Macmillan-Scott; as well as the irreplaceable Charles Anson and David O'Rourke.

Many friends have helped in different ways: Simon Bishop, Charlie Boxer, Emma Bridgewater, Helen Browning, Jonathan Buckley, Carla Carlisle, Antonio Carluccio, Sue Clifford, Priscilla Conran, Harry Cory-Wright, Tim Dee, Sheila Dillon, Montagu and Sarah Don, Martin Drury, Jo Fairley, Hugh Fearnley-Whittingstall, Simon and Lucinda Fraser, Katrin Hochberg, Patrick Holden, Glenn Horowitz, Mary Keen, William Kendall, Angela King, Robin Leach, John and Kate Leigh-Pemberton, Tom Maynard, Pip Morrison, Tom Oliver, Andrew Palmer, Anna Pavord, Dan Pearson, Thomas and Flora Pennybacker, Sorley Pennybacker, Johann Perry, Matthew Rice, Sigrid Rausing, Norman Rose, Jacob Rothschild, Peter Rumley, Craig Sams, Claire Spottiswoode, Phil Stocker, Penny Tweedie, Guy Watson, Peter Weeden, Claire Whalley, Kim Wilkie, Fred Windsor-Clive, and Sofka Zinovieff.

Others who have unstintingly given their assistance are: Tony Allison, Nicola Bannister, Peter Brandon, Betty Carman, Hadrian Cook, Nicholas

Cooper, George Ellis, Lorraine Flisher, Douglas Green, Paula Henderson, Mark Hoare, Jeremy Hodgkinson, Maurice Howard, Alastair Laing, Todd Longstaffe-Gowan, Tom Maynard, Nick Newell, Susan Pittman, Ernie Pollard, Lee Prosser, Jeremy Purseglove, Ben Raskin, Kirsty Righton, Margaret Richardson, Tony Singleton, Michael Zell.

Caroline Dawnay and Zoe Pagnamenta have been stalwart allies as ever. At HarperCollins in the UK, Susan Watt, Pria Taneja, Vera Brice, and Helen Ellis have worked their usual miracles. In particular I would like to thank Peter Wilkinson for drawing the maps.

In the US, at Viking, I would like to thank Barbara Campo, Francesca Belanger, Beth Tondreau, Kevin Doughton, Maggie Riggs, and above all Wendy Wolf; they have the great and irreplaceable gift of making the writing, editing, design and production of books seem important. No writer could ask for anything more valuable than that.

Derrick Bradbury's picture of Sissinghurst was identified only by chance. He very kindly had it photographed for this book. If there is anyone else who knows of images, artifacts, plans, or pictures of Sissinghurst, please get in touch with the author at adam@shiantisles.net.

Illustration Credits

Text photographs

Page iv, Derek Adkins; page viii, Jonathan Buckley; page 5, author's collection; page 7, Derek Adkins; page 9, © English Heritage. NMR Aerofilms Collection; page 15, author's collection; page 16, Country Life Picture Library ; page 18, Edwin Smith / RIBA Library Photographs Collection; page 19, Ian Graham; page 22, author's collection; page 29 (left), Edwin Smith /RIBA Library Photographs Collection; page 29 (right), author's collection; page 32, Country Life Picture Library; page 35, Ray Hallett; page 41, Kerry Dundas; page 51, Country Life Picture Library; page 55, Mary Stearns; page 57, Mary Stearns; page 58, author's collection; page 68, author's collection; page 79, author's collection ; page 82, author's collection; page 86, author's collection; page 89 (top and bottom) author's collection ; page 99, author's collection; page 111, author's collection; page 120, Mary Stearns; page 127, Peter Dear; page 131, Mary Stearns; page 140, J.E. Downward; page 148, author's collection; page 153, Peter Dear; page 160, author's collection; page 166, author's collection; page 169, Edwin Smith / RIBA Library Photographs Collection; page 173, author's collection; page 176, author's collection; page 178, Denney; page 181, author's collection; page 183, author's collection; page 185, National Trust / Derrick E. Witty; page 193, National Archives, London; page 198, author's collection; page 199, National Archives, London; page 200, author's collection; page 202, Derrick Bradbury; page 205, Centre for Kentish Studies, Maidstone; page 206, author's collection; page 207, Peter Dear; page 209, author's collection; page 210, P. Andre; page 213, author's collection; page 218, Mary Stearns; page 219, Mary Stearns; page 221, author's collection; page 222, Mary Stearns; page 225, author's collection;

page 236, C. Conte; page 239, author's collection; page 240, Swaine; page 245, author's collection; page 246, author's collection; page 248, author's collection; page 251, author's collection; page 253, author's collection; page 256, Kurt Hutton; page 259, author's collection; page 261, Cecil Beaton / Sothebys Picture Library; page 263, Roloff Beny; page 265, author's collection; page 271, NTPL / Penny Tweedie; page 272, NTPL/ Penny Tweedie; page 273, NTPL / Penny Tweedie; page 275, author's collection; page 284, NTPL / Penny Tweedie; page 285, author's collection; page 286, author's collection; page 297, author's collection; page 302, author's collection; page 319, author's collection; page 321, Mary Stearns

Color insert photographs
1. ©NTPL / Jonathan Buckley; 2. ©NTPL / Jonathan Buckley; 3. ©NTPL / Jonathan Buckley; 4. ©NTPL / Jonathan Buckley; 5. author's collection; 6. © Penny Tweedie; 7. ©NTPL / Jonathan Buckley; 8. ©NTPL / Jonathan Buckley; 9. ©NTPL / John Hammond; 10. ©NTPL / Jonathan Buckley; 11. ©NTPL / Jonathan Buckley; 12. ©NTPL / Penny Tweedie; 13. © Penny Tweedie; 14. KEO films.com Ltd 2008

Note on Sources

FOR THE EARLY HISTORY OF KENT, articles in the volumes of *Archaeologia Cantiana* are invaluable. Many are now online at www. kentarchaeology.org.uk.

Frans Vera's *Grazing Ecology and Forest History* (CABI Publishing, 2000) provides a new and fascinating perspective on the early environmental history of the Kentish forest. Oliver Rackham's *Woodlands* (Harper-Collins, 2006) ties Vera's suggestions into a more traditional English frame. William Anderson, in *The Green Man* (HarperCollins, 1990), is a source of rich speculation on the meaning and significance of that near-universal wood symbol, and G. H. Garrad, *A Survey of the Agriculture of Kent* (Royal Agricultural Society, 1954), provides a detailed account of the Kentish farmer's response to his environment. Henry Cleere and David Crossley, *The Iron Industry of the Weald*, 2nd ed. (Merton Priory Press, 1995), speculate fascinatingly on the Weald under Roman occupation and give a full description of the early modern iron industry.

J. K. Wallenberg's study *The Place-Names of Kent* (Uppsala, 1934) and K. P. Witney's *The Jutish Forest: A Study of the Weald of Kent, 450–1380 AD* (Athlone Press, 1976) are the classic accounts of the early medieval penetration of the Wealden forest around Sissinghurst. K. P. Witney's edition of *The Survey of Archbishop Peacham's Kentish Manors, 1283–85* (Maidstone: Kent Archaeological Society, 2000) takes that movement up into the high Middle Ages.

For Sissinghurst's social environment in the sixteenth century, see Michael Zell's *Industry in the Countryside: Wealden Society in the Sixteenth*

Century (Cambridge, 1994) and a volume of essays edited by him, *Early Modern Kent, 1540–1640* (Boydell Press, 2000). Maurice Howard, *The Building of Elizabethan and Jacobean England* (Yale, 2007), and Malcolm Airs, *The Tudor and Jacobean Country House: A Building History* (Sutton Publishing, 1995), combined with Caroline van Eck, *British Architectural Theory, 1540–1750* (Ashgate, 2003), describe the philosophical, political, and practical world in which the new Sissinghurst was made. For the use and aesthetics of the park around it, see the essays in Robert Liddiard, ed., *The Medieval Park: New Perspectives* (Windgather Press, 2007). Descriptions of Sir John Baker's murderous behavior can be found in *Foxe's Book of Martyrs*, which is online in a variorum edition at www.hrionline.ac.uk /johnfoxe/. Early modern histories of the Weald are William Lambarde, *A Perambulation of Kent* (London, 1570), John Philipott, *Villare Cantianum or Kent Surveyed and Illustrated* (1659), and the great Edward Hasted's *History of the County of Kent* (1790). The three-volume *History of the Weald of Kent* by Robert Furley (Ashford, 1871), although often muddly, is full of fascinating sidelights. Nigel Nicolson's short *Sissinghurst Castle: An Illustrated History* (National Trust, 1964) has remained in print for over forty years. Contemporary accounts of Elizabeth's progresses were gathered by John Nichols in the late eighteenth century. Many, including the list of those who came to stay at Sissinghurst in 1573, are now online at www2 .warwick.ac.uk/fac/arts/ren/projects/nichols/progresses/.

Papers of the Mann estate, including many relating to Sissinghurst, are kept in the Centre for Kentish Studies in Maidstone (U24). Quarter Session Records, detailing the Elizabethan park invasions, are there too. Accounts of the plot to destroy the ironworks at Hammer Mill are in the Staffordshire County Record Office. References are all available on www .a2a.org.uk.

A printed copy of the sermon by Robert Abbott, vicar of Cranbrook, *The holinesse of Chrisian [sic] Churches, or a Sermon preached at the consecration of the chappell of Sr. Iohn Baker: of Sussing-herst in Cranbrooke in Kent, Baronet* (London, 1638), is in the library of St. John's College, Cambridge. For papers relating to the sequestration of the Baker estates in the Civil War, see SP/19, 20, 23, and 28 in the National Archives in Kew. The probate Inventory of Dame Elizabeth Howard's possessions at Sissinghurst in 1694 is also there under PROB 5/3715.

Sissinghurst as an eighteenth-century prisoner-of-war camp is described in Francis Abell, *Prisoners of War in Britain, 1756–1815* (Oxford University Press, 1914), and referred to by Edward Gibbon in his *Journal*, ed. D. M. Low (Chatto & Windus, 1929). The Admiralty files in the National Archives contain the long and fascinating transcript of an "Examination of complaints of prisoners at Sissinghurst" (ADM 105/42) held in 1761, and, under ADM 97/114/2, "Letters to and from French prisoners held in England 1756–63," many of them at Sissinghurst.

C. C. R. Pile's short leaflet on *The Parish Farm at Sissinghurst Castle* (Cranbrook and Sissinghurst Local History Society, 1952) remains the best account of Sissinghurst Castle Farm as Cranbrook's "Old Cow." MAF 32/1022/101 in the National Archives contains the 1941 Farm Survey Records for Cranbrook in which Captain Beale's farm is revealed in all its perfection.

The Vita Sackville-West and Harold Nicolson years at Sissinghurst have been written about more than any other. Vita herself wrote *Country Notes* (Michael Joseph, 1939), and many collections of her *Observer* articles have been in print since the 1950s. Anne Scott-James's *Sissinghurst: The Making of a Garden* was published by Michael Joseph in 1975. Jane Brown's *Vita's Other World: A Gardening Biography of V. Sackville-West* (Viking, 1985) set Sissinghurst in wider context. Tony Lord, *Gardening at Sissinghurst* (Frances Lincoln, 1995), focused tightly on the garden here, bed by bed. Nigel Nicolson edited Harold Nicolson's *Diaries and Letters*, 3 vols. (Collins, 1966–68), and in 1973 published *Portrait of a Marriage* (Weidenfeld & Nicolson), about his parents' marriage and homosexual infidelities. His own autobiography, *Long Life* (Weidenfeld & Nicolson, 1997), describes among much else his own deep attachment to Sissinghurst. Two biographies of Harold (James Lees-Milne, *Harold Nicolson*, 2 vols. [Chatto & Windus, 1980–81], and Norman Rose, *Harold Nicolson* [Pimlico, 2006]), match two of Vita (Michael Stevens, *V. Sackville-West* [Michael Joseph, 1973], and Victoria Glendinning, *Vita* [Weidenfeld & Nicolson, 1983]).

Susan Mary Alsop wrote about Vita's mother in *Lady Sackville* (Weidenfeld & Nicolson, 1978).

Most of the manuscripts on which these books were based are now to be found in the Lilly Library in Indiana (Harold's and Vita's letters—www .indiana.edu/~liblilly) or at Balliol College, Oxford (the three million words of Harold's diaries).

Index

Page numbers in *italics* refer to picture captions.

Abbott, Robert, 191–92
Abery, Claire, 110, 112–13, 148
Acts and Monuments (Foxe), 165, 167
Addcock, Simon, 138
Addcok, Alice, 138
Æthelmod, 127
alders, 135
Allin, Edmund, 166–68
Allin, Katherine, 167, 168
Amherst, Earl, 94
Amiel, Barbara, 103
Angley, 118, 122, 125
Anglo-Saxons, 116, 122, 124, 125–26
apple orchard, 9

Bachelard, Gaston, 147
Baker, Chrysogna, 185, *185*
Baker, John (born c. 1488), 160–70, *160*, *169*, 173–75, *178*, 185–87, 191, 214
Baker, John (son of John), 165
Baker, John (son of Richard), 184, 185
Baker, Mary (wife of John), *193*
Baker, Mary (wife of Richard), 185
Baker, Richard, 160, 163, 165, 170–74, 176 78, 180, 182, 184–89, *185*, 190–97, *193*, 202, 225
Baker, Thomas, 159–60
Baker family, 139, 159–89, 234
Bannister, Nicola, 180–81, *183*
Bassuck, William, 203
BBC, 259, 283, 287

Beale, A. O. R. (Ossie), 14, 56, 58, 59–62, 132, 215, 217–18, *218*, *219*, 220–21, 225, 234, 257, *321*
farm diary of, 59–61
Beale, Donald, 215
Beale, John, 222
Beale, Louis, 217
beavers, 93
Bedgbury, 157, 186
Bedington, 188
beech trees, 81, 83–85, 122, *127*, 132, 193–94, 207, *207*, 208
Benenden, 3, 4, 122
Bentley, Richard, 197
Beowulf, 121, 125, 126
Berger, John, 39–40, 320
Bergson, Henri, 267
Berry, Wendell, 297, 318
Berryingden, 123
Bethersden, 133
Bettenham, 3, 50, 52, 55, *55*, 56, 59, 60, 75, 100–101, 118, 122–24, 132, 134, 212, 215, 217–21, 249, 257, 298
Beale with ewes at, *321*
Nigel's sale of, 101, 221, 298
pigs at, *120*
ring found near, 95
Bexley, 133
Biddenden, 4, 117, 184
Biddenden Road, *181*
Big Room, 17, 234
Birches Wood, *127*
birch trees, 81, 83, 84–85, 194
birds, 80–81, 109, 306
nightingales, 11–12, 312–13, 314

blackthorn, 82
Bletchenden, 129, 130
Bloomsbury Group, 27, 231–32, 252
Bodiam Castle, 244
Boles, Jack, 53
Boleyn, Anne, 161
Branden, 118, 123
brickmaking, 75, 77–79, 209, 213
Brissenden, 50, 52, 100–101, 118, 130, 220,
    257, 297–301, 309
British Hedgehog Preservation Society, 306
Brown, Capability, 196
Brown, Jane, 252, 264
Browning, Helen, 106, 107, 109
Bubhurst, 123, 130
Buckhurst, 118, 122, 125
Bull Wood, 207
Burghley, Lord, 187, 188
Bushell, Sally, 66, 98, 101, 105, 142, 229
Butler, Sam, 276–78
Butz, Earl "Rusty," 290

Cadaca (Kardarker) Ridge, 115–16, 119,
    121, 128
Camden, 118
Campaign to Protect Rural England, 151
Cannadine, David, 42
Canterbury, 130, 134, 138, 164
cants, 10–11
Carew, Francis, 188
Carluccio, Antonio, 149
Castle Residence, 211
cattle, 12, 133, 157, 221, 225
    Guernsey, 99, 217, 220, 221, 222, 223
Celtic ring, 95
Charing, 134, 137
Chart Hills, 117, 137
Chatsworth, 227
Cheeseman brothers, 126, 215
chestnut coppice, 127
Chittenden, 122–23
Civil War, 192, 208
Clarendon Park, 188
clay, 73–75, 76–79, 81, 273
Clifford, Linda (Linda Stearns), 59, 216,
    225
Clinton, Edward, 187
clothmaking, 157–58, 180, 184
Cobbett, William, 208
Codrington, Ursula, 47
Coleridge, Samuel Taylor, 303–4

Combewell, 129
Commenden (Comenden), 118, 298
Compton Wynyates, 163
Connolly, Cyril, 242
Conran, Priscilla, 149
Consilience: The Unity of Knowledge
    (Wilson), 310–11
Constantinople, 238
Coombes, Ginny, 142, 152, 278–79, 280
Copden (Copton), 118, 123, 129, 130, 134,
    161
Copper, Jack, 13, 17, 31, 46–47, 50, 53, 59,
    220, 255, 257
Cornwallis family, 210–11, 213, 215
Cottage Garden, 251, 252
Couert, Robert, 138
Country Life, 43, 252
Covent Garden, 223
Covent Garden Soup Company, 150
Covey, Amy, 271, 272, 274, 284
Cowdray House, Sussex, 188
Cow Field, 13, 56, 225, 272
cows, 133
    wild, 80
    see also cattle
Cranbrook, 121–23, 125, 128, 132, 139,
    157–59, 171, 172, 180, 182–84, 189,
    201, 214
    religion and, 165, 167, 168, 192
    Sissinghurst Castle Farm leased by,
        208–10, 315–17
Cranbrook church, 85, 88, 95, 136, 139,
    175, 191, 196
    bosses in, 85–88, 86, 94, 139
    James Stearns's funeral at, 224–25
    pediment from Sissinghurst courtyard
        in, 224–25, 225
Cranbrook Common, 129
Cromwell, Thomas, 161–62
Culpeper family, 157, 186, 189

Daily Telegraph, 287
Dalton, Hugh, 43
Datta, Alexis, 110–11, 112, 142
Dear, Peter, 109, 152–54, 272, 273, 274–75,
    275
Dearn, T. D. W., 209
De Berham, Elisia, 137–38, 139
De Berham, Richard, 137, 138
De Berham family, 136, 137–40, 161,
    162–63, 173

De Bikenorre, John, 136–37
Delos, 250, *251*
dens, 119, 120, 121, 128, 132
Depression, Great, 220
De Rude, William, 136
De Saxenhurst, John, 128–29
De Saxingherst family, 128–30, 136, 137
De Saxinherst, Galfridus, 129
Dictionary of National Biography, The, 42
Don, Montagu, 150
draft animals, 133
Dudley, Robert, Earl of Leicester, 187, 188

Edward I, King, 136–37
Edward VI, King, 161, 162
Edward VII, King, 238
Eleven Acre Wood, 207
Elizabeth, Queen, 17, 18, 165, 171, 182, 186–89
Elizabethan Tower, 20, 50, 84, 142, *148,* 149, 171, 174, 175, 178–81, 187, 188, 210, *210,* 212, 214, 250
    Harold, Nigel, Vita, and Ben under, *246*
    Harold and Vita on steps of, *261*
    plaque by Reynolds Stone to Vita under, *111*
    in prison-camp period, 198, *198*
    Vita's room in, 17, 233, 239–40, *248, 249,* 262–69
Ellis, Havelock, 267
Esher, Viscount, 44
Essex, 162
Euston, Earl of, 44
ewes, 133, *321*
Exhurst, 122
Exmoor, 101

Fairley, Jo, 149
farming, 291–97, 311, 318
    beauty and, 318–19
    organic, 144, 282, 284, 290–94, 299
    tourism and, 308–9
    in Tuscany, 307–9, 312
Farris, Gordon, 38
Faversham, 117
Fearnley-Whittingstall, Hugh, 151–52
Fifield, Peter, 264
Flishinghurst, 118
Floodgate (Fludgate) Wood, 134, 207
Fowler, John, 44
Foxe, John, 165, 167

Fraser, Simon, 113
Frazer, James George, 267
Freight, The, 123
Friezley, 118, 123
Frittenden, 75, 77, 78, 117, 118, 123, 166, 167–68, 209, 213, 272, 273
Frogmead, 13, 55, 134–36, *219,* 222, 274, 284
Furley, J. M., 81

"Garden, The" (Sackville-West), 267
Gibbon, Constance, 137
Gibbon, Edward, 201–2
Glassenbury, 118
Glendinning, Victoria, 238
Gloucestershire, 162
Glover, Jasper, 183
Godfrey, Richard, *176*
Golden Bough, The (Frazer), 267
gold ring, 95
Goldyng, Robert, 138
Goudhurst, 129, 157
Granary Restaurant, 31, 70, 106, 110, 141, 142–43, 151–52, 227, 278–81, 282
    Adam and Sarah's experience working in, 279–80
    farm and, 68–69, 71, 99–100, 113, 143, 151, 152, 278, 280, 282, 293
    National Trust and, 278, 280–81
Granby, Lord, 235
Grant, Duncan, 231
Graves, Robert, 311–12
Graylins Wood, 207
Green Man 1, 86–87, *86*
Green Man 2, *86, 87*
Greensand Hills, 91
Grimm, S. H., *198*
Grose, Francis, 140, 163, *166*
Guernsey cows, 99, 217, 220, 221, 222, 223
Guilford family, 186
Gunn, Thom, 268

Hadlow Down, 217
Hall, Mr., 5
Hall, Mrs., 134
Hammer Brook, 3–8, *5,* 11, 36, 39–40, 60, 73, 80, *82,* 93, 117, 124–26, 134, 136, 153, 172, 182, 193, 196, 214, 274
Hammer Mill, 4, 134, 182, 184, 194, 207, 257
Hammer Wood, 207

Hampshire, 162
Hardie, Philippe, 203–4
Hareplain, 122
Hartley, 122
Hartridge, 118
Haselden, 129, 130
Hasted, Edward, 159–60, *176*
Hawkridge, 118
haycarts, *7*
Hayter, Mrs., 220
hazel, 92
Hazelden, 122
Headcorn, 91, 117, 123, 129, 137
Heaney, Seamus, 126
hedgehogs, 304–6
Hemsted, 123, 186
Hemsted Forest, 122
Herth, Thomas, 138
Hidcote, 44
High Tilt, 118, 123
Hills, Ivan, 49–50
History and Topographical Survey of the County of Kent, The (Hasted), *176*
Hochberg, Katrin, 107, 142, 149
Hocker Edge, 118
Holden, Patrick, 289–96, 310, 312
Hollingbourne, 117
holly, 83, 85
Holmesdale, Viscount, 94
Holred, 129, 130
Homer, 313–14
Honeysett, Mrs., 46
honor, 319–20
hops, 13–14, *15*, 30, 55, 62, 73, 124, 131, 135, 157, 190, 212–14, 218–22, *219*, 257
Horneyold-Strickland, Mrs., 145
Horse Race, *9*, 56, 75, 106
Horse Race House, 212
Horticulture Week, 271
Hoskins, W. G., 150
Hungerden, 124, 126
hunting, 122, 130
hursts, 120, 121, 125

Ibornden, 122
ice ages, 80, 81, 135
Iden, 122
idiosyncrasy, 306
Ightham Mote, 162, *163*
Illich, Ivan, 294
ironworks, 182, 184

jackdaws, 116
James, Henry, 37
James, Margery, 298, 299
James, Thomas, 101, 298, 299
Jenkins, Simon, 287, 289
Jones, Jo, 110

Kardarker (Cadaca) Ridge, 115–16, 119, 121, 128
Karsh, Yousuf, 263
Keen, Mary, 103
Kendall, Will, 150
Kent, 3, 6, 19, 80, 81, 116–18, 127, 128, 132, 157, 158, 161–62, 164, 194, 282
Kent Archaeological Society, 94
Keppel, Alice, 238
Kew, 171
King's Meadow, 168
Kipling, Rudyard, 48–49, 85, 288
Knole, 18, 181, 190, 195, 201–2, 235–37, 238
    National Trust and, 43, 45, 49, 145
    Vita and, 18, 181, 235, 243–44
Knole and the Sackvilles (Sackville-West), *263*
Kreutzberger, Sibylle, 47, 260

"Land, The" (Sackville-West), 215
landscape:
    elegy rejected for, 314
    honorable, 319–20
    language and, 302–3
    place versus, 303–4
language, 301–2
Language Instinct, The (Pinker), 301
Larkin, Philip, 305, 306
Lascelles, Lord, 235
Lees-Milne, Jim, 24–25, 43, 162, 249–50
Legge Wood, 207
Leicester, Robert Dudley, Earl of, 187, 188
Levin, Bernard, 241–42
Lewis, Robert, 101, 298–301
ley lands, 121, 122
Light, Jonathan, 71–72, 98, 101–2, 104–7, 109, 141–42, 154, 226, 228, 229
Lime Walk, 20, *259*
Lincoln's Inn, 171
Little Bettenham, 220
Little Chart, 127–28, 137
Lloyd, Christopher, 34
Lodge Field, 13, 55, 180

Long Barn, 238, 239, 242, 244, 250
Lossenham, 138, 139, 159
Lovehurst, 118, 124
Lower Courtyard, 254
Lower Tassells, 272
Lupton, Tom, 270–71, 271, 274, 276
Lutyens, Edwin, 18, 253

MacDermot, Niall, 52
Maidstone, 134, 168, 171
Making of the English Landscape, The
  (Hoskins), 150
Mann, Edward, 204–6, 205, 315
Mann, Horatio, 315
Mann family, 209, 210
Maplehurst, 122, 125
Maplehurst Mill, 166
Mary, Queen, 161, 162, 164, 165, 197, 214
Mary Queen of Scots, 18
meadows, 133–36
meaning, 301–3
Medhurst, Alison, 21
Medhurst, Simon, 21–22
Middle Ages, 116–39, 156
Milestone Wood, 129
Milkhouse, 123, 129
moat, 139, 140, 153, 201
Moat Walk, 253
Moore, Charles, 287–89
Morgan, Shirley, 75–76
Moss Force, 303–4
Mottenden (Moatenden), 137, 138, 139, 159
Murray, Simon, 145, 146

National Trust, 42–45, 150–51, 180, 231,
  283, 296
  and Adam's return to Sissinghurst,
    65–68
  beliefs of, 43–44
  Exmoor and, 101
  Gardens Panel of, 69
  Granary Restaurant and, 278, 280–81
  Knole and, 43, 45, 49, 145
  meadows and, 136
  meeting for donor families, 144–47
  Sissinghurst farm and, 48, 49, 52, 54,
    63–64, 68–72, 98, 100, 101–7, 109,
    112, 113, 141–44, 150–52, 190, 226–
    29, 272, 276–77, 287–89
  Sissinghurst given to, 42, 45–54, 66, 67,
    288, 289

Stearns family and, 223, 224
Tower and, 262, 265
Waddesdon and, 103, 104
National Trust Enterprises, 110, 152
Neve, Frederick William, 214
Neve, George, 75, 94–95, 139, 211–12, 214
Newenden, 138
Nicolson, Ben (uncle of Adam), 26, 79,
  233, 239, 241, 244, 246, 254, 257
Nicolson, Harold (grandfather of Adam),
  17, 18, 19, 19, 20, 29, 174, 220, 231–34,
  237–38, 244, 246, 247–51, 248, 254,
  258, 259, 261, 261, 263, 268, 269, 283,
  320
  death of, 262
  Lees-Milne and, 25, 43, 249–50
  letters and diaries of, 26, 233, 268–69
  National Trust and, 45
  Nigel's book about marriage of, 232,
    240–42, 252
  Nigel's relationship with, 232–33, 234
  and purchase of Sissinghurst, 179,
    244–45, 245
  Sissinghurst gardens and, 77, 91, 175,
    234, 247–49, 250–51, 252–53, 259–60
  visitors and, 256–57
  Vita's death and, 20, 23, 262
  Vita's letters to, 243, 255, 265
  Vita's marriage to, 237–38
Nicolson, Juliet (sister of Adam), 2, 18, 19,
  21, 25, 36, 37, 53, 111
Nicolson, Molly (daughter of Adam), 153
Nicolson, Nigel (father of Adam), 5, 17,
  18, 19, 29, 30, 31, 35, 72, 79, 105, 106,
  112, 162, 174, 215, 237–38, 239, 244,
  246, 249, 254, 257, 262, 264, 268
  Adam's boyhood memories of, 2–6, 19,
    21, 24, 38
  Baker stories and, 168–69
  beech tree and, 84
  as biographer and publicist of his
    parents' lives, 231–34
  breakup of marriage, 23–24
  character of, 24–29
  farms sold by, 101, 221, 298
  Harold's relationship with, 232–33, 234
  illness and death of, 32, 34, 36–38, 63
  letters and diaries of, 26, 268–69
  memoir of, 28
  oak circle planted in memory of, 153, 153
  Portrait of a Marriage, 232, 240–42, 252

Nicolson, Nigel (*cont.*)
  Shirley Morgan and, 75–76
  Sissinghurst given to National Trust by,
    42, 45–54, 66, 67
  social life of, 27
  tidying-up habits of, 29, 64–65
Nicolson, Philippa (mother of Adam),
    17–18, *18*, 19, 26, 47, 50, 51, 53
  breakup of marriage, 23–24
Nicolson, Rebecca (sister of Adam), 19, 25,
    36, 111
Nicolson, Rosie (daughter of Adam), 65,
    153
Nicolson, Tom (son of Adam), *29*
nightingales, 11–12, 312–13, 314
Noah's Ark, 124–25
Nuttery, 21, 176, 252

oak, 88, 121, 131, 164
  bosses at Cranbrook church, 85–88, *86*,
    94, 139
  timber framing, 88–90, *89*
oak trees, 88, 91–93, 127, *127*, 131, 132, *140*,
    153–54, 182, 193–94, 207, 208, 272
  holly and, 83, 85
  memorial to Nigel Nicolson, 153, *153*
oast house, 14, *15*
Observer, 242, 259, 261
Odyssey (Homer), 313–14
Oliver, Tom, 151
organic farming, 144, 282, 284, 290–94,
    299
Otford, 134
oxen, 133, 213, *213*
Oxford, Earl of, 187, 188
Oxfordshire, 162

Paternoster Chophouse, 281
Pavord, Anna, 69
Peak, James, *206*
Peasants' Revolt, 156
Penshurst, 195
Pevsner, Nikolaus, 162
Philipott, Thomas, 191
Picture Post, 257
Pig Earth (Berger), 39–40, 320
pigs, 12–13, 119–20, *120*, 127–28, 131
Pinker, Steven, 301, 312
Piper, John, 18
place, landscape versus, 303–4
place-names, 117–25

Pluckley, 137
ponds, 74, 152–53, 172
Pope-Hennessy, James, 25
Porritt, Jonathon, 147
Portrait of a Marriage (Nicolson), 232,
    240–42, 252
Pratt, Jeffrey, 307, 308
Priest's House, 17, 50, 68, 147, 171, 175, 192,
    212, 250, 254
Private Eye, 242
Proby, Merry, 67
Proby, William, 67–68, 145
Protestantism, 156, 162, 165–68, 192
  Reformation, 161, 165, 166
Punnett, Shirley, 19, 23, 106

Rackham, Oliver, 30
Radclyffe, Thomas, 187
Rathbone, Jack, 45–46, 48, 50
Regional Planning Group, 154
Raven, Sarah, 32, 36, 64, 65, 98, 101, 104,
    105, 111–13, 148, 149, *153*, 274, 278–
    81, *284*, 287–89
  career of, 98, 114, 278
  redundancy, 301, 303
Reformation, 161, 165, 166
Reynolds, Fiona, 63–64, 72, 102, 145,
    150–51, 282, 283
Rhymers Lexicon, The (Loring), 266
Richards, Stuart, 152
ring, gold, 95
Rire, Le (Bergson), 267
Rogley, 122
Romans, 3–4, 81, 116
Romney Marsh, 138
Roots, Sarah, 142
rose, "Sissinghurst Castle," 177–78, 185
Rose Garden, 21, *148*, 250–51, *251*, 252,
    260
Rothschild, Jacob, 103–4, 144, 146
Rothschild, Serena, 103
Royal Society for the Protection of Birds,
    43
Rumley, Peter, 139, *173*
Ruthven, Jacqui, 111

Sackville, Catherine, 161
Sackville, Thomas (brother of Catherine),
    161, 202
Sackville, Thomas, 1st Earl of Dorset, 18,
    19

Sackville, Victoria, 235
Sackville-West, Robert, 6, 54, 114, 145, 146
Sackville-West, Vita, 20, 21, 23, 26, 46, 59,
　　70, 132, 139, 175, 184–85, 197, 206,
　　220, 231–51, 239, 240, 246, 248, 254,
　　256, 257–69, 261, 263, 281, 283, 320
　Beale and, 218, 220
　boots of, 169
　death of, 17, 20, 23, 42, 45, 48, 221, 262
　dressed as a basket of wisteria, 236
　"The Garden," 267
　gardening column of, 259, 261
　grandmother of (Pepita), 235, 266
　Harold's marriage to, 237–38
　Knole and, 18, 181, 235, 243–44
　Knole and the Sackvilles, 263
　"The Land," 215
　letters to Harold from, 243, 255, 265
　as mother, 233–34
　name of, 249
　National Trust and, 45
　Nigel's book about marriage of, 232,
　　240–42, 252
　note written about visitor, 214
　plaque from Reynolds Stone to, 111
　rose discovered by, 177–78, 185
　"Sissinghurst," 70, 245–47
　Sissinghurst farm and, 257
　Sissinghurst gardens and, 49, 77, 91, 142,
　　234, 247, 252, 259–60, 267
　Sissinghurst purchased by, 17, 161, 171,
　　179, 202, 215, 234, 244–45
　Tower room of, 17, 233, 239–40, 248,
　　249, 262–69
　Trefusis and, 238–43, 267, 269
　visitors and, 256–57, 256
St. Levan, John, 145
St. Michael's Mount, 145
Samoa, 300
sand, 73, 74–75, 126, 299
Saville, Sue, 67, 104–5, 145, 229
Saxons, 3, 122, 125
scale, 309–10
Schwerdt, Pam, 47, 260
Scott, John Murray, 235
Sevenoaks, 238, 242
Seven Years' War, 197
　Sissinghurst as prison camp during,
　　197–206, 198, 200, 202
Sex and Character (Weininger), 267
Sheffield Park, 100

silt, 73, 74–75, 126, 299
Sinkhurst, 124
Sissinghurst:
　Adam's boyhood memories of, 1–24
　Adam's return to, 32, 63–68, 111
　admiration patches at, 231
　aerial view from the east, 9
　aerial view from the northeast, 251
　back of, in medieval times, 166
　Baker family and, 139, 159–89, 190–95,
　　193, 196, 197, 234
　as brand, 63–64
　chapel at, 191–92
　cold at, 23–24, 254
　courtyard at, circa 1787, 176
　de Berham family and, 136, 137–40, 161,
　　162–63, 173
　decline of, 190–211
　de Saxingherst family and, 128–30, 136,
　　137
　east front of the south range, 32
　in eighteenth century, 196–208
　emotional bonds to, 276–77
　farm at, see Sissinghurst Castle Farm
　financial reserves of, 105, 110, 112
　front range of, during World War II, 58
　gardens at, see Sissinghurst Castle
　　Garden
　gateway in, 163, 174, 178, 209
　history of the area, 73–96, 115–40,
　　156–59
　house at, 16, 17–19, 23–24, 34, 48–52, 54
　meadows at, 134–35
　name of, 125–26, 198, 206
　National Trust ownership of, 42, 45–54,
　　66, 67, 288, 289
　in nineteenth century, 208–11
　park pale at, 180–82, 181, 194, 207
　pediment from courtyard, 224–25, 225
　plan of, in Elizabethan era, 173
　plan of, 1930s–'90s, 253
　Priest's House at, 17, 50, 68, 147, 171, 175,
　　192, 212, 250, 254
　as prison camp, 197–206, 198, 200, 202
　profits of, 142–43, 152
　public visitors to, 30–31, 32, 48, 49, 100,
　　112, 141, 142, 152, 155, 231, 256–57,
　　262, 277–78, 282, 283, 309
　restaurant at, see Granary Restaurant
　romanticism and, 282–83, 286, 288
　in seventeenth century, 190–95

Sissinghurst (cont.)
    sitting room in the southern end of the
        front range, 51
    in sixteenth century, 17, 156, 157,
        161–89, 183
    soils at, 73–79, 106, 108–9, 126, 134,
        273
    South Cottage at, 17, 20, 46, 50, 68, 79,
        139, 171, 210, 210, 212, 250, 254
    southern end of the front range, 16
    timber framing at, 88–90, 89
    Tower at, see Elizabethan Tower
    Vita's purchase of, 17, 161, 171, 179, 202,
        215, 234, 244–45
"Sissinghurst" (Sackville-West), 70, 245–47
Sissinghurst Castle Farm, 48, 179
    Adam's vision for, 54, 59, 62, 63–64,
        68–72, 97–114, 155, 190, 226–30, 274,
        282, 284–85, 287, 292–93
    bed-and-breakfast at, 226, 275, 282, 284
    Beale's diary for, 59–61
    changes implemented at, 270–86
    Cranbrook parish's renting of, 208–10,
        315–17
    farmers at, 54–55, 70–71
    Farm Survey Record for, 56–59
    hedges and ditches at, 302
    intentions versus outcomes, 284–85
    map of, 275
    National Trust and, 48, 49, 52, 54, 63–
        64, 68–72, 98, 100, 101–7, 109, 112,
        113, 141–44, 150–52, 190, 226–29,
        272, 276–77, 287–89
    orchard in, 9, 274–75, 283, 286, 319
    organic farming at, 144, 282, 284
    in 1960s and '70s, 12–16, 30–31, 34
    restaurant and, 68–69, 71, 99–100, 113,
        143, 151, 152, 278–81, 282, 293
    shop of, 99–100, 106, 113, 143, 151, 152
    significance of, 286–96
    television series about, 283, 287
    vegetable garden in, 272–74, 272, 273,
        282, 284, 284, 297
    in Victorian era, 75, 211–14
    view of the buildings at, 41
    Vita and, 257
Sissinghurst Castle Garden, 17, 20–21, 32,
    34, 48, 52, 54, 71, 148, 149, 151, 175,
    177, 250–53, 256, 258–60
    Cottage Garden, 251, 252
    Delos, 250, 251

    Harold and, 77, 91, 175, 234, 247–49,
        250–51, 252–53, 259–60
    Lime Walk, 20, 259
    Nuttery, 21, 176, 252
    Rose Garden, 21, 148, 250–51, 251, 252,
        260
    Vita and, 49, 77, 91, 142, 234, 247, 252,
        259–60, 267
    White Garden, 37, 149, 175, 177, 251,
        252, 253, 254, 259–60
Sissinghurst House Case, 195
Sizergh Castle, 145
Smarden, 117, 137
Smith, John, 44
Smyth, Ethel, 262
Snoad, 118
Society for the Protection of Ancient
    Buildings, 42
Soil Association, 106, 107, 108, 109, 142,
    143, 149, 152, 225–26, 284
soils, 73–79, 106, 108–9, 123, 126, 133, 134,
    159, 273, 299
South Cottage, 17, 20, 46, 50, 68, 79, 139,
    171, 210, 210, 212, 250, 254
Southwark, 162
Speenhamland system, 208
Spencer House, 144–45
Spring Garden, 252, 253
Staffordshire, 171
Stag Hounds, 214
Staniforth, Sarah, 147
Staplehurst, 117, 122–23, 124, 164
Staples, Mrs., 17, 50
Stark, Freya, 266
Stearns, Catherine, 216, 225
Stearns, James, 12, 14, 55–56, 58, 59, 109,
    131, 217, 221–25, 222, 226
    death of, 216–17, 224, 226
Stearns, Linda, see Clifford, Linda
Stearns, Mary, 31, 131, 216, 217, 218, 219,
    220, 223–24, 225
Stearns, Pat, 12, 55, 216–17, 225, 226
Stearns, Stanley, 59, 62, 220, 221, 222,
    223
Stearns family, 55
Stein, Gertrude, 103
Stevenson, Robert Louis, 300
Stocker, Phil, 107–9, 143
Stone, 129, 130, 161
Stone, Reynolds, 111
Strachey, Lytton, 231

Studies in the Psychology of Sex (Ellis), 267
Sturry, 117
Summerson, John, 162
Sunday Times, 241–42
Surrey, 188
Sussex, 159, 161–62, 217, 278
Sutton Valence, 117
Swing Riots, 208

Taylor, George (director of Kew Gardens), 46, 48
Taylor, George (gardener), 46
Tempest, George, 197
Thackray, Caroline, 142
Thomas, Edward, 118–19
thorn thickets, 82–83, 85, 93
Thorpe, John, 174
Tilgeseltha, 123
Tolehurst, 118, 124
tourism, farming and, 308–9
Tower, *see* Elizabethan Tower
Tower Lawn, 252
trees:
    beech, 81, 83–85, 122, 127, 132, 193–94, 207, *207*, 208
    birch, 81, 83, 84–85, 194
    birds and, 80–81
    oak, *see* oak trees
    willow, 83, 85
    see also woods
Trefusis, Violet, 238–43, 267, 269
tug-of-war in the orchard, *22*
Tunlafahirst (Tolehurst), 118, 124
Tuscany, 307–9, 312
Tyntesfield, 146

Ulcombe, 91
Upper Courtyard, 20, 252

Vass, Jack, 258, 260
Vera, Frans, 90, 92, 121
Verlaine, Paul, 18

Wadd, 122, 207
Waddesdon, 103, 104
Wallace Collection, 235
Wallenberg, J. K., 119
Walpole, Horace, 177, 182, 197, 303
Walston, Oliver, 289–96, 297, 310
Warwickshire, 163
Watson, Guy, 149–50

Weald, 3–4, 16, *41*, 85, 90–91, 95, 116–17, 128, 130–32, 136, 156–60, 162, 168, 182, 185, 194, 300
    in ancient times, 90, 91–92
    farming in, 99
    meaning of word, 85, 122
    place-names in, 117–25
Weeden, Peter, 281
Weininger, Otto, 267
Wellesley, Dottie, 215, 244, 266
Well Fields, 56, 195
West, Rebecca, 242
Westgate, 134
wheat, 55, 132, 157, 290, 292, 299
    threshing of, 57
White Garden, 37, 149, 175, 177, *251*, 252, 253, 254, 259–60
Whitegate Farm, 190
White Goddess, The (Graves), 311–12
Whitsunden, 118, 207
Wilkie, Kim, 151
Wilkinson, Peter, *173*, *253*, *275*
Wilkinson, Sue, 280–81
willow trees, 83, 85
Wilmshurst, John, 215
Wilmshurst, William, 215
Wilmshurst, William, Jr., 215
Wilsley, 118
Wilson, Edward O., 310–11, 312
Wimpole, 44
wood, 85, 121, 131–32, 213
    see also oak
Wood Bird/Dragon, 86, 87–88
Wood God, 86, 87
woodman, 10
woods, 81–85, 90–94, 106, 115, 121–23, 126, 131–32, 154, 193–94, 207–8
    Adam's boyhood memories of, 8–11, 115
    original wildwood, 90, 91–92
    place-names and, 120–21
    see also trees
Woolf, Leonard, 254–55
Woolf, Virginia, 231, 245, 262
World War II, 43, 257–58
Wye, 117

Xenophon, 268

Yew Walk, 21, 250–51, *251*, 252, 254